a synopsis
of American
History

a synopsis of American History

Fourth Edition

VOLUME ONE
Through Reconstruction

Charles Sellers
Henry May
University of California at Berkeley

Neil R. McMillen
University of Southern Mississippi

RAND McNALLY COLLEGE PUBLISHING Company/Chicago

10 9 8 7 6 5 4 3

Fourth Edition

Preface

A Synopsis of American History is a brief summary, with an emphasis on politics, designed for those who are beginning the study of the subject. Our purpose in offering a much briefer book than the average textbook is not to cut down the amount a student reads, but to increase the diversity. The *Synopsis,* together with the *Berkeley Readings in American History* and other materials, should help a student to get some idea of the vast diversity of American historical writing and to experience some of the excitement of close, first-hand study of historical sources. At the same time, one can acquire some knowledge of the chronological order without which history makes no sense. The very brief chapter bibliographies are restricted to books that are readily available and readable, and they provide no more than a bare introduction to the study of each period.

In our opinion, political history affords the clearest organization of American history. Surprisingly often, American politics reflect with fair accuracy underlying tendencies in economic, social, and intellectual life. In general, we have said little about social and intellectual history, not because we consider these fields unimportant, but because they are best studied in primary sources and specialized books and because they do not lend themselves to summary.

To supplement the political emphasis, 17 essays on "Conflicting Historical Viewpoints" are included. These point out areas of past and present political controversy and show the development of historical thinking about some of the critical events in American history.

In reducing this big story to such a small space, we have found it impossible to avoid expressing opinions. While we have tried to keep partisanship to a minimum, we have allowed ourselves to suggest interpretations. Appropriate reading in other books—the whole purpose of the *Synopsis*—should enable students to accept or reject our interpretative statements.

We wish to thank Professors Richard B. Morris, Harold Hyman, William E. Leuchtenburg, Martin Sherwin, Richard Abrams, and Thomas B. Jones, who in one edition or another read all or parts of this book and made many valuable suggestions.

In its first two editions, the *Synopsis* was the work of Charles Sellers (Chapters 1–15) and Henry May (Chapters 16–31). Neil McMillen joined the enterprise in 1974, assumed responsibility for the third and fourth revised editions and wrote the essays on "Conflicting Historical Viewpoints."

A *Synopsis of American History,* Fourth Edition, is available as a single volume or as a two-volume set. In the two-volume set, Chapters 1–16 comprise Volume One, *Through Reconstruction;* Chapters 15–32 comprise Volume Two, *Since the Civil War.*

C.S.
H.M.
N.R.M.

Contents

Preface   v

1. Beginnings, 1607–1700   1

2. Britain's North American Empire, 1660–1763   14

3. A New Society   24

4. Toward Revolution, 1763–1775   37

5. Independence Achieved, 1775–1783   49

6. A Nation Emerges, 1780–1788   58

7. Federalists and Republicans, 1789–1800   73

8. The Jeffersonian Republic in a Threatening World,
   1800–1823   85

9. The Market versus the Agrarian Republic   101

10. Depression Decade: Sectionalism and Democracy,
    1819–1828   115

11. The Jacksonian Era, 1828–1840   125

12. Romanticism, Reform, Slavery   140

13. Manifest Destiny and Sectional Conflict, 1840–1852   157

14. A House Dividing, 1843–1860   171

15. The Civil War, 1861–1865   185

16. Reconstructing the Union, 1865–1890   197

Name Index   207

Subject Index   213

Essays: "Conflicting Historical Viewpoints"

1. What Caused the American Revolution and How
   Revolutionary Was It?   44

2. How Democratic Was the Constitution?   69

3. What Caused the War of 1812?   97

4. What Was Jacksonian Democracy?   137

5. How Brutal Was Slavery?   151

6. What Caused the Civil War?   181

7. Was Reconstruction a Tragic Era?   205

Special Lists

1. Events Leading to the Revolution   36

2. Presidential Elections and Major Events, 1789–1800   72

3. Presidential Elections and Major Events, 1800–1823   84

4. Presidential Elections and Major Events, 1816–1828   114

5. Presidential Elections and Major Events, 1828–1840   124

6. Presidential Elections and Major Events, 1840–1852   156

7. Presidential Elections and Major Events, 1852–1860   170

8. Presidential Elections and Major Events, 1860–1865   184

9. Events of Reconstruction   196

Maps

1. The American Revolution   48

2. Westward Movement   90–91

3. The Transportation Revolution to 1860   100

4. The Trans-Mississippi West after the Kansas-Nebraska Act
   (1854)   163

Beginnings
1607–1700

1

When Christopher Columbus broke through the water barrier to the New World and became the first European to set foot on San Salvador, he opened a momentous chapter in the history of the Old World as well as the New. Already, a static and status-bound Europe was responding to new intellectual stirrings, growing trade, and competition among emerging nation-states in overseas exploration and commerce. The dramatic European discovery of the New World frontier accelerated these beginning currents of change into a four-hundred-year revolution. The very knowledge of the existence of seemingly limitless space and resources in America set off a prolonged economic boom, quickened the spirit of enterprise, generated mounting pressures against the rigidities of the social order, and hastened Europe toward the modern world of individualism, capitalism, and liberal democracy.

The development of America took place in the midst of this profoundly important transformation of the Atlantic world toward modernity. The central characteristics of the emerging "modern" epoch, as the term is used here, were the increasing importance of individual autonomy and the growing faith that men could win secular salvation—wealth and "happiness"—through individual enterprise. By the nineteenth century, when modernity in this special sense reached its fullest development, this emphasis on the individual had given rise to the social philosophy known as *liberalism*. In its original meaning, liberalism was the conviction that the good of everyone would be served if all were left as free as possible to pursue their individual ends. In the economic sphere, liberal doctrines lent support to *laissez faire* capitalism. In the political sphere, liberal doctrines encouraged a majoritarian democracy with protection for the rights of minorities.

ENGLAND DISCOVERS THE NEW WORLD

Curiously enough, the area that became the United States was the last major segment of the New World frontier to be exploited by Europeans. During the sixteenth century, the Spanish expended their enormous colonizing and exploitative energies in bringing most of Central and South America under their control, while the Portuguese began developing an empire in Brazil. In the northern latitudes, French fishermen on the Grand Banks and Jacques Cartier on the St. Lawrence laid the foundations upon which French Canada would be built. But the intervening expanse of temperate and fertile country lay untouched through most of the sixteenth century while England slowly made ready for overseas enterprise.

English colonization in America differed in character and consequences from that of other European nations in several crucial respects. England was closer to having a tradition of individual rights and social mobility, and Englishmen exhibited earlier and more fully that spirit of individual enterprise that was to be a major force in the modernization of the European world. Henry VII and Henry VIII had destroyed the power of the feudal nobility, already weakened by the War of the Roses, and had established a strong centralized state. In so doing, the Tudor monarchs had encouraged the growth of the business middle classes, the merchants and entrepreneurs who were to be major agents of the modernizing process. Moreover, Henry VIII had welcomed the Protestant Reformation in England, and Protestant theology, with its spiritual individualism, reinforced the individualistic, enterprising spirit of English middle-class life. All of these influences culminated in a burst of national vigor and creativity in the late sixteenth century under the last of the Tudors, Elizabeth I. It was at this point that Englishmen turned their eyes toward the New World.

A second crucial difference between England and the other major colonizing nations was that England entered upon her colonizing ventures as a poor country. Though the Elizabethans dared to challenge the might of Catholic Spain, they were only on the threshold of holding major-power status, and the Queen's treasury had not sufficient funds to support the New World ventures that seemed vital to England's grand strategic design. Private enterprise had to be enlisted, and Englishmen responded to this national purpose with a mixture of patriotism, Protestant religious zeal, thirst for adventure, and greed.

Sir Humphrey Gilbert, one of the first individual colonizers, died in his effort to found a colony in Newfoundland in 1583. Gilbert's half-brother Sir Walter Raleigh then took up the task. But the colonists he planted on Roanoke Island in present North Carolina in 1585 gave up and returned to England after a year, and a second group of settlers sent out in 1587 disappeared before a relief expedition reached Roanoke three years later. These failures demonstrated that a colonizing venture was beyond the financial capacity of any single individual. Raleigh solved this problem by organizing a "joint-stock company" to finance his second colonial venture. The joint-stock device, forerunner of the modern corporation, dated back to the time of Henry VIII when English merchants had pooled their capital and shared the risks of trade with Russia by buying shares in the "stock" or capital of the self-governing Muscovy Company. Applied to America, this device not only made English colonization possible, but insured that it would be carried out under the direction of private entrepreneurs seeking private profits as well as national ends.

The private entrepreneurial aspect of English colonization and the individualistic character of English society interacted with the New World environment to produce important consequences. Everywhere in the New World, the absence of established institutions left men free to build new social orders, and rich resources afforded a field for enterprise that led English Americans toward individualism and modernity.

The ready source of gold and silver that the Spanish found in their America reinforced the authoritarian social structure they had brought with them. The fur trade played a like role in French America. The English colonizers at first also sought gold or a northwest passage that would open to them the Pacific and the riches of the fabled Orient. They, too, attempted to impose on their colonies a rigid form of social organization designed to promote corporate rather than individual ends. But their New World, the temperate zone of North America, yielded no ready riches. Instead, it proved superbly fitted for the humbler pursuits of farming, fishing, and trade, tasks better adapted to individual than corporate enterprise.

Paradoxically, the English colonies flourished because they failed in their original corporate aims and thus left fields of enterprise for individual Englishmen. It was under these circumstances that English America surged into the forefront of the Atlantic world's drift toward modernity. This movement, with interesting variations, can be seen in the two colonial societies established in the first half of the seventeenth century, one on Chesapeake Bay and the other in New England.

THE CHESAPEAKE COLONIES: VIRGINIA AND MARYLAND

Following Queen Elizabeth's death in 1603, her successor, James I, made peace with Spain, thus freeing English manpower and resources for American ventures. In 1606, King James issued charters to two joint-stock companies to colonize the land that Raleigh had named Virginia in honor of the virgin Queen Elizabeth. The more important of the two Virginia companies, with headquarters at London, promptly sent out an expedition. Reaching Chesapeake Bay in April, 1607, after a voyage of four months, the hundred-odd adventurers proceeded up the great river that they named for King James and founded the first permanent English settlement in the New World at Jamestown.

Hunger, hostile Indians, and disease took many lives in the early years before the settlers learned to cope with the strange environment. At one point the colony was almost abandoned. Much trouble arose from the organization and aims of the enterprise. Anxious for quick profits from gold or a northwest passage, the settlers were slow to settle down to the mundane agricultural labor necessary for the colony to sustain itself. Their reluctance arose partly from the fact that all the original settlers were employees of the company and their labor was exacted under military discipline by an autocratic governor.

By 1618, officials of the Virginia Company frankly recognized that there would be no quick profits and shifted to a policy of making Virginia so attractive to immigrants that it would grow rapidly and yield eventual profits through the company's control of trade. The famous "headright" system was inaugurated whereby a person received fifty acres for every individual he transported to America. The "cruell lawes" of former years were replaced by the "free lawes" of England, and the settlers were authorized to send delegates to a representative assembly. In 1619, as the first representative body in the New World, the democratically elected Virginia House of Burgesses organized itself on the model of the English House of Commons and claimed the right of local self-government.

The shift in company policy was a graceful adaptation to social fact: the fortunes of the colony were increasing only as men found opportunity to pursue their individual ends rather than the corporate ends of the company. John Rolfe, best known as the Virginian who helped gain peace with the Indians by marrying Pocahontas, daughter of the local chieftain, made a greater contribution to Virginia by developing, around 1613, a strain of Indian weed tobacco that achieved instant popularity in England. As the craze for tobacco in England created a flourishing market and high prices, Virginians poured all their energies into growing tobacco for individual profit, and company enterprises were left to languish.

The company made one final effort to recruit immigrants to man its corporate enterprises, but the cost of promotion was too great, and the lure of tobacco quickly drew the new workers away. The company fell into factional bickering, and in 1622, after the death of Pocahontas' father, a new and more bellicose chieftain led the Indians in a devastating massacre of the English settlers, extending to the very gates of Jamestown. This disaster so discredited the company that the King revoked its charter in 1624, and Virginia became henceforth a royal colony. While the governor and his council were appointed by the crown, the Virginians' representative assembly was left unmolested, and the King interfered in Virginia affairs less than the company had.

The high profits from tobacco brought quick recovery from the effects of the Indian massacre and made Virginia a land of opportunity for the disadvantaged and discontented. The poorest Englishman could come as the indentured servant of a Virginian who would pay the ocean passage. Labor was so dear and land so cheap that, when the three to five years of servitude were through, he or she could often buy a farm, plant tobacco, and perhaps even acquire indentured servants of his or her own. The most enterprising and affluent of the early settlers accumulated both labor and land in abundance by importing indentured servants and acquiring headrights in the process. While these more successful planters filled the offices of colony and county government, Virginia society remained so fluid during most of the seventeenth century that the planters could not be said to constitute an aristocracy or ruling class.

For one class of immigrants, the Virginia environment produced not self-fulfillment but enslavement. In 1619, the year of the first representative assembly in British North America, a Dutch trading ship dropped anchor at Jamestown with the first cargo of Africans. The original English settlers had brought with them the traditional European prejudice against black men, but there was no provision in English law for treating Negroes differently from other indentured servants. However, it was easier to take advantage of blacks. Torn forcibly from their African cultures and languages, they had few means of resisting oppression in the alien culture of Virginia. Conspicuously distinguishable from European servants, they could not run away and melt into the free population. Gradually, masters began holding black servants for life and claiming the labor of their children. By the middle of the seventeenth century, Virginia law was modified to define a separate status of permanent and absolute slavery for Africans. America was to be a land of opportunity for Europeans only. In fact, it was through the exploitation of cheap black labor in the tobacco fields that some white Virginians began to amass great fortunes in the later seventeenth century.

While white men flourished in Virginia, a similar pattern of colonial life was being established under very different auspices farther up the shores of Chesapeake Bay. In 1632, King Charles I, successor of James I, granted to George Calvert, Lord Baltimore, proprietorship of the feudal domain of Maryland lying between the Potomac River and the fortieth parallel. The Calverts were a noble Catholic family who envisioned Maryland as a refuge for their fellow Catholics from Protestant England. The first settlement was established at Saint Mary's in 1634, and soon both Protestants and Catholics were immigrating to Maryland to grow tobacco in emulation of the Virginians.

Lord Baltimore enjoyed absolute political power and ownership of the soil, but in order to attract settlers and make the colony a success, it was necessary to share both soil and power with the inhabitants. Large manorial grants were made to some men, mostly Catholics, who presided over large numbers of servants and tenants and came to constitute a kind of gentry. Most of the population were yeoman farmers, perhaps employing a few servants and leasing their lands from the proprietor on a basis nearly equivalent to ownership in return for a nominal quitrent. The Calverts appointed a governor, but eventually allowed the inhabitants to elect an assembly that soon asserted its right to initiate legislation. The most notable piece of legislation was the Act of Toleration of 1649, assuring religious liberty to both Protestants and Catholics.

NEW ENGLAND: PLYMOUTH AND MASSACHUSETTS BAY

Meanwhile, far to the north of the Chesapeake colonies, a different kind of English colonization was taking place on the less hospitable coast of New England. The New England colonies were a direct outgrowth of a renewal of religious conflict in England. The more thoroughgoing Protestants had never been satisfied with the moderate English Reformation as it was institutionalized in the Church of England. Calling themselves Puritans, they demanded a further purification of the English church through the elimination of bishops and the simplification of church services. The essence of Puritanism was a heightened sense of God's sovereignty and man's dependence on divine grace, and the Puritans strove zealously to live strictly in accordance with God's will.

Queen Elizabeth's astuteness had prevented the growing Puritan spirit from causing trouble during her reign, but her successors, the Stuart monarchs James I (1603–1625) and Charles I (1625–1649), invited conflict. James bluntly told the Puritans that they would either conform to the usages of the Church of England or be "harried out of the land." His son Charles married a French Catholic princess and supported efforts to compel religious conformity.

Early on, James harried one little band of particularly fervid left-wing Puritans out of England to Holland. Not finding Holland to their liking, these Pilgrims turned their eyes toward America. With support from a group of London merchants, they and additional recruits from England set sail in 1620 in the *Mayflower* bound for Virginia. Poor navigation brought them to the American coast at Cape Cod, and rather than brave further winter storms on the Atlantic, they established nearby the settlement of Plymouth. Before landing they subscribed the Mayflower Compact, an agreement to govern themselves by majority will that was inspired by radical Puritan notions of church government. The Pilgrim settlement at Plymouth developed into a small agricultural colony, which was important as the first English community in New England but was soon overshadowed and eventually swallowed up by a larger Puritan migration.

The main Puritan migration to New England was made possible when a group of well-to-do and influential leaders obtained from King Charles in 1629 a charter for the Massachusetts Bay Company authorizing settlement in the area north of the Plymouth colony. In a bold move, the leaders resolved to make this charter of a joint-stock company the constitutional basis for a holy commonwealth beyond the King's reach by moving charter and company officers across the Atlantic. All over England, Puritans subscribed funds and volunteered themselves, and in the summer of 1630, a fleet of seventeen vessels carried nearly a thousand people to establish a series of towns around Boston harbor. As conditions for Puritanism worsened in England, these original settlers were followed by thousands more. Within little more than a decade, New England had twenty thousand people.

However foreign the Puritans' ideals may seem to later generations, their enterprise for a holy commonwealth was certainly one of the nobler dreams that men have entertained. If one accepts the Puritans' premises that God is sovereign, that man's primary duty is to do His will, and that the major issue of life is whether one receives God's grace, then it is hard to resist their conclusion that society should be constructed around a divine plan for salvation.

The Puritans' theory of civil government was similar to their "congregationalist" theory of church government, and both were based on the idea of covenant. A true church was a group of the "visible elect" (those who appeared by their lives to be true recipients of God's grace) who had entered into a covenant with God and each other to obey the divine will and establish a church to preach His word. It was then the business of the church members to choose as minister a man especially qualified by character and education to interpret divine will. This theory contained an element of democracy in that all members participated in the covenant, the choice of a minister, and the admission of new members; an element of aristocracy in that the minister once chosen should be accorded the authority due his special qualifications for interpreting God's will; and an element of monarchy in that God's will was sovereign.

The Puritans similarly believed that their holy commonwealth was founded on an implicit covenant with God and each other and that civil magistrates derived their authority from their special qualifications for interpreting God's will for the society. The Puritan commonwealth took its form from the corporate charter of the Massachusetts Bay Company. The stockholders or "freemen" of a joint-stock company met annually as a "Great and General Court" to decide major company policies and to elect the company's executive officers, a "governor" and a board of "assistants." When the Puritan leaders transferred the charter from England to Massachusetts Bay in 1630, only a handful of magistrates, the governor John Winthrop and a few freemen of the company who were also assistants, went along.

In their zeal to protect the religious objectives of the holy experiment, these few magistrates sought at first to make all rules, judge all cases, and govern alone. But within a year, a number of the leading settlers demanded a voice in government, and the magistrates decided that henceforth all church members should be considered freemen and allowed to attend the annual General Court to elect the governor and assistants. Within three years, the General Court had forced the magistrates to concede it a share in the lawmaking power. As the population increased and the General Court became unwieldy, the practice was adopted of having the freemen in each town elect two deputies to represent them in the General Court. The evolution of the General Court as a representative legislative body was completed in the 1640s when the deputies and magistrates began meeting separately.

The Puritan commonwealth was theocratic in the sense that God's will was sovereign, but not in the sense that ministers were given direct political power. The real power of the clergy arose from their authority as interpreters of God's will. With respect to civil matters, this function was ordinarily performed by the magistrates, but when they disagreed with the deputies, the magistrates could usually call the powerful authority of the clergy to their support. Everyone believed that it was the duty of the state to support the church, to require church attendance by members and nonmembers alike, to enforce a strict morality, and to do anything else that would increase the chances of salvation for every member of the community.

The pattern of settlement reflected the religious aims of the holy commonwealth. Individuals were not permitted to buy land wherever they wished. The General Court insisted on compact settlement in contiguous towns. When population increase warranted, the General Court would authorize a group of people to settle a new town adjacent to one already established. Families were given house lots in a compact village within the town's boundaries from which they went daily to work the outlying agricultural lands they were allotted. The church was located in the village center, and villagers and the town and church officials were encouraged to guard, warn, and reprove each other against moral lapses. Everyone was allowed to participate in the town meeting, which elected town officials and decided town policy.

Deeply believing that a trained intelligence was required to discern God's will, the Puritans were zealous advocates of education. The family was the basic educational unit. Every father was required to see that his children and servants mastered reading, writing, and arithmetic and that the boys learned a trade. Fathers were responsible, too, of course, for the religious and moral training and behavior of their families. In 1647, the General Court ordered every town of fifty houses to maintain an elementary school, and some of the larger towns supported public secondary schools as well.

Puritan theory required not only a decently educated general population but also a highly educated magistracy and clergy. Over a hundred graduates of Oxford and Cambridge came to Massachusetts Bay in its first decade to fill this need. In 1636, the General Court established at Cambridge a college modeled on the English universities and named after John Harvard, a young English clergyman who bequeathed to it his library and half his estate. Bright boys from ordinary farm families attended Harvard, and about half of the graduates became ministers.

RHODE ISLAND, CONNECTICUT, NEW HAMPSHIRE

It was inevitable that the holy commonwealth's efforts to maintain social discipline and a uniform doctrine would lead to friction in a population filled with gifted, intense, and devout individuals. The most embarrassing troublemaker in the early days was a brilliant young minister named Roger Williams, who challenged the principle of religious uniformity. Williams was really a radical Puritan who had arrived at the modern principle of separation of church and state on the not so modern ground that enforcement of religious uniformity impeded the soul in its search for religious truth. Such a view clearly threatened the commonwealth, and Williams' close friend Governor Winthrop warned him of his impending arrest in time for him to escape. Making his way south to Narragansett Bay in 1634, he became the father of the colony of Rhode Island, where he proclaimed the policy of complete religious freedom and inaugurated a democratic system of self-government. Receiving a charter from the English government in 1644, Rhode Island attracted dissenters from Massachusetts and Europe, flourished as a farming and trading community, and was a thorn in the sides of its orthodox Puritan neighbors.

Another New England colony came into being when the strongminded Reverend Thomas Hooker and members of his congregation in Cambridge became excited over the fertile Connecticut River Valley, a hundred miles inland from the Massachusetts Bay settlements. Rivalry between Hooker and the other leaders probably figured in the fact that the magistrates departed from their rule of compact settlement and allowed the Cambridge people to go. Traveling overland in 1636, Hooker's followers founded Hartford and organized their own colony of Connecticut on the model of Massachusetts Bay. Other Puritan groups founded settlements at Saybrook and New Haven on the coast and maintained an independent status for a quarter of a century before merging with Hooker's valley settlements as the united colony of Connecticut.

Massachusetts Bay sought to maintain control over the sporadic settlements that grew up to its north. In 1679, the towns beyond the Merrimac River obtained a charter making them the separate royal colony of New Hampshire, but the Maine area beyond continued to be ruled from Boston.

ENGLISH STRIFE AND AMERICAN AUTONOMY

The Stuart monarchy of Charles I had little liking for the stiff-necked independence of Puritan New England, but Charles had his hands too full with Puritanism in old England to undertake any punitive measures across the broad Atlantic. English Puritans had become increasingly important leaders in Parliament's struggle against the arbitrary policies of the Stuarts. The long and bitter conflict culminated in civil war in the 1640s. Oliver Cromwell's Parliamentary army defeated the royalist forces, King Charles was beheaded in 1649, and Cromwell became the dominant figure in a Puritan Commonwealth.

Under these circumstances, the English colonies on the Cheasapeake Bay and in New England had been left to develop as they pleased. The Virginians cared little who ruled in England so long as they were left alone to grow tobacco and pursue their individual fortunes. In Maryland, however, the Protestant majority took advantage of the English Civil War to overthrow the Calverts and the Catholic ruling class and to repeal the Act of Toleration.

The New Englanders became more independent than ever. The leaders of Massachusetts Bay regarded their holy commonwealth as "a city set upon a hill," a model that England and eventually the whole world would follow. The early success of the Puritan cause in the English Civil War reinforced their faith that they were leading the way to a world organized under the will of God. With redoubled zeal to maintain a pure and undefiled commonwealth, they sought to eliminate religious error wherever it appeared. The Quakers caused the Puritans the greatest trouble. These adherents of the Religious Society of Friends represented a kind of radical Puritanism of lower-class origin that enjoined each person to follow the divine promptings of the "Inner Light" in his or her own soul. Antiauthoritarian, the early Quakers felt impelled to bear witness to their faith in the most hostile places, and many of them came to Massachusetts Bay for this purpose. Although they were banished, they returned at the first opportunity. The authorities tried whipping, then cutting off ears, then the threat of hanging, but still the banished Quakers returned. Finally four were hanged.

But suddenly, New England lost its sense of cosmic significance. The Puritan Commonwealth collapsed in England, and the Stuart monarchy returned to power in the Restoration of 1660. The new Stuart king, Charles II, restored Maryland to the Calverts and sought to strengthen his control over the other colonies, but the habit of independence had become so deeply ingrained that he encountered strong resistance. Though the New England magistrates and clergy ceased their persecutions and grudgingly began to tolerate Quakers, Anglicans and other dissenters, they stubbornly sought other ways to maintain their autonomy and power in loyalty to the ideal of the holy commonwealth. But by now, this ideal was being weakened from within as well as from without.

PURITANISM VERSUS MODERNITY

The Chesapeake colonists had reacted to the New World environment and the lure of profits from tobacco culture by moving easily and happily toward a society of individual enterprise and liberal institutions. In New England, an equally autonomous society had developed, but here institutionalized Puritanism was a brake against the pull of the New World environment toward modernity.

In emphasizing God's sovereignty and man's dependence, Puritanism (only somewhat more forcibly than Protestantism generally) was profoundly antagonistic to the modern spirit of optimism and confident individualism. Yet at the same time, Puritanism gave a powerful psychological impetus to individual striving. The Puritans were "moral athletes" who believed that "right living" was the best evidence (although no guarantee) that one enjoyed God's grace. Right living included working as hard and being as successful as possible in whatever worldly calling or business God had placed one. With these convictions, it was not surprising that Puritans were highly successful in their temporal pursuits, especially under the favoring circumstances offered by the New World environment.

Despite its scarcity of fertile soil, New England prospered from the beginning. The cod fisheries developed early into a source of profit. Even greater opportunities were opened up by trade with the English colonies in the West Indies. These tropical islands devoted themselves exclusively to the production of tobacco and sugar for the European market, and New England hastened to supply them with foodstuffs, lumber, and livestock. In the process, the New Englanders built a flourishing merchant marine, and this in turn stimulated a shipbuilding industry.

By the middle of the seventeenth century, the Puritan colonies contained a growing class of successful and wealthy merchants and entrepreneurs. Such men found it increasingly difficult to put salvation ahead of wordly prosperity and to feel helplessly dependent on the grace of an omnipotent God. They did not consciously part from orthodoxy, but nevertheless there was a gradual ebbing of the intense piety that had sustained the early commonwealth. This became apparent when the children of the first generation of church members increasingly failed to give sufficient evidence of God's grace to be received into full membership themselves. Stubbornly retreating before the relentless tides of heterodoxy and secularism, the churches compromised; to retain influence, they opened their membership under a "halfway covenant" to those baptized children of church members who led exemplary lives and accepted the orthodox doctrines but who were still unable to testify to a convincing subjective experience of grace. Having thus blurred the distinction between the "elect" and all others, some churches soon went even further by permitting communion without public confession of faith.

Meanwhile, some of the more successful and less pious New Englanders began to argue that religious persecution discouraged immigration and hampered growth and prosperity. These men also chafed under the orthodox leadership and disapproved of the continued defiance of royal authority. Thus when the British government finally lost patience with Massachusetts Bay, it found some allies among the Puritans. In 1684, Charles II annulled the Massachusetts charter, and the following year his brother and successor, James II, placed all the New England colonies, along with recently acquired New York and New Jersey, under the Dominion of New England. All legislative bodies were suspended, and the Dominion was arbitrarily ruled by a royally appointed governor, Sir Edmund Andros, and his council. But James's equally arbitrary rule at home was arousing opposition. When the King was overthrown in the "Glorious Revolution" of 1688, a series of popular demonstrations ousted the Dominion authorities in the American colonies.

In 1691, the Massachusetts Bay authorities had to accept from the new English monarchs William and Mary a charter that seriously compromised the ideal of the holy commonwealth. The legislative power of the General Court was restored, but henceforth the governor was to be royally appointed, and property ownership replaced church membership as a qualification for voting. Under the new charter, the anticlerical elements gained increasing political influence and finally succeeded even in taking control of Harvard College.

The clergy sought to stem the ebbing of their spiritual and political authority by ever more fervent reminders of God's power and wrath and unwittingly contributed to the Salem witchcraft hysteria of the early 1690s. Before this frenzy subsided, two dogs and nineteen innocent people died on the gallows, an old man was pressed to death by rocks, and some 150 others awaited (but would not suffer) a similar fate. Although belief in witches was almost universal throughout Christendom and although Europe was only then emerging from three centuries of witch mania, the revulsion against the Salem outrages further undermined the prestige of the orthodox leadership. In all likelihood, the New England hysteria owed more to tensions resulting from a changing social and political order than to clerical excesses, but the tragic episode was another major setback for the Puritan hierarchy. By the turn of the century, the social and political leadership of the Puritan colonies was clearly passing into the hands of the enterprising merchant class that constituted the advance guard of modernity.

FOR FURTHER READING

A. L. Rowse's *Elizabethans and America* (1949), and Samuel Eliot Morison's *The European Discovery of America* (1971) are notable introductions to English explorations. Wallace Notestein describes *The English People on the*

Eve of Colonization, 1603-1630 (1954).* The authoritative account of the early colonies is Charles M. Andrews, *The Colonial Period of American History* (4 vols., 1934-1938).* The early history of the Chesapeake colonies is traced in Wesley Frank Craven's, *The Southern Colonies in the Seventeenth Century* (1949); and Philip L. Barbour ably describes *The Three Worlds of Captain John Smith* (1964). Darrett B. Rutman provides a good introduction to the faith and practice of *American Puritanism* (1970); and Edmund S. Morgan's *Visible Saints* (1963) helps to explain the transformation of the Puritan commonwealth into a Yankee province. Other major works include Perry Miller's classic two volume study of *The New England Mind* (1939, 1953)* and Samuel Eliot Morison's volumes on the *Builders of the Bay Colony* (1930)* and *The Intellectual Life of Colonial New England* (1956).* There is no substitute, however, for the splendid contemporary account written by Governor William Bradford, *Of Plimouth Plantation, 1620-1691* (1966).* Edmund S. Morgan has written a brief biography of Governor John Winthrop under the title of *The Puritan Dilemma* (1958);* Robert Middlekauff surveys three generations of Puritan intellectuals in *The Mathers* (1971); and John Demos examines family life in Plymouth colony in *A Little Commonwealth* (1970). Chadwick Hansen has analysed *Witchcraft at Salem* (1969), as has M. L. Starkey in *The Devil in Massachusetts* (1949).

----

*Available in paperback edition.

Britain's North American Empire 1660–1763

2

Before 1660, Englishmen had little or no conception of a colonial empire. The isolated American settlements were rarely thought of, and the British government had been too distracted by political chaos to devise any systematic scheme of beneficial relations between colonies and mother country. The end of civil strife brought a new interest in America. Under the Stuart Restoration, the whole North American seaboard, from Maine south to Spanish Florida, was organized for settlement and exploitation, and an emerging theory of empire began to be embodied in a set of colonial policies.

THE PROPRIETARY COLONIES

The expansion of English settlement in North America was prompted partly by a desire to gain strategic advantages against other colonizing nations and partly by a desire to reward favored courtiers who had sided with the Stuarts during the Civil War. In 1663, Charles II granted a group of eight English noblemen the vast domain stretching south from Virginia to the borders of Spanish Florida. This grant of Carolina was modeled on the proprietary grant of Maryland to the Calverts, and the eight Lords Proprietor were given title to the soil as well as political authority over the area. Carolina already contained a small population that had spilled over from Virginia into the area of Albemarle Sound. In 1670, an expedition from the British West Indies colony of Barbados established another settlement several hundred miles down the coast at Charleston.

Anxious to encourage immigration and make profits from rising land values, the Proprietors promised religious toleration and adopted a liberal land system, including headrights. Settlers in each of the two settled sections were allowed to elect an assembly and make laws in conjunction with a governor and council appointed by the Proprietors. Coastal sandbars blocked off the northern settlements from good ocean transportation, and this area came to be populated by small landowners whose isolation and independent-mindedness made them difficult to govern. The southern settlements around Charleston, on the other hand, quickly developed profitable staple productions for export, first deerskins and naval stores and then rice and indigo. Great plantations grew up on the tidal estuaries, and the planters came to constitute a tightly knit ruling class. They had their headquarters in Charleston, where they spent the malarial summer months in breeze-swept town houses.

While Carolina was a buffer against the Spanish to the south, the British were eliminating another competitor farther north: the Netherlands, the European nation most like England in the enterprising qualities of its people. Early in the sixteenth century, the Dutch merchant marine dominated the spice trade with the Far East. Though their Far Eastern ventures absorbed so much of their slender resources and manpower that they had little left for the New World, the Dutch were interested in finding a more direct water passage to the spice islands through North America. It was the search for such a northwest passage that led Henry Hudson in 1609 up the river that bears his name.

The Hudson River proved to be no northwest passage, but it did lead into the heart of the fur-rich Iroquois country, and by 1624, the Dutch had established trading posts that grew into the colony of New Netherland. New Amsterdam at the tip of Manhattan Island became a cosmopolitan trading center; a scattering of Dutch farmers spread out over Long Island, Staten Island, and across the Hudson from Manhattan; along the Hudson vast manors were granted to wealthy patroons who exercised feudal authority over their tenants. Yet the preoccupation of the Dutch with the Far East, the authoritarian patroonship system, and the petty tyranny of its governors prevented New Netherland from flourishing like its English neighbors.

The English resented this Dutch intrusion into what they regarded as their domain. In 1664, Charles II granted the area between the Delaware and Connecticut rivers to his brother, the Duke of York, who ascended the throne in 1685 as James II. James promptly organized a fleet and sailed for New Amsterdam, which surrendered without a shot. He found his proprietary domain, which he renamed New York, to be larger than he desired, and he transferred the area lying between the Delaware and the Hudson to two of his favorites as the proprietary grant of New Jersey. The New Jersey proprietors later divided the grant into eastern and western sections and sold their rights to other proprietors; West Jersey eventually came into the hands of a group of Quakers who included William Penn.

William Penn was responsible for filling one of the last gaps in the co..,inuous band of English settlement along the Atlantic coast of North America. The son of a British admiral who was a close friend of the Duke of York, Penn was converted to Quakerism and spent time in prison for his religious convictions. On missionary tours of continental Europe, he began dreaming of a refuge in America where not just Quakers but the persecuted and poor of all sects and countries could live in peace. The Stuarts had owed Penn's father a large sum of money, and this debt helped persuade Charles II to grant the son in 1681 the province of Pennsylvania, extending west and south from the Delaware River to Maryland.

Penn promptly began advertising his province, offering complete religious freedom, representative government, and the most generous land policy of any of the American colonies. The quick response from English Quakers, Welshmen, and persecuted German sects made Pennsylvania the most rapidly growing and populous area in British America. Penn himself went there in 1682 to stay several years, laid out the city of Philadelphia between the Delaware and Schuylkill rivers, and inaugurated a government that enforced the most humane code of laws in the world. Separate assemblies were provided for the Philadelphia area and the area of the "Three Lower Counties" of Delaware below Philadelphia; both had the same governor who was appointed by the Proprietor. The preponderant Quakers continued for decades to govern the province in the generous spirit of Penn's "Holy Experiment," and Pennsylvania became for European liberals the preeminent symbol of a tolerant and prosperous New World society.

Thus by 1682, Great Britain's North American empire had been almost completely rounded out. Georgia, the last remaining American colony of Great Britain, was not established until 1732. In that year, a group of English philanthropists persuaded the British government to appoint them Trustees of the area south of the Savannah River to be used as a refuge for imprisoned debtors and the unemployed. The leading Trustee and first governor, James Oglethorpe, sailed with a contingent of settlers in 1733 and founded Savannah. While the benevolent Trustees tried to insure a moral society of small farmers by limiting each settler to fifty acres of land and prohibiting the importation of rum and slaves, these restrictions had to be relaxed to enable Georgia to compete for settlers with its prosperous neighbor, South Carolina. However, the colony remained only a small outpost against Spanish Florida.

The failure of the Georgia restrictions was merely the final demonstration that corporate purposes, however high minded, could not survive among Englishmen in the New World. This lesson was forced upon the Virginia Company early, and the holy commonwealth of the Puritans resisted it only somewhat longer. The proprietary colonies founded after 1660 all promised religious toleration, representative government, and cheap land—policies designed to attract settlers by guaranteeing individual rights and opportunity. The characteristics of Englishmen and the free environment of the New World led irresistibly toward a society permeated with the spirit of individual enterprise.

THE NAVIGATION ACTS AND THE COLONIAL ECONOMY

While the proprietary colonies were eschewing corporate purposes in the New World, officials in London were developing a series of policies designed to implement the larger corporate purposes suggested by an emerging concept of British empire. These policies were based on the theory of political economy known as *mercantilism* that was generally accepted throughout Europe. Mercantilism presupposed that nations were engaged in a continuous struggle for supremacy. Economic strength was valued for the military and strategic advantages it yielded and was to be measured primarily by the accumulation of bullion. As nations lost gold and silver by buying things from other nations, the most self-sufficient nations were considered the strongest and healthiest.

Colonies held an important place in mercantilist thinking. No one questioned that colonies should exist to benefit the mother country, which they could do by furnishing those non-European commodities—like sugar, tobacco, rice, molasses, cotton, indigo, naval stores, and furs—that the mother country would otherwise have to buy from a rival nation. Colonies could also contribute to the prosperity of the mother country by providing a market for its manufactures. Finally, an extensive trade with colonies would support a large merchant marine, and in a period when merchant ships and seamen were easily converted to naval purposes, this increased the fighting strength of the mother country.

These mercantilist principles were applied to the British colonies through a series of Acts of Trade and Navigation passed by Parliament between 1660 and 1672 and augmented by subsequent legislation. The Navigation Acts contained three major requirements: (1) All trade between England and her colonies must be carried in British boats. (2) All European goods imported into the colonies—with a few special exceptions—must pass through England, thus benefiting the English businessmen who handle these items of foreign manufacture. (3) Certain "enumerated articles" produced by the colonies (primarily tobacco at first, but later nearly every export) must be shipped first to Britain or British colonies, even if destined for ultimate resale in other European countries.

The exclusion of Dutch merchantmen from the Chesapeake tobacco trade and the loss of the direct European market for North American tobacco contributed to a period of stringency in Virginia and Maryland in the late seventeenth century. Yet the effects of the Navigation Acts were by no means uniformly bad for the Americans, who, at least until the end of the French and Indian War (1763), generally agreed that the advantages of the loosely administered British imperial policy outweighed its disadvantages. The British colonies were given a monopoly of the tobacco market in the mother country, and bounties were paid to colonial producers of indigo and naval stores. The exclusion of foreign built and owned ships from the trade between England and the colonies was a great boon to the New England shipbuilding industry and merchant marine. Indeed, the Navigation Acts were the "cement of empire," a positive force that bound colony to mother country.

Certainly by the first half of the eighteenth century, the colonial economy was in a highly prosperous state. European demand for tobacco, sugar, rice, indigo, and naval stores rose even faster than the production in the southern and West Indian colonies could expand. As these colonies grew and concentrated ever more exclusively on the profitable staples, they provided an ever greater market for wheat, flour, ground vegetables, salt fish and meat, lumber, and livestock from the middle colonies and New England. Philadelphia and Baltimore became flour milling and exporting centers, and New York exported the furs brought into Albany by the far-ranging Iroquois.

New England produced few or no staples for the mother country and at first did not seem to fit the mercantilist prescriptions for usefulness. But the New Englanders quickly made themselves indispensable to the operation of the imperial economic system. Carrying provisions from the mainland to the West Indies, they picked up cargoes of sugar and then proceeded to England where they loaded their vessels with manufactured goods for America. In another variation of this "triangular trade," they brought molasses from the West Indies to New England, manufactured it into rum, took the rum to West Africa and traded it for slaves, and then carried the slaves for sale in the West Indies or the southern colonies. Similarly they carried Chesapeake tobacco or Carolina rice to England, bringing back manufactured goods. Prospering greatly from this trade and from shipbuilding and fisheries, New England also became the heaviest consumer of British manufactured goods.

As the colonial economy matured, British officials found additional regulations necessary to maintain mercantilist aims. To prevent New England rum makers from importing their supplies from non-English sources, Parliament passed the Molasses Act in 1733, levying a prohibitive duty on foreign molasses or sugar imported into British possessions. But New England evaded the duty by systematic smuggling, and the rum trade continued to flourish. To prevent colonial producers from competing with British manufacturers, Parliament passed a series of acts between 1699 and 1750 forbidding colonists to export woolen cloth and beaver hats or to expand their production of finished iron products.

The most serious economic problem of the colonies, money supply, was greatly aggravated by British restrictions that grew out of the mercantilist preoccupation with bullion for the mother country's treasury. Because gold and silver coin was the only recognized money and because the colonists could neither import British coin nor mint their own, they had to rely on Spanish coin acquired in the West Indian trade. Even this was an unstable money supply for it was constantly drained away to offset colonial trade deficits with England. Thus, there was never an adequate money supply for an intercolonial exchange of goods and services.

Under these circumstances, the colonial governments finally resorted to issuing paper money. These issues were to be redeemed within a certain period and were accompanied by new taxes designed to yield a sufficient fund to pay for redemption. But if too much paper money were issued or if redemption were delayed, the paper money depreciated in value and creditors complained. Moreover, colonial paper money was worthless in England and caused trouble to English merchants who tried to collect from American debtors. The British government first sought to remedy the situation by instructing the colonial governors to veto all but the most soundly backed paper money issues. This failing, Parliament in 1751 forbade the New England colonies, where the worst abuses occurred, to issue any further paper for payment of debts.

ADMINISTERING THE EMPIRE

While British officials were groping toward a concept of empire, administrative agencies for colonial planning and control were haphazardly evolving in the British government. Soon after the Restoration, the King's principal advisory body, the noble Privy Council, designated a committee known as the Lords of Trade to consider colonial matters. But not until the Glorious Revolution of 1688 and the accession of William and Mary did colonial officials in London seriously consider the creation of a centralized empire of politically uniform and dependent colonies directly supervised by the imperial government. A supplementary Navigation Act in 1696 set up a system of admiralty courts in America to enforce commercial regulations and punish smugglers. This same legislation created in England a Board of Trade and Plantations (a group of bureaucratic experts on colonial matters) to advise the Privy Council through the Lords of Trade. While the Board of Trade had little direct power, it did attain considerable importance as the one agency of the British government that systematically considered all colonial matters. Gradually and over many years, the Board of Trade was able to implement some consistent policies of colonial control.

One basic aim of the Board was to convert all the corporate and proprietary colonies into royal colonies. This process, begun with Virginia in 1624 and New Hampshire in 1679, became a deliberate objective upon the accession of William and Mary. Massachusetts Bay, Plymouth, and Maine were organized into the province of Massachusetts under a royal governor in 1691. That same year the Calverts' Maryland proprietary was royalized, and in 1692, Penn's Pennsylvania and Delaware suffered the same fate. But the new policy was too weak to withstand the political influence of such powerful Proprietors: Penn's domain was restored within two years, and the

Calverts finally got theirs back after being converted to Protestantism in 1715. Despite these setbacks, the colonial converters persevered, extracting East and West Jersey from their Proprietors and uniting them as the royal province of New Jersey in 1702. The Carolina Proprietors gave up South Carolina in 1719, North Carolina ten years later, and in 1752 Georgia fell under royal control. Only the strong English respect for property and charter rights enabled Connecticut and Rhode Island to maintain their corporate status, and Penn and the Calverts to regain their domains.

The British government had several means of control over a royal colony. Most important was appointment of the governor who was sent out with a set of detailed instructions drafted by the Board of Trade and who had an absolute veto over the acts of the colonial assembly. Moreover all colonial legislation was sent to the Board of Trade for careful scrutiny, and anything objectionable could be disallowed by the Privy Council. The Privy Council was also a court of appeal from decisions of colonial courts.

Through these means, the Privy Council and the Board of Trade sought to restrain the provincial governments from acts harmful to either English merchants or the royal prerogative. But this restraint was not burdensome. Sir Robert Walpole, who became the king's chief minister in 1721, believed that it was to England's interest to let the colonies flourish without interference; and his policy of "salutary neglect" continued until the 1760s.

Under these circumstances, the provinces became virtually self-governing. All had a similar form of government. Except in Rhode Island and Connecticut, which continued to elect all their officials, and in Massachusetts, where the assembly elected the council, the governor and his council were appointed by the king or the Proprietor for indefinite terms. The council sitting with an elected lower house formed a bicameral assembly. The assembly could convene only when called by the governor, who could suspend its sessions or dissolve it at will. The governor's veto could not be overridden. But whatever the governor's legal authority, he had practical difficulties in resisting the assembly's will. Lax imperial administration, either through design or neglect, permitted colonial assemblies gradually to exercise powers and privileges that in practice, though not by law, shifted the center of colonial control from the executive to themselves. Although intended to be dependent assemblies, they became, in effect, little Houses of Commons and claimed broad Parliamentary authority over local affairs. They particularly insisted on the well-established English principle that citizens could be taxed only by consent of their representatives. The governors were paid by the colonies, and an assembly's refusal to levy taxes or appropriate funds for the governor's salary was a powerful political weapon.

Disputes between governors and assemblies were legion. Often incompetent, invariably caught between the conflicting demands of the London officials and the local assemblies, the governors could satisfy neither group. The ablest among them achieved some success only through the astute distribution of favors and by horsetrading with leaders of the assembly. At times, a governor could fill his council with influential provincials who would side with him against the lower house. But except in the few areas of special concern to the Privy Council, the assemblies usually had their way.

As the decades wore on, Americans increasingly assumed that they had an inalienable right to self-government through their assemblies. The recurrent disputes with the governors taught them political sophistication and political skills that were to be invaluable when this right was challenged. Serious conflict with Crown and Parliament was to be avoided only so long as imperial authorities did not demand that colonial practices coincide with imperial policies.

THE ANGLO-FRENCH WARS

While the English colonies were growing strong and prosperous along the eastern seacoast of North America, the French were developing a different kind of empire to the north and inland. In 1608, one year after the founding of Virginia, Samuel de Champlain began a French settlement at Quebec on the St. Lawrence River. For years Champlain devoted himself to exploring the interior far up the St. Lawrence and into the Great Lakes country and to developing a flourishing fur trade with the Algonquin and Huron Indians of the region. The French fur traders were soon joined by a band of dauntless Jesuit missionaries who ranged far and wide over the wilderness of the north country preaching Christianity to the Indians. By the middle of the seventeenth century, there was a narrow zone of agricultural settlement along the St. Lawrence where humble French *habitants* worked peasant-style on the manorial grants of a rather down-at-the-heels class of feudal *seigneurs*.

Despite the numerical weakness of the French in America, their vigorous exploration and the good relations they had achieved with their Indian allies made them a formidable barrier to English westward expansion. Only the powerful Iroquois confederation in upper New York, hostile to the French-oriented Huron and Algonquin tribes, shielded Dutch New Netherland and the English colonies from contact with the French. But after the rise of Louis XIV in the 1660s, the French pushed their Canadian enterprise more vigorously and assisted their Indian allies in making war on the Iroquois. Meanwhile Louis sought to make France the dominant power in Europe as well as to expand her colonial empire in America and other parts of the world. England joined a series of alliances designed to block French ambitions, and the result was a series of four great wars (1689–1763) fought mainly in Europe but also between the French and English in America.

In the first three encounters—King William's War, 1689–1697; Queen Anne's War, 1702–1713; King George's War, 1744–1748—the French and their Indian allies raided the New England and New York frontiers. Beginning with Queen Anne's War, the Spanish were allied with the French, so that there was skirmishing along the southern as well as northern British frontier. The only American territorial change that resulted from the first three wars was the transfer of Nova Scotia, Newfoundland, and the Hudson Bay country in the far north from France to England in 1713.

Meanwhile, during the intervals of peace, the French moved into the Mississippi Valley behind the English settlements. Around 1700, they set up posts in the Illinois country on the northern Mississippi and established themselves at Biloxi and Mobile on the Gulf Coast near the great river's mouth. New Orleans was founded as the capital of French Louisiana in 1718.

The final phase of the conflict between Britain and France in North America, the French and Indian War (known in Europe as the Seven Years' War), began when a group of Virginians sent agents across the Appalachians and into the upper Ohio Valley for the purpose of Indian trade and land speculation. The French responded by building a chain of small forts on the upper Ohio. Young George Washington, sent out in command of a force of Virginia militia in 1754, arrived barely too late to prevent construction of Fort Duquesne at the forks of the Ohio on the site of later Pittsburgh. He was driven off by the French, and the war began though it was not officially declared for two more years.

All the major European powers were quickly drawn into the fighting. At first things went badly for the British in America and elsewhere. General James Braddock's army was routed within a few miles of Fort Duquesne, throwing the whole frontier open to several years of pounding by the French and Indians. The British seemed to have no overall strategy, and the colonies could not be persuaded to contribute very loyally or enthusiastically to the war effort. Delegates from eight of the colonies, meeting at Albany in 1754, approved Benjamin Franklin's far-sighted plan for intercolonial defense and unity, but this early plan for voluntary union failed to win the support of either the crown or the colonial assemblies. (Its implications, however, were not lost on a later generation of rebels who during the imperial crisis that followed the war with France would again entertain plans for a closer union.)

The situation changed dramatically in 1757 when the vigorous William Pitt assumed direction of the British war effort. Making the conquest of Canada his paramount aim, Pitt organized a series of offensives that culminated in the capture of Quebec by General James Wolfe in 1759. By the time the war ended in Europe, the British were victorious everywhere. In the Peace of Paris (1763), Britain gained French Canada and Spanish Florida, as well as acquisitions in India and elsewhere. Louisiana was transferred from France to Spain.

No one had more reason to rejoice than the British Americans. Suddenly freed from the greatest threat to their security, they now looked west upon an unbounded arena of opportunity lying open to their enterprise. It did not yet occur to them that their new security and confidence might weaken their attachment to the mother country whose emergence as the world's most powerful nation they were now so loyally celebrating.

FOR FURTHER READING:

The final volume of Charles M. Andrews, *The Colonial Period of American History* (4 vols., 1934–1938)*; Oliver M. Dickerson, *The Navigation Acts and the American Revolution* (1951); and Michael Kammen, *Empire and Interest* (1970) are significant analyses of British policy and administration. Jack P. Greene has studied the struggles between colonial governors and assemblies in *The Quest for Power: The Lower House of Assembly in the Southern Royal Colonies, 1689–1776* (1965). And in *"Unite or Die"* (1971) Harry M. Ward has analyzed intercolonial relations from 1690 to 1763. *The Middle Colonies* (1938) are described in a volume by Thomas J. Wertenbaker. Catherine O. Peare has written a good biography of *William Penn* (1957)*; and Frederick B. Tolles deals with the changing role of Philadelphia's Quaker merchants in *Meeting House and Counting House* (1948).* Francis Parkman's *France and England in America* (8 vols., 1851–1892)* is still the classic account of the development of French Canada and the great struggle for empire in North America. The final phase of that struggle and the period after the French and Indian War are delineated magisterially in Lawrence H. Gipson's *The British Empire before the American Revolution* (15 vols., 1936–1970).

---

*Available in paperback edition.

A New Society

3

Within the loose institutional framework of Britain's North American empire, a distinctly new kind of society had been taking shape. Inside this new society, European man was being subtly altered. "What then is the American, this new man?" the French immigrant Crèvecoeur was asking by the 1770s.

THE AMERICANS

Crèvecoeur's American, in the first place, belonged to a numerous and rapidly multiplying people. The American population grew from about a quarter of a million in 1700 to two and a half million by 1775. The majority of these Americans were of English origin. But English immigration slowed in the latter part of the seventeenth century, and the continuing predominance of English stock owed much to the fecundity of Anglo-American mothers.

The spectacular population increase of the eighteenth century was also based on a quickening of non-English immigration. Since the founding of Pennsylvania in the 1680s, Penn's advertising attracted a steadily mounting flow of impoverished peasants from the war-ravaged states of the German Rhineland. By the 1770s there were around two hundred thousand of these industrious German farmers in the North American colonies, and in Pennsylvania they constituted a third of the population.

An even larger tide of immigration began flowing in the first decades of the eighteenth century from Ulster in northern Ireland. These Protestants of Scottish origin, called Scotch-Irish by their descendants to distinguish them from the indigenous Catholic population of the rest of Ireland, had been transplanted to Ulster in the early seventeenth century as part of the English government's campaign to subdue Ireland. By the beginning of the eighteenth century, they were suffering from English restrictions on Irish trade and industry, increasing farm rents, and various civil disabilities against their staunch Presbyterianism. Under these circumstances, Scotch-Irish by the thousands crossed the Atlantic. Concentrated along the frontier as pioneer farmers and aggressive Indian fighters, they made up one-twelfth of the entire population by the 1770s.

Smaller groups from Europe included the Dutch and the French Huguenots. New Netherland had eight thousand Dutch residents at the time of its transfer to English control, and their descendants remained a substantial segment of New York's population. The Huguenots, or French Protestants, began leaving France when the revocation of the Edict of Nantes in 1685 ended religious toleration in that predominantly Catholic country. They did not come to America in large numbers, but their enterprising qualities made many of them successful and prominent. Probably the largest number came to South Carolina, where they were quickly assimilated to Anglicanism and emerged as a major element of the mercantile-planting elite.

Whether English or non-English, the European immigrants of the eighteenth century came mainly from the lower or middling orders of Old World society. Probably half or more of the settlers in the middle colonies crossed the Atlantic as indentured servants. Some were actually kidnapped and sold to America by dealers in human merchandise. Thousands more—orphans, pauper children, and prisoners—were sent abroad by public authorities. Not a few of them chose emigration as a welcome alternative to long imprisonment or execution for minor offenses. Some forty thousand English convicts were transported to North America in the six decades before the Revolution, and in Maryland, convicts made up the bulk of the servant class.

But whatever their legal status, most Europeans who embarked on the long voyage to America were the younger and more vigorous people from their home communities. Once free of indenture, even the lowliest among them was free to rise. Colonel John Lamb, a wealthy merchant and prominent political leader in New York in the 1770s, was the son of a man who had been taken from the gallows in England and transported to America, where he established himself as a solid citizen and laid the basis for his son's later success.

The African slaves, however, came most unwillingly and had no chance to rise, whatever their vigor or ability. By the late seventeenth century, the very prosperity of the European immigrants was creating a growing demand for cheap and easily exploited labor. This demand Yankee and European ship captains hastened to supply. Slavery became established in all the colonies, but the readiest market for the black men and women who survived the horrors of the middle passage from Africa or the West Indies was found in the southern states. There large gangs of Africans could be employed efficiently in the exhausting but routine plantation tasks of tobacco, rice, and indigo culture. By the eve of the Revolution, there were about 600,000 blacks in British North America. In South Carolina they comprised nearly half of the population; in Virginia, fully 40 percent.

AMERICAN ENVIRONMENTS: NEW TOWNS AND THE OLD WEST

The acceleration of immigration and economic activity in the eighteenth century created a diversified society in the American colonies. Towns began to play an increasingly important role in colonial life. The early upsurge of commercial activity in New England was accompanied by a trend toward urbanization as Boston, Newport, and Salem became flourishing trading centers. Philadelphia and New York emerged later as major urban centers but eventually outstripped their predecessors. By the 1770s, Philadelphia's population of nearly forty thousand made it the second largest city in the British empire. New York was the second biggest city of British North America followed by Boston, Charleston, and Newport, the last having a population of around seven thousand. The Chesapeake tobacco country, where ocean-going ships could sail directly up to the individual planter's wharf for trade, was the only area that did not develop a major urban center.

Though the colonial towns never contained more than a tenth of the total population, they exercised great influence. Here were published the newspapers, pamphlets, and almanacs that were almost the only means of general communication in the colonies. Here flourished the artisan class of shoemakers, weavers, hatters, cabinetmakers, and adepts of countless other trades who produced most of the colonists' needs. Here sat the principal courts, and here the lawyers emerged as an influential professional group. The towns in short became the focal points of the economic, intellectual, and political life of the colonies.

While towns were developing along the coast, the pressure of the population increase was forcing a line of settlement far inland. In this hinterland or "Old West," a new kind of society took shape by the middle of the eighteenth century. The distinguishing characteristic of this settlement was that it lay beyond the "fall line," the point where the rivers descended over rapids into the level coastal plain and became navigable. In the absence of good roads or other transportation facilities, the Old West lay too far inland to produce goods for market, and thus became an area of pioneer subsistence farming, isolated from the coastal settlements and the Atlantic world. Nevertheless, to those who peopled it, the Old West seemed an agrarian paradise where the ease of acquiring farms of their own promised a degree of security, well being, and independence that would have been unthinkable in the land-hungry Europe they had left behind.

New England's Old West included the northern and western hill towns and lay away from the coast and the deep inland extension of coastal society along the navigable Connecticut River. The old Puritan pattern of town planting broke down in New England as the provincial governments began disposing of blocks of new towns to land speculators who in turn sold farms to actual settlers.

South of New England, New York's Hudson River was a magnificent highway north into the interior. The Mohawk River, flowing east from the Great Lakes country into the Hudson at Albany, afforded the colonies' only easy avenue through the Appalachian mountains to the Ohio and Mississippi valleys. But fur-trading interests blocked settlement along the Mohawk until the early eighteenth century when the British government sponsored the resettlement of a large number of Germans above Albany.

The main current of German settlement flowed through Philadelphia and on inland to fill the broad and fertile lower valley of the Susquehanna. Beyond the Susquehanna, it washed up against the series of Appalachian ridges that run from the northeast through central Pennsylvania. Diverted down the valleys to the southwest, the Germans settled interior Maryland and crossed the Potomac into Virginia. Here some drifted southeast of the first great Appalachian range, the Blue Ridge, into the rolling Virginia Piedmont, but the main current moved on southwest up the Shenandoah Valley behind the Blue Ridge. By the 1750s, some Germans were pushing southeast from the upper Shenandoah across the Blue Ridge and down into the North Carolina Piedmont.

The German migration was followed and overlapped by the migration of the more aggressive Scotch-Irish. The Scotch-Irish filled in the gaps left by German settlements and then surged beyond them to the west and south. In Pennsylvania these hardy Indian fighters crossed ridge after ridge and filled valley after valley until by the 1770s they were on the waters of the Ohio occupying the area around Pittsburgh. Farther south, in the Carolinas, the Scotch-Irish pushed the Piedmont frontier up against the mountains; while in Virginia they pressed southwest through the mountain valleys toward the headwaters of the Tennessee River.

COLONIAL SOCIETY

The people of the Old West—the Yankee farmers of the New England hill towns, the Germans on the Mohawk, and the Germans and Scotch-Irish in their great curve southwest against the Appalachians from the Susquehanna to Georgia—soon complained of grievances against the older colonial settlements along the coast. The older areas continued to dominate the provincial governments by refusing to give the new settlements the representation to which their population entitled them. In Pennsylvania, the three oldest counties had only a third of the province's population but elected two thirds of the assemblymen. The frontiersmen complained that unrepresentative,

Quaker-dominated assemblies were indifferent to such western problems as the need for an aggressive policy against the Indians. The most extreme case of indifference to frontier needs occurred in South Carolina where the new settlements were separated from the old coastal planting society by a wide belt of sandhills. Though the up-countrymen in the new settlements came to be a majority of the free population, the low-countrymen not only refused them any representatives whatever in the assembly, but also neglected to provide them with courts or local law-enforcement officers.

Not remarkably, the failure to give representation or consideration to the rapidly growing frontier settlements led to sporadic tensions and occasional outbreaks of violence. As early as 1676, Nathaniel Bacon led an armed rebellion in Virginia against the governor, Sir William Berkeley, who had ruled the province autocratically for twenty-five years in alliance with the wealthiest planters. Similar tensions among New Yorkers figured in Jacob Leisler's rebellion at the time of the Glorious Revolution. Great landlords periodically faced mob violence from their tenants in New York, New Jersey, and elsewhere. There was a bitter struggle between debtor and creditor interests in Massachusetts over an inflationary Land Bank scheme in the 1740s. In 1764, the Paxton Boys, an armed mob of frontiersmen, marched on Philadelphia in anger at the pacific Indian policy of the eastern-dominated Pennsylvania assembly. The most spectacular of these outbreaks occurred in North Carolina where the oppressive policies of the local ruling class finally goaded the people of the interior into systematic mobbing of the courts. The governor had to march an army against the insurgents, or the Regulators, as they called themselves, and in a ragged engagement at Alamance in 1771, dispersed them.

The tension between the old and new settlements was only a phase of a more general tension that accompanied the emergence of somewhat sharper class distinctions in the eighteenth century. The Englishmen who came to the New World in the seventeenth century had brought with them the traditional European notion that men should defer to their betters in a society of ranks and orders. Old World distinctions, however, made little sense in a fluid society of mobile individuals, and consequently, class and property qualifications for voting were almost unknown in the early assemblies. Yet the very atmosphere of equal opportunity that eroded Old World notions made for new forms of inequality. In an environment of growing wealth and expanding opportunities, social and economic disparities widened as some men inevitably became more successful than others. Eventually, a disproportionate share of wealth from trade and commercial farming fell into the hands of the most enterprising New England merchants and southern planters. As a result, the relatively simple society of roughly equal yeomen in the seventeenth century became a more highly stratified and differentiated society in the eighteenth.

This process was abetted by the British government, which actively encouraged the growth and political influence of a colonial elite. After the Glorious Revolution London authorities replaced religious qualifications for voting with a property qualification in the new Massachusetts charter, and property qualifications became general in the colonies. Usually a voter had to be a "freeholder," the owner of fifty acres or a town lot. Royal governors generally sought to secure the support of the wealthiest colonials by bestowing important appointments and other favors on them. The provincial councils became the political strongholds of the very rich, while the assemblies were usually controlled by the merely well-to-do. Thus the eighteenth-century provincial governments were generally dominated by a local ruling class, the wealthiest members of which sometimes sided with the governors in disputes with the assemblies.

Yet too much can be made of socio-economic conflict in eighteenth century America. Unquestionably, this was a "deferential society." Marked by extremes in standards and styles of life, fundamentally elitist in character, it was governed by men of privilege whose influence was usually, though not invariably, derived from wealth and property. Pre-Revolutionary America compared very favorably to older and more highly structured contemporary Europe. Although hardly democratic by twentieth century standards, this highly mobile New World society offered remarkably broad economic opportunities, relatively little poverty, and much class fluidity. Except for the anomaly of slavery, there was no real social stratification in the Old World sense. Even the property restriction on suffrage was hardly restrictive in a society of extensive land ownership. In some colonies, where the franchise was open to a vast majority of free male adults, there is evidence to suggest that suffrage was more widespread than the willingness to use it. To be sure, this remarkable breadth of franchise owed much to the availability of inexpensive land and very little to either constitutional theories or modern democratic notions. Even in a society that readily acquiesced to government by gentlemen, colonial rulers could not entirely ignore the needs and aspirations of the general population. Certainly, few historians would argue today that class tension was a principal, or even an important, cause of the Revolution. By the 1760s and 1770s, most scholars now agree, the Americans had already made significant progress toward a more representative social and political order.

THE ENLIGHTENMENT

By the eighteenth century, the Atlantic world's advance into modernity had produced a new climate of thought known as the Enlightenment. The men of this optimistic age believed that a benevolent Creator had laid down certain "natural laws" regulating all phenomena for the purpose of producing human happiness. Men, it was believed, had been endowed by the Creator with powers of observation and reasoning that would enable them to understand and live by these natural laws and thus achieve happiness.

This faith of the Enlightenment received a strong impetus from Sir Isaac Newton's description of the physical world (*Principia Mathematica,* 1687) as a harmonious system of bodies regulated by simple natural laws. Another English thinker, John Locke, most persuasively applied the Newtonian kind of analysis to the moral and political spheres. In *An Essay Concerning Human Understanding* (1690), Locke analyzed the processes of observation and reasoning that enabled man to understand what kinds of behavior were conducive to happiness or, in other words, consistent with the Creator's natural laws for human behavior. Following Locke, thinkers of the Enlightenment exalted "reason" as the faculty that could lead man toward virtue, happiness, and perfection. Analyzing politics (*Two Treatises on Government,* 1689), Locke maintained that natural law ordained a government that rested on the consent of the governed and that respected the inherent "natural rights" of all.

Enlightenment thought was the theoretical expression of the emerging spirit of modernity. Though British North America was too young and too busy a society to give much attention to metaphysical speculation, its people, at the forefront of the movement into modernity, gladly embraced Lockean ideas as explaining what already seemed to them self-evident. Many of the better educated drifted gradually and often unconsciously from the tenets of orthodox Christianity toward *Deism,* the worship of a wise and kindly, but impersonal Creator who is best served by right living.

The influence of Enlightenment thought can be seen everywhere in eighteenth-century American life. The esthetic principles of rational simplicity, order, and balance were exemplified in the "colonial" or "Georgian" architecture of the period. American writers imitated the simple elegance of the English authors Addison and Steele and sought to persuade their readers by rational argument.

The Enlightenment gave a great impetus to the maturing cultural and intellectual life of the colonies. Beginning with the Boston *News-Letter* (1704), newspapers sprang up everywhere; by 1765 there were twenty-five, and every colony except Delaware and New Jersey had at least one. A hungry market developed for pamphlets on every conceivable topic. Artisans organized clubs for discussion and intellectual self-improvement. Booksellers flourished, many gentlemen developed fine private libraries, and following the example of an enterprise launched by Benjamin Franklin in Philadelphia, subscription libraries were established in most of the towns.

By placing such a high value on intellect, the Enlightenment reinforced the religious impulse toward higher education. This combination of influences resulted in the creation of nine colleges by the 1770s. Harvard (1636) was joined by Virginia's William and Mary (1693); Connecticut's Yale (1701); and the Philadelphia Academy, which was originally founded as a secondary school by Benjamin Franklin and became in the 1750s the most modern and secular of the colonial colleges. Five other new colleges owed their founding most immediately to a great religious movement that seemed at first to oppose the spirit of the Enlightenment and modernity.

THE GREAT AWAKENING

The drift toward modernity had steadily eroded the seventeenth-century piety that the settlers had brought to all the early colonies and of which Puritanism was merely the most intense form. Religious observances were as strictly enforced in early Anglican Virginia as in New England, but the prosperity from tobacco soon converted Anglicanism into a bland and undemanding adornment of Virginia's genial country life. It was this kind of Anglicanism that became the "established" or official religion, supported by public taxation, in all the southern colonies and the three lower counties of New York. Anglican religious zeal was apparent only where the missionaries sent out by England's Society for the Propagation of the Gospel were at work and in New England where the Anglicans were an unpopular minority. Perhaps the most conspicuous example of the erosion of piety in the New World was the quick conversion of the Huguenots, those French counterparts of the Puritans, to the polite Anglicanism of the South Carolina planter class. Even the Pennsylvania Quakers, growing wealthy as a result of godly industry, frugality, and honesty, arrived at a point where the counting house seemed to overshadow the meeting house.

The decline of piety can be clearly traced among the theologically sophisticated and articulate Puritan Congregationalists of New England. By the end of the seventeenth century, the Reverend Cotton Mather, the last great defender of the orthodox order, was talking more about the necessity of right living in this world than about man's dependence on God for salvation in the next. The wealthy Boston merchants who founded the Brattle Street Church in 1699 did not require an account of conversion for full membership and chose a minister who preached a "free and catholic" version of Christianity emphasizing morality over piety. As the eighteenth century advanced, the most influential ministers in Boston, Charles Chauncy and Jonathan Mayhew, drifted into the "Arminian" heresy, which diminished human dependence on God by regarding humans as capable of contributing to their own salvation by right living.

But a people conditioned to piety did not adjust easily to the clear, rather bland atmosphere of the dawning Enlightenment. The embers of the old intense faith still smoldered and, in the 1730s and 1740s, were fanned into a bright blaze of religious enthusiasm that burned up and down the length and breadth of the colonies. This American Great Awakening was only part of a general movement in the Protestant world including such parallel phenomena as an upsurge of Pietism in Germany and the Wesleyan revival in England. Beginning as an effort to reassert the earlier extreme piety against the rationalism and optimism of the Enlightenment, these awakenings appealed frankly to the emotions and ended by unconsciously accommodating Christianity to the modern spirit.

The American Great Awakening began in different places. As early as the 1720s, the Reverend Theodore J. Frelinghuysen touched off emotional revivals of religious feeling among the Germans in New Jersey's Raritan Valley. Nearby a group of ardent Presbyterian ministers began trying to stimulate intense religious feeling in place of the cold formalism of Calvinist orthodoxy. And at Northampton, Massachusetts, in 1734, a gifted Congregationalist minister, Jonathan Edwards, stirred up a series of revivals by his powerful appeals to the religious emotions. All of these streams merged into a general revival movement throughout the colonies when England's great evangelist George Whitefield made the first of his American tours in 1739–1740.

The Great Awakening was emotional, popular, and anti-intellectual. The revivalists were often poorly educated, and their fervent exhortations sometimes touched off extravagant reactions—barking, having the "jerks," falling down—by their audiences. Revivalists maintained that a heart open to the divine spirit was more important than a highly trained intellect, and they stirred up much strife by accusing conservative, educated clergymen of spiritual coldness. People responded with enthusiasm, and the more popular Protestant denominations, the Baptists, the "New Light" Presbyterians, and later the Methodists, grew enormously as a refreshing religious pluralism swept across the colonies. In appealing for an emotional response to God's grace, the revival preachers often unconsciously suggested that salvation was available to all and that man played an important part in the process. The Methodists came to espouse these Arminian (and modern) heresies quite consciously.

Despite its anti-intellectual character, the Great Awakening prompted the establishment of three colonial colleges designed to train ministers for revivalist wings of the sponsoring denominations: the Presbyterians' College of New Jersey (Princeton, 1746), the Baptists' College of Rhode Island (Brown, 1764), and the Dutch Reformed Rutgers (1766). Two other colonial colleges were founded under nonrevivalist church auspices: Anglican King's College in New York (Columbia, 1754) and Congregationalist Dartmouth (1769), which began as an Indian school in New Hampshire. For all of its anti-intellectualism, this eighteenth century resurgence of religious enthusiasm contributed mightily to the nation's educational development.

The Awakening had as one of its major leaders the most gifted intellectual in colonial America, Jonathan Edwards. This brilliant Congregationalist minister burned with a personal sense of God's majesty and power that would have been exceptional even among the first-generation Puritans. But he also had an understanding of the intellectual implications of Newtonian-Lockean thought that was equaled by few if any of his generation in either Europe or America. In a series of treatises, he impressively utilized the most advanced thought of his day to reconstruct the old Puritan vision of God. In a very real sense, this remarkable theologian was a transitional figure, a bridge between two ages, who sought to recast and modernize Puritanism in the light of eighteenth century rationalism.

Few in Edwards' generation really understood what he was trying to do. His fellow revivalists gladly adopted his advanced principles of human psychology, which recognized the importance and legitimacy of emotion. But most Americans had moved too far into modernity to share, even in seasons of religious exaltation, his vision of the beauty and fitness of God's awful sovereignty and sinful man's helpless dependence on the miracle of divine grace.

"THIS NEW MAN"

Crèvecoeur's "new man," then, was a product of New World opportunity, whether the opportunity to acquire a farm of his own in the Old West, to grow rich planting tobacco, to trade with the West Indies, or to achieve dignity and independence as an artisan in one of the growing colonial towns. He welcomed the optimistic tendencies of Enlightenment thought as something his New World experience had made self-evident. In politics, he stoutly defended the English tradition of individual rights and aspired to control the representative institutions of provincial government in the interest of his group. In religion, he tended consciously toward Deism or Arminianism if educated; otherwise he reveled in the emotionalism of the Great Awakening while moving less consciously away from the orthodox piety of his fathers.

"The American, this new man," may be seen in his most fully developed form in the *Autobiography* of Benjamin Franklin. This son of a Boston candlemaker sat in Cotton Mather's congregation as a boy, assimilated Enlightenment thought while working on his brother's newspaper and while sowing wild oats in London, and returned to win wealth and prestige as a Philadelphia printer while still in his forties. Retiring from business, this wise, humane, and practical man spent the rest of his life in scientific experiments that explained the nature of electricity, in developing a host of practical devices and projects for the benefit and improvement of his fellow citizens, and in public service culminating with attendance at the birth of a new nation.

The fascination of Franklin lies largely in the fact that he showed to perfection so many traits that were characteristic of his fellow countrymen.

"*He* is an American," wrote Crèvecoeur, "who, leaving behind him all his ancient prejudices and manners, receives new ones from the new mode of life he has embraced, the new government he obeys, and the new rank he holds. . . . Here the rewards of his industry follow with equal steps the progress of his labor. . . . Here religion demands but little of him. . . . The American is a new man, who acts upon new principles; he must therefore entertain new ideas, and form new opinions. From involuntary idleness, servile dependence, penury, and useless labor, he has passed to toils of a different nature, rewarded by ample subsistence.—This is an American."

FOR FURTHER READING:

J. Hector St. John de Crèvecoeur recorded his impressions of American life in the eighteenth century in *Letters from an American Farmer* (1782).* European immigrants to America in the colonial period are described in Marcus Lee Hansen, *The Atlantic Migration, 1607–1860* (1940)*; while Abbott Emerson Smith's *Colonists in Bondage* (1947) deals with indentured servants. The development of slavery and of white men's attitudes toward black men in America are analyzed in Winthrop D. Jordan, *White over Black: American Attitudes toward the Negro, 1550–1812* (1968). Daniel J. Boorstin presents a suggestive interpretation of the unique institutions and attitudes that emerged in the New World environment in *The Americans: The Colonial Experience* (1958).* The development of colonial towns is described in Carl Bridenbaugh, *Cities in the Wilderness, 1625–1742* (1938).* The best introduction to the Old West, as well as to Frederick Jackson Turner's famous "frontier thesis," is the first three chapters of his volume of collected essays, *The Frontier in American History* (1920).* The Old West of the southern colonies is described, along with the tidewater societies of Virginia and South Carolina, in Carl Bridenbaugh's *Myths and Realities: Societies of the Colonial South* (1952)*; Wilcomb Washburn's *The Governor and the Rebel* (1957) is a recent critical interpretation of Bacon's rebellion. Richard M. Brown examines the *South Carolina Regulators* (1963). Leonard W. Labaree's *Conservatism in Early American History* (1948)* traces the growing influence of the upper classes in colonial politics, while Carl Bridenbaugh deals with the mechanic classes of the towns in *The Colonial Craftsman* (1950). Jackson T. Main's *Social Structure of Revolutionary America* (1965) and Robert E. Brown's *Middle-Class Democracy and the Revolution in Massachusetts* (1955) are major revisionist studies of colonial social, economic, and political developments. The intellectual and theological transformation of New England Congregationalism may be fol-

---

*Available in paperback edition.

lowed in Conrad Wright, *The Beginnings of Unitarianism in America* (1955)*, Alan Heimert has written an arresting interpretation of *Religion and the American Mind: From the Great Awakening to the Revolution* (1966). Edward H. Davidson's *Jonathan Edwards* (1968) is a brief biography, and Perry Miller's *Jonathan Edwards* (1949)* is a brilliant interpretation of his thought. Carl Van Doren has written the best biography of *Benjamin Franklin* (1941),* but a sense of Franklin's quality is best derived from his own fascinating *Autobiography* (many editions).*

---

*Available in paperback edition.

EVENTS LEADING TO THE REVOLUTION

British Actions		American Actions
Revenue (Sugar) Act—laying duties for revenue.	**1764**	
Stamp Act—revenue stamps.	**1765**	Mob action. Nonimportation agreements.
Repeal of Stamp Act. Declaratory Act—asserting right of Parliament to legislate for colonies in all respects.	**1766**	Nonimportation suspended.
Townshend duties—revenue duties on various articles.	**1767**	Mob action. Nonimportation agreements.
Repeal of Townshend duties, except duty on tea.	**1770**	Boston Massacre. Suspension of nonimportation.
	1772	Committees of correspondence organized.
Tea Act—giving East India Co. monopoly of colonial tea trade.	**1773**	Mob action. Boston Tea Party.
Intolerable acts: 1) closing port of Boston. 2) restricting self-government in Massachusetts. 3) allowing royal officers to be tried in England. 4) allowing royal troops to requisition private buildings for quarters. Quebec Act—continuing non-representative government in Quebec, tolerating Roman Catholicism in Quebec, and incorporating Ohio Valley in Quebec.	**1774**	First Continental Congress 1) rejects Galloway's plan of union. 2) adopts Continental Association, establishing committees of safety to enforce commercial nonintercourse with England. 3) encourages Massachusetts to establish revolutionary government and prepare for military defense.
Lexington-Concord — British troops skirmish with Massachusetts militiamen.	**1775**	Committees of safety seize control. Second Continental Congress —appoints Washington to command continental army at Boston.

Toward Revolution
1763–1775

4

At the close of the French and Indian War in 1763, the inhabitants of British North America considered themselves patriotic and loyal British subjects. Under British rule, the colonies had become flourishing and prosperous societies, affording to ordinary individuals well-being and opportunities without parallel in Europe and perhaps anywhere in previous human history. The British navigation laws had, by and large, fostered colonial prosperity; British fleets and armies had defended colonials against their Spanish, French, and Indian enemies; and a benevolent (or careless) home government had allowed them to develop representative institutions and to regulate their domestic affairs with only minor interference. Nourished on the British Whig tradition stemming from the Glorious Revolution of 1688, the American colonists thought of their political rights and liberties as British rights and liberties.

Yet within twelve years, these same loyal British subjects were at war with the mother country. Although their relations with Britain until 1763 were relatively harmonious, the crisis of the next dozen years taught them that they had long since developed a deep attachment to the society they were creating in the colonies. Somewhat to their own surprise they learned that they really valued the British connection only as far as, and as long as, it was compatible with their desire to preserve and perfect their free and semiautonomous American society. In one of history's most notorious instances of bad timing, British officials had chosen to tighten the lax administration of the Empire at the very moment when Americans were beginning to feel their own separate identity. Colonial cries of imperial "despotism" and "oppression" were doubtless unwarranted, but the stiffening of British policy was at best untimely.

THE NEW IMPERIAL POLICY

When Britain emerged victorious from the great Anglo-French wars, there were a number of conditions that supported a new and more vigorous imperial policy. First, King George III, enthroned in 1760, was an ambitious and conscientious monarch who desired to play a larger role in governmental affairs than had his predecessors. Through manipulation of royal patronage and maneuvering of Parliamentary elections he tried to reestablish the royal influence that earlier monarchs had exercised by right. Unfortunately, the King and his ministers proved to be less flexible and astute in dealing with the colonists than their easygoing predecessors had been. Yet probably any British ministry would have sought to strengthen the imperial system at this time. During the war, the colonists had irritated the British by their reluctance to furnish troops, supplies, and money and in too many cases had actually prospered by trading with the enemy. Moreover, the Empire had been greatly enlarged, and more efficient regulation seemed necessary everywhere if the colonial territories were to serve their purpose of benefiting the mother country.

The most pressing immediate problem was that of revenue to pay off the crushing debt incurred during the war and to support the increased costs of defending and administering the enlarged empire. Compared with English landowners, the colonists were virtually untaxed, and in London it seemed only fair that they should bear some of the heavy tax burden required for the defense of American territory.

The new imperial policy that grew out of these conditions was inaugurated by the ministry of George Grenville in the years 1763–1765. A permanent military force was established in the American colonies, the control over Indian relations was transferred from the colonial governments to imperial officials, settlement on the western frontier was restricted and placed under imperial regulation, and the colonial assemblies were forbidden to issue paper money. Particularly important was the Revenue Act of 1764 (often called the Sugar Act) that for the first time avowedly levied import duties for revenue rather than regulation of trade and provided machinery insuring that the duties would really be collected.

Most disturbing was the duty on molasses from the French West Indies. For years New England merchants had been evading an earlier duty levied under the Molasses Act of 1733 in order to import molasses for manufacture of rum. The new molasses duty was half of the old, but it was rigorously enforced, and the effect was to cripple the flourishing commerce of New England. Shocked by the sudden vigor of imperial control after decades of "salutary neglect," the colonists quickly took the position that they could not rightfully be taxed except by their own representatives.

Either underestimating the strength of colonial opposition or not caring how strong it was, Grenville pushed through Parliament in 1765 the even more provocative Stamp Act. This measure required the colonists to purchase revenue stamps and affix them to all kinds of legal and commercial documents, newspapers, almanacs, playing cards, dice, and liquor licenses. This was taxation (without representation) in a highly visible and odious form. Moreover, it offended most those who were most influential in shaping colonial opinion—merchants, lawyers, printers, and tavern keepers. An explosion of protest indicated not only how averse the colonists were to taxation of any kind, but also how attached they were to the representative tradition of British Whiggery and to the home rule they had enjoyed with so little interference.

Colonial mobs blocked a sale of stamps and intimidated stamp agents into resigning. A more effective reaction, in the long run, was a nonimportation agreement sponsored by the colonial merchants that led to a boycott of British goods. This had such an effect on British manufacturers and exporting merchants that Parliament was persuaded in 1766 to repeal the Stamp Act. But Parliament did not surrender its claim to tax the colonists, for repeal was accompanied by a Declaratory Act asserting Parliament's right to legislate for the colonies in any and all respects.

That this was no idle claim was shown the very next year, 1767, when Charles Townshend, Chancellor of the Exchequer, pushed through Parliament the so-called Townshend Acts levying duties for revenue on a new class of previously untaxed articles. The new taxes were rendered more unpalatable by provisions for further strengthening the enforcement and collection machinery and by the stipulation that revenues from the act would be used to pay the salaries of royal officials in the colonies, thus robbing the colonial assemblies of their most potent weapon, the power to withhold salaries from uncooperative royal officers. Again the Americans resorted to mob action and the proven weapon of nonimportation, and again, in 1770, Parliament backed down, repealing all the duties except the one on tea.

Most of the colonists were willing to accept this action as settling the controversy, and the next few years were a period of prosperity and relative peace between colonies and mother country. Except for New England merchants and, later, wealthy Virginia planters—two of the most powerful and articulate segments of the population—the trade regulations adopted after 1763 imposed no significant hardship on the colonial economy. Yet the British ministers were badly deceived if they supposed that imperial relations were as cordial as they had once been. During the seven years of controversy, the Americans had become increasingly conscious of their separate identity and common interest. They had been able to defy the home government successfully, and they were now more committed than perhaps they themselves realized to the principles of self-government without Parliamentary intervention.

THE RADICALS

Especially dangerous to continued harmony was a small but well-organized and ably led group of American "radicals" who, since the 1760s, had opposed any British effort to tax or regulate colonial affairs. Most of these radicals were the men who had led the more violent phases of the agitation against the Stamp Act and the Townshend duties, and their hostility toward the British was often combined with a democratic resentment toward their more aristocratic fellow Americans. In Virginia, for example, Patrick Henry's radical opposition to the Stamp Act was simultaneously a challenge to the control of the House of Burgesses by the most conservative wing of the planter oligarchy. In Boston the radical leader Samuel Adams, though strongly backed by the wealthy merchant John Hancock, drew most of his support from mechanics and shopkeepers who welcomed an opportunity to strike at aristocratic Bostonians with close royal ties. Charleston mechanics and other "middling" types constituted most of the radical group in their city, although their leader was the young aristocrat Christopher Gadsden.

Americans of every social level had joined in the protest against the Stamp Act and Townshend duties, but the wealthier and more conservative of them had been dismayed by the excesses of mob action. These more conservative American Whigs were satisfied when Parliament repealed all the offensive duties except the one on tea, while the radicals insisted on continuing the agitation against the tea duty. The most dangerous of the radical leaders was that superb organizer, agitator, and propagandist Samuel Adams. Through his control of the Boston town meeting, Adams kept Boston in an uproar even as quiet returned to other areas. By exploiting incidents like the "Boston Massacre" of 1770 (where an unruly crowd goaded a small party of British soldiers into firing and killing three persons), Adams poured out a constant stream of distorted propaganda designed to keep the colonists alarmed over encroaching British tyranny.

Simultaneously, Adams and his allies were creating a radical organization. Operating from his base in the Boston town meeting, Adams induced other Massachusetts towns to establish "committees of correspondence" to promote intercolonial resistance to imperial policy. The idea spread and, shortly, dissident Virginians urged the establishment of a provincial committee of correspondence in every colony. Naturally these committees came to be dominated by men with relatively radical attitudes. While the radicals were unable to dispel the complacency that prevailed in the prosperous years 1770–1773, they created an organization that could seize the initiative whenever an opportunity arose.

THE SECOND CRISIS

Opportunity came when the British ministry of Lord North, in all innocence, undertook to aid the British East India Company by pushing through Parliament the Tea Act of 1773. The company was given the exclusive privilege of selling its tea directly to American consumers without paying the English export tax, thus increasing the company's profits, lowering the price of tea to Americans, eliminating widespread smuggling and evasion of the Ameri can tea duty, and depriving American importing merchants of any share in the tea trade.

The resentment of the conservative American merchants drove them again into alliance with the radicals, and the radicals made the most of this opportunity to renew violent agitation. Convinced that the British were using lower tea prices to seduce Americans into surrendering their liberties, the radicals again resorted to mob action which was climaxed by the famous Tea Party in Boston. Boarding the vessels that had arrived with East India tea, Samuel Adams' followers dumped Boston's entire consignment overboard. These defiant and destructive acts were shocking to many Americans, but patriot leaders and the public in general agreed that to accept the Tea Act was to risk conceding Parliament's right to tax the colonies for revenue.

The British government, on the other hand, was now convinced that only punitive action could bring the rebellious colonists to heel. Promptly, Parliament passed a series of four "Coercive Acts" (known to Americans as the "Intolerable Acts"), closing the port of Boston until the Bostonians paid for the tea they had destroyed, drastically reducing the representative and self-governing features of the Massachusetts provincial government, allowing royal officials to be tried in England when accused of crimes in the colonies, and permitting the British army to requisition American buildings as quarters. However logical and necessary these measures appeared to a London government faced with colonial insubordination, they confirmed American suspicions of Britian's despotic designs. A fifth measure followed that, although not punitive in nature nor actually one of the Coercive Acts, proved no more tolerable to the colonists. Through the Quebec Act of 1774, Parliament added to the Canadian province western territory claimed by several of the colonies, continued the autocratic rule in Quebec that had prevailed under the French, and afforded complete religious toleration to the province's Catholic population.

These measures threw the radical propaganda machine and committee organization into high gear. "The cause of Boston is the cause of all British America" was the message trumpeted everywhere during the spring and summer of 1774. Food, fuel, and money were collected for the relief of the beleaguered Bostonians, local nonimportation agreements sprang up on all sides, and a proposal for a continental congress to coordinate resistance won quick endorsement from the assemblies or from extralegal meetings of the assemblymen in most of the colonies.

THE FIRST CONTINENTAL CONGRESS

In September, 1774, an extralegal Congress of delegates from every colony except Georgia assembled in Philadelphia. Because the delegates had been chosen at the height of the anti-British excitement following the Intolerable Acts, the already organized radicals gained a majority in the Congress over the confused and unorganized conservatives. Nevertheless, the conservatives were ably led and made a strong fight for moderate measures. The most promising conservative proposal was Joseph Galloway's plan for establishing a colonial union under a royally appointed president-general and a council representing the colonial assemblies, with the latter having power to legislate for the colonies and to veto Parliamentary legislation affecting the colonies. But when the Congress narrowly refused to endorse this plan, the radicals were given a green light to proceed with more aggressive measures.

After a hard fight, they persuaded Congress to adopt the Continental Association, a detailed plan for nonimportation, nonconsumption, and nonexportation of goods between the colonies and Great Britain. To enforce the plan, Congress authorized every county or town to elect extralegal committees of safety. These committees were to circulate the Association among all citizens for endorsement and then to single out violators for boycott and for denunciation as "enemies to the rights of British America." Goods imported in violation of the Association could be seized, and the work of the local committees was to be coordinated in each colony by a provincial Congress and a provincial committee of safety.

During the winter and spring of 1774–1775, the radicals began vigorously implementing this revolutionary scheme in every colony. A drastic decline in British imports quickly demonstrated the Association's effectiveness as an instrument of economic warfare; it was probably even more important as an instrument of political persuasion and coercion.

While nearly all Americans favored efforts to secure concessions from the British government, perhaps only a minority supported the aggressive tactics of the radicals. Many were decidedly hostile to any action that threatened to break the British connection, and many more were simply confused or indifferent. But the Association and its committee system gave the organized and purposeful radicals a highly efficient means of committing the passive and often hostile majority to their program.

Though the committees were supposed to be elected, they were frequently in fact self-constituted bodies of the local radical leaders and in some cases were merely the old committees of correspondence continued under a new name. Where public denunciation failed to secure compliance with the Association, committees did not hesitate to employ threats and even physical violence. As the revolutionary crisis deepened, the committees increasingly assumed the powers of government, fixing prices, levying fines, and taking charge of local militia units.

Yet radical control was far from complete by the spring of 1775. The mercantile and officeholding aristocracy put up strong opposition in the northeastern port towns; up-country Carolina farmers were disposed to side with the royal governors against the provincial politicians who had oppressed them in the past and who were now leading the radical movement; and everywhere there were wide areas still so unexcited over British oppression that the radicals had made little headway. An additional impulse was needed and once again Samuel Adams' Massachusetts radicals supplied it.

WAR

British "despotism" was anything but a remote and idle threat to the Massachusetts radicals during the winter and spring of 1774–1775. As part of the British plan to crush the spirit of insubordination in Massachusetts, additional troops were sent to Boston, and their commander, General Thomas Gage, was designated military governor of the province. With the endorsement of the Continental Congress, the radicals took the momentous step of establishing a revolutionary provincial government under the old suspended charter and began training troops and collecting military supplies.

The inevitable clash came on the morning of April 19, 1775, when General Gage sent a detachment of British soldiers from Boston to seize the powder and arms that had been collected at nearby Concord and to arrest Samuel Adams and John Hancock. Warned by Paul Revere and William Dawes, the farmer "minutemen" of Lexington and Concord boldly challenged the British regulars, and by the time the harassed soldiers had run the gauntlet of farmers' muskets on the road back to Boston, they had lost 273 dead, wounded, and missing.

Instantly the radicals sent special riders flying through the colonies with exaggerated accounts of the massacre of innocent Massachusetts farmers by bloodthirsty British soldiers. Everywhere there was a burst of patriotic indignation, enabling the radical-dominated committees of safety to gain complete control. Royal governors were driven from their posts, troops were drilled, and royal forts and powder magazines were seized.

On May 10, a Second Continental Congress was hastily assembled in Philadelphia. As a gesture to the timid, this radical-dominated body sent an "Olive Branch Petition" to the king as a final appeal for a peaceful settlement. When this petition was refused, the last vestiges of loyalty to the crown dissolved. Rapidly, a once-respected monarch was becoming, in Tom Paine's memorable words, a "royal brute." With all other acceptable avenues of resistance now closed, Congress prepared for war. The thousands of armed New Englanders who had rushed to besiege Gage's redcoats from the hills overlooking Boston were taken under the aegis of the Congress. And George Washington, who came to Philadelphia in the blue uniform of the Virginia militia, was named to command the emerging continental army.

What Caused the American Revolution and How Revolutionary Was It?

Nineteenth-century historians rarely quarreled about the origin and nature of the Revolution. The war for American independence, they concluded, was a just and truly revolutionary struggle against the tyrannical and reactionary British imperial system. The colonial triumph ushered in a new era of human liberty, brotherhood, and democracy. Indeed, to George Bancroft, author of the authoritative and justly celebrated History of the United States *(12 vols., 1834–1882), the Americans were God's chosen people and their Revolution was part of the "grand design of Providence," a noble prelude to the "regeneration" of humankind.*

In the 1890s, the patriotic distortions of this traditional view were challenged by two "schools" of historical interpretation: the imperialist and the progressive. Influenced by a turn-of-the-century spirit of Anglo-American accord, such imperialist historians as Charles McLean Andrews (The Colonial Background of the American Revolution *[1924]) were more critical of colonial behavior than English policy. The quarrel with England, they argued, could be interpreted correctly only within the broad context of the British empire as a whole. Examining the imperial as well as the colonial point of view, they sympathetically concluded that the British Trade and Navigation Acts were not oppressive and that Parliament's efforts to tax the Americans were justifiable.*

While imperialist scholars sought for the origins of the Revolution in political and constitutional issues within the empire, the progressives focused on social and economic issues within the colonies themselves. Products of the reform mentality of the late nineteenth and early twentieth centuries, these liberal scholars addressed not only the question of home rule but the question of who should rule at home. Indeed, as Carl Becker, the greatest of the progressive historians, expressed it (History of Political Parties in the Province of New York *[1909]) the American Revolution was actually two revolutions in one. The first, an external revolution, involved a conflict of economic interests between Great Britain and the American colonies. The second, an internal revolution, involved a class conflict between the "haves" and "have-nots" of colonial society. Such distinguished historians as Lawrence Gipson* (The British Empire before the American Revolution *[15 vols., 1936–1970]) and Merrill Jensen* (The Founding of a Nation, *[1968]) still analyze the Revolution from the imperialist and progressive persuasions. But in recent decades new directions in historical thought have challenged these older viewpoints. In the 1950s, for example, so-called consensus historians, apparently mirroring the conservatism of the Cold War period, disputed progressive notions of class conflict. Arguing that American society was far more democratic, affluent, and fluid than the progressives had believed, such consensus histories as Robert E. Brown's* Middle-Class Democracy and the Revolution in Massachusetts *(1955) and Daniel J. Boorstin's* The Genius of American Politics *(1953) concluded that the Revolution was essentially a conservative movement waged to protect traditional American rights and liberties from a changing and increasingly arbitrary British policy.*

Edmund S. Morgan (The Birth of the Republic *[1956]), Bernard Bailyn* (The Ideological Origins of the American Revolution *[1967]) and other scholars who stress the causal importance of ideas have also discounted internal social and economic cleavage theories. Colonial patriots, Bailyn wrote, although not unmindful of their pocketbooks, were genuinely alarmed by the changing course of imperial policy and deeply affected by the antiauthoritarian tradition of English thought. Possessed of "real fears, real anxieties, [and] a sense of real danger," they viewed their opposition to Parliamentary taxation as a struggle of liberty against the corrupting force of power. Thus the new intellectual history has returned to the nineteenth-century conclusion that constitutional rights and lofty ideals lie at the heart of the American revolution. Although embracing neither Bancroft's patriotic and religious excesses, nor his undue criticism of British policy, it finds the old master correct when he argued that the colonists revolted in the name of liberty.*

Recently, radical or New Left scholars have contributed yet another dimension to the debate. Not without justice they indict their fellow historians for overemphasizing the attitudes and behavior of social and economic elites to the neglect of the great mass of human society. In the radical view the Revolution can be correctly interpreted only from "the bottom up," the vantage point of colonial nonelites. Regardless of the perspective, however, there is little likelihood of unanimity of historical opinion.

FOR FURTHER READING:

John C. Miller's *Origins of the American Revolution* (1943)* offers a narrative overview of the events leading to conflict, and John R. Alden has assessed the role of *The South in the Revolution, 1763–1789* (1957). Both J. Franklin Jameson, *The American Revolution Considered as a Social Movement* (1926) and A. M. Schlesinger, Sr., *The Colonial Merchants and the American Revolution* (1918), are dated but still command attention. J. R. Pole's *Political Representation in England and the Origins of the Ameri-*

---

*Available in paperback edition.

can Republic (1966) is a work of great importance, and Pauline Maier's *From Resistance to Revolution* (1972) provides a new synthesis of the role of colonial radicals in the development of hostilities. Bernhard Knollenberg traces *The Origins of the American Revolution;* Edmund S. and Helen M. Morgan brilliantly analyze *The Stamp Act Crisis* (1953); Hiller B. Zobel surveys *The Boston Massacre* (1970); and Benjamin W. Labaree details *The Boston Tea Party* (1964). John C. Miller's *Sam Adams* (1936) is a readable biography of an important figure.

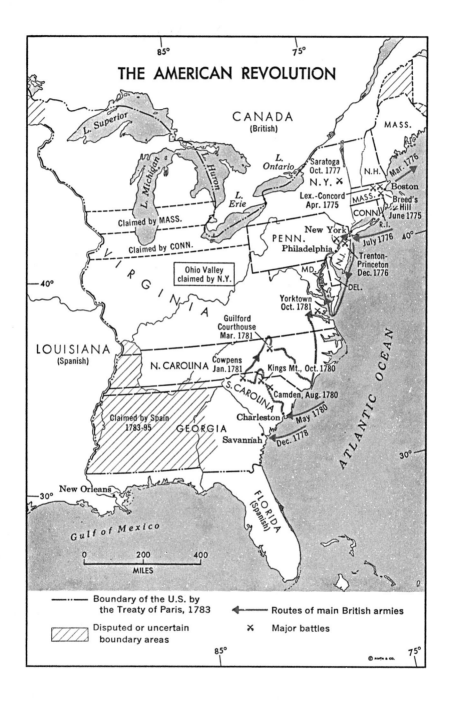

THE AMERICAN REVOLUTION

85° 75°

CANADA
(British)

L. Superior

MASS.

L. Michigan

L. Huron

L. Ontario

Saratoga
Oct. 1777

N.H.

Mar. 1776

N.Y. ✕

Boston

L. Erie

Lex.-Concord
Apr. 1775

MASS.
CONN.

Breed's
Hill
June 1775

Claimed by MASS.

New York

R.I.

Claimed by CONN.

PENN.

July 1776 40°

Philadelphia

N.J.

Trenton-
Princeton
Dec. 1776

Ohio Valley
claimed by N.Y.

MD.

V I R G I N I A

40°

DEL.

Yorktown
Oct. 1781

Guilford
Courthouse
Mar. 1781

LOUISIANA
(Spanish)

N. CAROLINA

Cowpens
Jan. 1781

Kings Mt., Oct. 1780

Camden, Aug. 1780

S. CAROLINA

Claimed by Spain
1783-95

GEORGIA

Charleston

May 1780

Savannah

Dec. 1778

A T L A N T I C   O C E A N

30°

New Orleans

30°

FLORIDA
(Spanish)

Gulf of Mexico

0   200   400
MILES

—··— Boundary of the U.S. by
the Treaty of Paris, 1783

◀━━━ Routes of main British armies

▨ Disputed or uncertain
boundary areas

✕ Major battles

85° 75°

Independence Achieved
1775–1783

5

THE FIRST YEAR OF WAR

The military struggle began slowly, and during the first year no really decisive engagements occurred. In June, 1775, shortly before Washington arrived to take command of the poorly organized American forces on the hills surrounding Boston, General Gage managed to drive his besiegers from one of their strongest positions, Breed's Hill. But the misnamed Battle of Bunker Hill cost the British some 40 percent of their force, and these frightful losses demonstrated that the Americans could not easily be dislodged. During the months that followed Washington methodically converted his untrained militiamen into a disciplined army and tightened the ring around the British.

With Gage's army encircled in Boston, the ebullient Americans undertook, during the winter of 1775–1776, a two-pronged offensive against Canada. The valiant forces led by Richard Montgomery and Benedict Arnold surmounted great hardships and won some early successes; but in the end the reluctance of the Canadian population to join the rebellion forced a retreat.

In the first year of the war, perhaps the most important struggle was within the colonies themselves. Because neither the British nor the American leaders were prepared to compromise, few doubted that the issue could be resolved by means short of full-scale war. But many colonists remained deeply loyal to the British and, despite the coercion of the Revolutionaries, unwilling to wage open war against the mother country. Nearly one hundred thousand of these Loyalists were forced into exile, while those who remained suffered ostracism, disfranchisement, confiscation of property, and other penalties for their loyalty to the King. Still, the American Revolution produced none of the wholesale imprisonments or executions of dissidents that have marked other revolutions, and the penalties imposed on the Loyalists do not seem disproportionate to the threat they represented to the success of the Revolutionary cause.

In March, 1776, General Gage finally abandoned the increasingly difficult task of holding Boston and sailed away with his army and hundreds of Loyalists to the British stronghold at Halifax, Nova Scotia. His departure did not mark a decisive American victory, but instead the approaching end of a year of stalemate in which each side had consolidated its position and prepared for the real struggle yet to come. During that fortunate year of respite a new American nation animated by fresh and exciting ideals had been coming to birth.

"CONCEIVED IN LIBERTY"

Until months after the Revolutionary War began, few Americans admitted that they sought independence from England. Yet the pressure of events increasingly forced them into independent acts and steadily prepared them for an open break.

The question of independence was connected in an indirect, but important, way with the acceleration of democratic tendencies inherent in the Revolutionary movement. While "home rule" was the primary issue in the Revolution, a political upsurge of the "lower orders" raised the important secondary issue of *who* should rule at home?" The Liberty Boys who rioted against the Stamp Act or the Townshend duties were making a bid for political status. Perhaps more important, the Revolutionary agitation opened an avenue by which ambitious men of the "middling sort"—Samuel Adams, Patrick Henry, and their counterparts in other colonies—could rise to power and influence. The Revolutionary movement offered such "new men" an opportunity to gain power by espousing radical measures and appealing indirectly to the inchoate democratic aspirations of those heretofore without influence in government.

The success of these "new men" was due in considerable measure to a favorable climate of ideas. The Revolutionary era was one of those periods in history when ideas have had great consequences. All Americans, including the most conservative and aristocratic, believed that the Glorious Revolution of 1688 and its great Bill of Rights had guaranteed to every British citizen certain rights—especially rights of "liberty" and "property"—upon which no monarch or government could rightfully infringe. The colonies pegged their opposition to the New Imperial Policy on the claim that it was an arbitrary violation of these rights. "Liberty and Property" became the slogan of the Revolutionary movement.

These Whig slogans carried democratic implications that could be applied to government within as well as without the colonies. When the colonial leaders argued for the Whig principle of "no taxation without representation" in imperial relations, it required no great imagination for inadequately represented Americans to apply the same argument to domestic affairs or even to expand it into the more general principle that government should be representative of the governed, meaning all the governed.

These democratic implications of the British Whig tradition were powerfully reinforced by the larger stream of thought of the Enlightenment. Confident that the Creator desired human happiness, the men of the eighteenth century were drifting toward the notion that all men were equal in their "natural rights" and that the only just end of government was to maintain a state of society in which every man could enjoy his rights to the fullest possible extent. Since liberty was the most precious of these rights, government should be restricted to the smallest possible compass that would enable it to keep individuals from invading each other's liberty, and since all men were potentially rational, government should rest on the consent of the governed. The second of John Locke's *Two Treatises on Government* (1689) was a most trenchant justification of revolution on the basis of the natural rights argument.

During the later stages of the Revolutionary crisis, the colonial leaders broadened the basis for their claim to autonomy from their rights as British citizens, according to the Whig tradition, to their rights as men, according to the natural rights tradition. Directly or indirectly, Americans were thinking in Lockean terms as they decided for revolution, drafted their Declaration of Independence, and established a new governmental system.

This is not to say that the Americans rebelled against England because they deliberately sought to extend democracy at home. Rather, large segments of the population rallied to the movement for colonial autonomy more enthusiastically than they might otherwise have done because they were aroused by the democratic implications of Revolutionary rhetoric. Moreover, in the process of creating broad support for their movement, the Revolutionary leaders were compelled to seek the participation of groups that had previously played little part in public life. Consequently the new provincial congresses that were organized in the early months of the war had a far broader membership than the colonial assemblies and councils that they succeeded.

This rise of the lower orders affected the ways in which members of the old colonial ruling group reacted to the Revolutionary crisis. Many of them were alarmed into being Loyalists. A larger number (conservative Whigs) continued to furnish leadership to the Revolutionary movement but resisted independence. They hoped to win colonial autonomy while restoring the British connection as a means of preserving the predominance of gentlemen within the colonies. A third segment of the gentry (radical Whigs) were so deeply infected with the Revolutionary ideology that they worked closely with the "new men" who spoke for the lower orders, espousing independence and paving the way for a new distribution of political power.

It was this last group of men, especially Richard Henry Lee of Virginia and Samuel and John Adams of Massachusetts, who controlled the Continental Congress in the early years of the war. On the question of independence, they were aided by the drift of events. The British government showed little disposition to conciliate the Americans and every disposition to wage vigorous war against them. The importance of aid from Britain's ancient enemy France became increasingly apparent, and it was hoped that independence might pave the way for a French alliance. Finally, Americans of all classes were gradually beginning to sense the exciting possibility of building a new and independent society based on natural rights and the implicitly democratic principles of Revolutionary rhetoric. How rapidly this feeling had spread was demonstrated by the tremendous public response to Thomas Paine's pamphlet *Common Sense,* published in January, 1776. Advocating both independence and democracy, Paine's slashing pamphlet sold several hundred thousand copies.

Paine did not create the sentiment for independence; he merely crystallized an unspoken but rapidly growing attitude. Once catapulted into the arena of open debate, the idea of independence rapidly overcame conservative opposition. On July 2, the Continental Congress resolved that "these United States are, and of right ought to be, free and independent states"; two days later the Declaration of Independence was adopted.

Drafted by Thomas Jefferson, with the help of Benjamin Franklin and John Adams, this memorable document was for the most part a long and exaggerated catalogue of British violations of American rights. Designed in large part as propaganda for world consumption, the Declaration offered no subtle interpretations of events. It was the hapless George III, not Parliament, the source of most colonial grievances, who was made the villain of the piece. What made the Declaration a momentous factor in history, however, was its opening section, which distilled in a few sentences of enduring prose the essence of the Lockean, natural rights theory of government: "We hold these truths to be self-evident, that all men are created equal, that they are endowed by their Creator with certain inalienable Rights, that among these are Life, Liberty, and the pursuit of Happiness. That to secure these rights, Governments are instituted among Men, deriving their just powers from the consent of the governed. That whenever any Form of Government becomes destructive of these ends, it is the Right of the People to alter or abolish it." Much of subsequent American history was to be a working out of the implications of the principles so ringingly enunciated here.

THE NEW STATE CONSTITUTIONS

By the time the Declaration of Independence was adopted, four of the colonies had already applied its liberal principles in the drafting of new state constitutions. Shortly, all the other states followed suit, except Rhode Island and Connecticut which continued to operate under their unusually liberal colonial charters. The very drafting of written constitutions was unprecedented and significant. With British authority destroyed, Americans were free to perform in literal fact the act that lay at the root of all legitimate government according to Lockean theory: they entered into a "social contract." The new state constitutions were conceived of as voluntary compacts among all the people creating governments of limited and explicitly defined powers. In several states, the people elected special conventions to draft the fundamental compacts; in several others, the constitutions were submitted for popular ratification; but in a majority of cases, the existing provincial congresses themselves drafted and promulgated the new constitutions.

However adopted, the new constitutions uniformly reflected the distrust of governmental power, and especially executive power, that arose from the Enlightenment's liberalism and from the colonists' experience with British authority. Most states followed the distinguished example of Virginia by including a Bill of Rights specifying in detail those rights of the citizen—freedom of speech, freedom of the press, trial by jury, and the like—that no government could rightly abridge. All the constitutions sought to minimize the danger of arbitrary power by building "checks and balances" and a "separation of powers" into the very structure of government. The executive, legislative, and judicial functions were exercised by separate bodies, and, except in Pennsylvania and Georgia, the legislature was divided into two houses that were expected to act as checks on each other.

The "checks and balances" principle, however, was tempered, by memories of the long struggles between the colonial assemblies and the royal governors. The new constitutions made the legislatures dominant and the governors—in most cases, elected annually by the legislatures and denied veto or appointive powers—relatively impotent.

Along with restrictions on the power of government, the new constitutions also manifested a marked tendency toward more representative government. Both of these impulses were reflected in the common provision that the voters should exercise close supervision over the legislators through annual elections. Although the state constitutions did not grant universal white manhood suffrage—and Massachusetts actually raised its property qualifications for voting—these new charters generally extended the privilege of voting, either by reducing the colonial freehold (property) requirement or by opening the polls to most taxpayers. While it would be easy to exaggerate the internal changes wrought by the rebellion, it seems certain that these new constitutions and the Revolutionary circumstances that produced them brought additional political democracy to the Americans.

THE ARTICLES OF CONFEDERATION

As the Continental Congress still had no regular constitutional authority, it began working on a plan for a confederation that would provide sufficient powers to conduct the war and to unite the states once victory was achieved. After protracted debate, the Articles of Confederation were finally approved by Congress in 1777, though a dispute over the western lands claimed by some of the states delayed final ratification until 1781.

The Articles of Confederation established not a government, but a confederation of sovereign states. Because the Revolution was being fought to abolish central control and because liberty was deemed safe only when government was kept close to where the governed could watch it, the Confederation was given only the powers to: (1) conduct foreign affairs by negotiating treaties and making war and peace, (2) control Indian affairs, (3) set standards of coinage, weights, and measures, (4) settle disputes among the states, and (5) conduct a postal service. It could not raise money or troops except by requisitions on the states. It had no power to make laws binding individual citizens and no means of enforcing its will on either citizens or states. Each state was to have a single vote in the Confederation Congress, the votes of nine states were required to approve all important measures, and the Articles could be amended only with the approval of Congress and the legislature of every state. The Articles did not even provide an executive agency to carry out whatever policies Congress might succeed in adopting.

THE CAMPAIGNS OF 1776–1777

The Declaration of Independence had just been adopted and the constitution-making process was well under way in the states and the Congress when the British launched the American war in earnest. In July, 1776, the greatest military force Britain had ever sent abroad sailed into New York harbor in hundreds of ships carrying 32,000 soldiers under the command of Sir William Howe. Anticipating the British strategy, Washington had moved his army to the vicinity, but his greatly outnumbered forces were easily pushed off Long Island, out of Manhattan, steadily through New Jersey, and across the Delaware River into Pennsylvania.

While Washington was probably no great military genius, his courage and tenacity under these disheartening circumstances kept his army intact and the American cause alive. Wisely avoiding decisive engagements, he waited until the British ceased offensive operations for the winter, and on Christmas night, 1776, he daringly ferried his troops back across the Delaware and fell upon unsuspecting British forces at Trenton and nearby Princeton, New Jersey. With these small but brilliant victories to buoy American hopes, he went into winter quarters at Morristown.

The following summer of 1777 was the time of greatest military peril for the infant American nation. From Canada, General John Burgoyne launched a British offensive by way of Lake Champlain toward Albany and the lower Hudson Valley. Sir William Howe had the opportunity to move up the

Hudson from New York City to join Burgoyne and cut the colonies in two. Instead, the indecisive Howe succumbed to the temptation of occupying the rebel capital at Philadelphia, brushing aside what resistance Washington's outmanned army was able to offer at the Battle of Brandywine.

Freed from the threat of Howe to their rear, the American commanders in the Hudson Valley, Horatio Gates and Benedict Arnold, were able to put up a stubborn resistance against Burgoyne's advance from the north. Far from his base of supply and harassed on every side by farmer militiamen, the British commander was finally forced to surrender his entire army at Saratoga in October, 1777. The importance of this victory and the narrowness of the American escape from a crushing military catastrophe cannot be exaggerated. Thanks to a combination of British lethargy and American valor, it now appeared for the first time that the rash bid for independence might succeed.

THE FRENCH ALLIANCE AND
THE SOUTHERN CAMPAIGNS

Yet even the victory at Saratoga could not make up for the feebleness of the American war effort. Driven from Philadelphia to York, Pennsylvania, Congress struggled ineffectually during the winter of 1777–1778 with the problems of supply and funds as the paper money with which it was trying to finance the war became more and more worthless. Meanwhile, cold and hunger in the winter camp at Valley Forge decimated Washington's ill-fed, ill-clothed, ill-paid army.

Across the Atlantic, however, the Saratoga victory was bearing fruit. From the beginning of the conflict, the Americans hoped that France would avenge her recent defeat at British hands by giving them aid. As soon as independence was declared, the Congress sent Franklin to Paris to seek an alliance. The French government proved willing to furnish supplies and funds secretly, but it wanted assurance that the Americans had a real chance of winning before siding with them openly. Saratoga furnished this assurance, and in February, 1778, the treaty of alliance was signed. As a result, France's ally Spain was also pulled into the war with Britain, and soon afterwards, the Netherlands were drawn into the conflict because of their insistence on continuing trade with the French and the Americans. Spain and the Netherlands furnished much-needed loans for the American war effort, but France became the main source of both the money and the munitions that enabled the Americans to keep fighting. In addition, the French sent an army and a powerful naval force without which victory would not have been possible.

Military activity was at a stalemate for a year following Saratoga as the British prepared for another offensive, this time aimed at the southern colonies. Landing at Savannah, Georgia, in December, 1778, the British army under the aggressive Lord Cornwallis easily took Charleston and occupied most of South Carolina. When the Americans finally marched against him in August, 1780, they were soundly defeated at Camden; and Cornwallis was able to push his invasion northward. By this time, however, the American forces in the South were under the able command of Nathanael Greene. At King's Mountain and at Cowpens, severe defeats were inflicted on contingents of Cornwallis' army, and in March, 1781, the British army sustained heavy losses in a hard-fought but inconclusive battle at Guilford Court House, North Carolina. The seriously weakened Cornwallis, despairing of subduing the vast and hostile southern interior, withdrew his army to Yorktown on the peninsula between the York and James rivers in tidewater Virginia, where he waited to be evacuated by the British fleet.

But it was not the British fleet that appeared. By a miracle of good fortune and good timing, Washington and the French commanders were able to march the combined Franco-American army down from the north just as the French fleet appeared off the Virginia coast. Thus caught between a hostile army and a hostile navy, Cornwallis had no alternative but to surrender on October 17, 1781.

THE TREATY OF PEACE

Cornwallis' surrender finally convinced the British that the effort to subdue the Americans was too difficult and too expensive to continue. Although the British armies had usually been able to advance at will and to defeat American armies when they could catch them, such success brought them little closer to their goal. The country was too vast, the population was too deeply committed to resistance, and the cost of supporting a large army three thousand miles away was becoming an intolerable burden on an already debt-ridden treasury. The debacle at Yorktown forced Lord North to resign his ministry, and a new ministry came to power prepared to treat with the Americans.

Already, John Adams, Benjamin Franklin, and John Jay were in Europe to negotiate a peace treaty, but a settlement was delayed for some time by the crosscurrents of international politics. The Franco-American alliance committed each party to continue fighting as long as the other was fighting, and the Franco-Spanish alliance committed France to continuing the war until Spain won Gibraltar from England. This seemed to mean that the Americans could not make peace with England until Spain regained Gibraltar. But when the American commissioners uncovered evidence that the French were arranging that the Spanish and British control the northern and southern portions of the American land between the Allegheny Mountains and the Mississippi, the Americans felt absolved of their obligation to negotiate in concert with the French.

Seeing an opportunity to detach the Americans from French influence, the British accepted an American proposal for separate Anglo-American negotiations. By thus playing off one power against the other, the American commissioners won an exceedingly favorable treaty. Besides recognizing the independence of the United States, the British also acquiesced in giving up a generous extent of territory, stretching from the Atlantic to the Mississippi and from the Canadian border on the north to the Florida border on the south. These terms were agreed upon by late 1782, but peace did not come officially until Spain and France ended hostilities in early 1783. In this general settlement, Florida was transferred from Britain to Spain to compensate for Spain's failure to win Gibralter.

FOR FURTHER READING:

John C. Miller's *Triumph of Freedom* (1948),* and John R. Alden's *A History of the American Revolution* (1954) are useful general accounts of the American Revolution. There are two excellent briefer military histories of the war: Howard Peckham, *The War for Independence* (1958),* and Willard M. Wallace, *Appeal to Arms* (1951).* Also excellent for military and naval history are two biographies: Douglas S. Freeman, *George Washington* (7 vols., 1948–1957), and Samuel Eliot Morison, *John Paul Jones: A Sailor's Biography* (1959).* William C. Stinchcombe has written about *The American Revolution and the French Alliance* (1969); and in *The Peace-makers: The Great Powers and American Independence* (1965), Richard B. Morris analyzes the maneuvers that led up to the Treaty of Paris. For the political thought that influenced the development of new political institutions during the Revolutionary years, see Carl L. Becker, *The Declaration of Independence* (1922)*; and Clinton Rossiter, *Seedtime of the Republic* (1953), which has been republished in two volumes under the titles *The First American Revolution*＊ and *Political Thought of the American Revolution.*＊ William Nelson's *American Tory* (1961), and Wallace Brown's *The Good Americans* (1969) supplement the standard account of *The Loyalists in the American Revolution* (1902) by C. H. Van Tyne; while Bernard Bailyn brilliantly delineates *The Ordeal of Thomas Hutchinson* (1974). Elisha P. Douglass, *Rebels and Democrats* (1955),* describes the conflict between the democratic-minded and the elite-minded in the formation of the new state governments; Jackson T. Main analyzes *The Upper House in Revolutionary America* (1967); and Merrill Jensen offers a controversial analysis of the drafting of *The Articles of Confederation* (1940).* Charles S. Sydnor describes the political leadership of the Virginia gentry in *Gentlemen Freeholders* (1952; republished as *American Revolutionaries in the Making*＊).

---

*Available in paperback edition.

A Nation Emerges
1780–1788

6

The new nation brought into being by the Revolution covered a thinly populated but vast expanse of territory six times the area of England and Wales combined. Ninety-five percent of its three million people lived in the countryside. Most of them were near the seacoast, but even here they were so dispersed that there were only six cities with over eight thousand inhabitants. Philadelphia, with some forty thousand, was largest, followed by New York, Boston, Charleston, Baltimore, and Salem. Transportation facilities from one part of this far-flung republican empire to another were rudimentary, and communication was so infrequent that the letters carried by the postal service amounted to only one per capita per year.

Nevertheless, the shared experience of the Revolution had given Americans a sense of national pride and optimism about the future of their experiment in liberty. But because not all Americans agreed what that future should be, the 1780s were a decade of conflict.

THE AGRARIAN-MINDED AND
THE COMMERCIAL-MINDED

One fundamental division was between what might be called the *agrarian-minded* and the *commercial-minded* portions of the population. The great majority of the people were small farmers. Measured against the Europe that they or their peasant forebears had left behind—the Europe of arbitrary government, heavy taxes, military conscription, state churches, and rigid social distinctions—America seemed a virtual paradise. In America, the dream of land ownership, the key to security, independence, and dignity, could be realized by the great majority.

To these small landowners, secure on their acres, far from cities, often illiterate or semiliterate, the American utopia was already at hand. Provincial and typically adhering to the more orthodox brands of Protestantism, they regarded the farmer's way of life as morally superior to all others. They were deeply suspicious of cities, of change, and of those ambitious and probably evil men in cities who grew rich by commercial manipulations. This agrarian mystique was also shared in good part by many southern planters and by many of the great landlord families in New York's Hudson Valley.

Less numerous but equally influential were the men who saw America's future in terms of general economic growth and national strength. This commercial-mindedness was centered in the cities and especially among the merchant and professional classes, the best educated and most cosmopolitan parts of the population. Included also were a good many farmers and planters who lived close enough to transportation and cities to produce commercial crops for foreign and domestic markets.

The division between the commercial-minded and the agrarian-minded merged into the other major division in the politics of the 1780s: there was a tendency for the agrarian-minded to be democratic-minded and for the commercial-minded to resist democratic tendencies. However, the two alignments did not coincide completely. Thomas Paine, for example, was among the most effective advocates of both democracy and commercial expansion, while much of the leadership for the agrarian forces was provided by elitist gentlemen from the great landholding families.

With some important exceptions, then, the political struggles of the 1780s involved two rough groupings. On one side were those who favored leadership by gentlemen, vigorous and more centralized government, and policies designed to foster national strength and economic growth through encouragement to enterprising businessmen. On the other side were men resentful of any pretensions to superiority, deeply suspicious of all government, and mistrustful of even their own elected representatives. They consequently wanted government kept as decentralized as possible, as inactive and inexpensive as possible, and subject to the check of frequent and democratic elections.

CONFLICT WITHIN THE STATES

The state governments were the principal arenas of conflict between the two groups. The conflict was in part a straight struggle for control, as in Pennsylvania where displaced conservatives warred unrelentingly against the ultrademocratic constitution of 1776 and the power it gave to western farmers and the lower orders of Philadelphia.

Religion was frequently another divisive issue. In New England (outside Rhode Island where religious freedom had always prevailed), the Congregationalists were persuaded to surrender only part of the exclusive privileges they had enjoyed by law before the Revolution; but in New York and the southern states, the members of the formerly established Anglican church were reduced to an equal footing with those other denominations. In Virginia, the Anglicans of the wealthy and conservative tidewater area managed to stave off this movement until 1786 when James Madison's coalition of liberal gentry, back-country Baptists, Methodists, and Presbyterians pushed through the legislature Jefferson's Statute for Religious Freedom.

The greatest cause of alarm to conservatives was the democratic legislatures' apparent disregard for property rights. In some states, property-minded men fought against wholesale confiscations of the property of Loyalists; and they were even more alarmed by the movement for debtor laws and state-issued paper money.

Paper money had been used during the colonial period with both good and bad results, but the collapse of the Continental currency during the Revolution had utterly discredited the whole idea with merchants and creditors. Yet the return to a specie (gold and silver) currency at the end of the Revolution, the collapse of the brief boom that followed, and the ensuing depression of 1785–1786 produced a severe deflation. People who had borrowed money during inflationary times found that they had to repay their debts in money that was worth much more than the money originally borrowed and at a time when money of any kind was hard to obtain.

Under the pressure of desperate debtors, seven state legislatures authorized issues of paper money, while in several other states, creditors and merchants barely averted such demands. The paper issues were relatively beneficial where taxes were levied to support them, but in other instances, the old story of rapid depreciation was repeated. Some states tried to compel creditors to accept the paper money in payment of debts; and creditors were said to flee the state of Rhode Island to avoid payment in depreciated paper.

The conflict became most violent in Massachusetts, where debtors and small farmers of the interior simply could not find enough of the scarce specie to pay their debts and heavy state taxes. As the courts began imprisoning large numbers of defaulting debtors or foreclosing on their farms, armed mobs started breaking up sessions of the courts. By the winter of 1786–1787, the interior was swarming with a virtual insurrectionary militia whose principal leader was a Revolutionary veteran named Daniel Shays. Finally, a state army of four thousand men marched into the area and quelled the disorders after a series of minor skirmishes. But meanwhile exaggerated accounts of "Shays's Rebellion" had further alarmed property-minded conservatives in all the states.

PROBLEMS OF THE CONFEDERATION

Already, in the early 1780s, conservative men sought to erect a bulwark against the localism and democratic irresponsibility of the states by strengthening the Confederation government. Under the leadership of Robert Morris, a Philadelphia merchant who had grown wealthy from war contracts, they had persuaded Congress to appoint full-time executives to superintend departments of finance, war, foreign affairs, and marine. Morris himself became superintendent of finance, but exercised great influence in all areas. Continental paper money was abandoned, and Morris sought to finance the government by borrowing, partly from American citizens. In the process, he encouraged the creation of a powerful class of public creditors who had a vested interest in a government strong enough to pay its debts.

Yet the Confederation government could neither pay its debts nor effectively carry on its ordinary operations as long as it had to depend for income on voluntary contributions by the recalcitrant states. Morris' whole program hinged on getting the states to approve the "Impost of 1781," a proposed amendment of the Articles of Confederation that would give Congress the power to levy limited import duties to pay the Confederation debt. But Rhode Island refused to ratify, and all further efforts to give Congress any taxing power failed to get the required unanimous approval of the states. Meanwhile, the coming of peace dissipated the atmosphere of emergency, and the drive to add vigor to the Confederation government stalled.

Through the mid-1780s, national-minded men could only grumble helplessly at the impotence of the Confederation in many areas. Lacking any means of enforcing its policies either on the states or directly on their citizens, the Confederation was unable to deal effectively with unseemly quarrels among various states over boundaries, western lands, and state-levied tariffs and trade restrictions.

The Confederation's weakness was most evident in foreign relations. Partly because the United States could not enforce uniform commercial regulations in its own territory or threaten uniform retaliatory regulations against other countries, it was unable to secure favorable commercial treaties with the leading European powers. More serious, Spain and Great Britain threatened the territorial integrity of the new nation in the Southwest and Northwest respectively.

Spain had lost Florida to Great Britain at the end of the Seven Years' War in 1763, but had gained formerly French Louisiana (the entire western watershed of the Mississippi and the "island" of New Orleans east of the river). Then, in 1783, Spain regained Florida, making her the dominant power on the southwestern borders of the United States. Moreover Spain would not be bound by the 31° northern boundary of Florida specified by the Anglo-American treaty, but occupied territory north of that line and claimed the greater part of the Southwest. These claims she actively buttressed in the 1780s by gaining control over the southwestern Indians and restricting the Mississippi River trade through New Orleans. When the Confederation proved powerless to protect new settlements in the Tennessee-Kentucky area against the Indians or to secure them a right to trade down the Mississippi, many of the settlements sought the protection of Spain, and for a time there was a serious danger that the western settlers would cooperate in making the entire Southwest Spanish territory.

Great Britain understandably treated her former subjects with great contempt, closing her West Indian possessions to American trade, restricting American trade with England, refusing to enter negotiations for a commercial treaty, and not even sending a minister to the new nation. Most threatening of all, she continued to occupy military posts along the northern frontier within territory she had ceded to the United States, and from these posts she retained dominion over the Indians of the northern Ohio Valley and encouraged them to resist the advance of American settlement.

The British found justification for these actions in the failure of the American states to live up to their obligations under the Treaty of Paris. Congress technically complied with the treaty by urging the states to restore confiscated property to Loyalists, but it could not force the states to do so. Nor could it prevent the states from violating the treaty by impeding the collection of debts that Americans owed to British merchants. The Confederation authorities could counter British complaints on these points only by demanding payment for several thousand slaves that the British armies had carried away from the southern states.

THE CONFEDERATION AND THE WEST

For all its weaknesses, the Confederation had one magnificent achievement to its credit: the creation of a great national domain west of the Appalachian Mountains and the formulation of a system for land sales and territorial government by which this West and later Wests would become a spectacularly expanding "empire for liberty."

Even before the Revolution, pioneers had crossed the mountains to form pockets of settlement in a few areas. New Englanders had moved up and across the Connecticut River to populate the green hills of Vermont. Resisting the claims of New York and New Hampshire to the area during the Revolution, Ethan Allen and his "Green Mountain Boys" created an independent republic that was not admitted as one of the United States until 1791.

Farther south, other pioneers had established themselves on the upper waters of the Ohio River in the Wheeling-Pittsburgh area, and still others had pushed southwestward through the valleys of the Virginia mountains to found the Watauga settlement on the headwaters of the Tennessee River in what was to become the northeastern corner of Tennessee. During and immediately after the Revolution, these outposts became staging areas for further advances of settlement into the country north of the Ohio, through Cumberland Gap into the Bluegrass region of what would later be central

Kentucky, and over the Cumberland Plateau into the Nashville basin of what would later be central Tennessee.

Seven states laid claim to various parts of the trans-Appalachian empire. Virginia, making the most of the vague boundaries specified by its colonial charter, claimed Kentucky and all the territory north of the Ohio River. New York had a shadowy claim to the Ohio Valley resting on Indian treaties, while Massachusetts and Connecticut argued that their boundaries extended indefinitely westward, cutting across the Virginia claim. Farther south the two Carolinas and Georgia asserted that their boundaries extended all the way to the Mississippi.

Even before the war was over, under heavy pressure from landless states, Congress had urged that these western claims be ceded to the Confederation to create a great common domain. Virginia led the way in 1781 by offering its lands north of the Ohio, and by the end of the 1780s all except one of the landed states had followed suit. Georgia finally ceded its western lands in 1802, while, in 1792, Virginia passed the sovereignty over its remaining western territory directly to the new state of Kentucky that was created from it.

Congress lost no time in providing for land sales and a governmental system in the new public domain. The Ordinance of 1785 established a "rectangular" system of survey. Land was to be divided into squares one mile from north to south and one mile from east to west. "Townships" six miles square were to be laid off, each of which would contain thirty-six one-mile-square (640 acres) "sections." As the line of settlement advanced, these sections were to be auctioned off to the highest bidders, with a minimum price of two dollars an acre.

A year earlier, in the Ordinance of 1784 (drafted by Thomas Jefferson), Congress had declared that territorial governments in the public domain should evolve as quickly as possible into new states fully equal to the original states. The process by which this was to happen was altered by the so-called Northwest Ordinance of 1787, adopted to meet the wishes of the Ohio Company, a group of New England land speculators who were promoting a settlement in the Muskingum Valley of what was to become southeastern Ohio. The Ordinance of 1787 established a Northwest Territory in the area north of the Ohio and east of the Mississippi rivers; this area was to be administered first by a governor appointed by Congress. When the population of the territory reached five thousand, the people were to elect a representative assembly and a nonvoting delegate to Congress. Eventually the Old Northwest was to be divided into not less than three and not more than five states, and when the population of any of these proposed states reached sixty thousand, it could be admitted to the union on an equal footing with the original states. During the territorial stage, civil liberties and religious freedom were guaranteed, a system of free public education was called for, and slavery was excluded. Thus Congress laid down the pattern of territorial evolution by which the United States was to become a continental nation of equal states.

THE MOVEMENT FOR A STRONGER GOVERNMENT

Although many Americans may have been satisfied with the limited successes and modest potency of the Confederation, others grew steadily more disgusted with its weakness and more desperately determined to secure a strong national government in its place. The unpaid public creditors constituted a standing lobby for change. Merchants wanted a uniform commercial policy that could force concessions from the great trading nations. The artisan class and infant manufacturers wanted a uniform tariff policy that would protect them from the competition of British manufactures. The elite of many of the states dreaded the possibility of popular control. Creditors and men of wealth cried out for protection against debtor legislation, paper money, and the assaults of the unpropertied on property. Frontiersmen demanded more vigorous defense against the Indians and their British and Spanish abettors. And the more cosmopolitan and national-minded patriots wanted their country to assume a position of greater strength and dignity among the nations of the world.

As the 1780s wore on, events pushed some of these national-minded elements into an almost revolutionary mood. Robert Morris' drive to strengthen the Confederation from within had stalled when the urgency of war was removed in 1783; and all further attempts to remedy the inadequacy of the Articles by amendment failed. More important, the brief economic boom that followed peace collapsed into a commercial and financial depression in the mid-1780s, and inevitably merchants, financiers, and artisans began to think that their distress was related to the Confederation's weakness. As a result of the depression, the panic of conservative men over paper money and debtor legislation reached its peak; and in the autumn of 1786, the conservatives' worst fears of the lower orders and anarchy seemed confirmed by the exaggerated accounts of Shays's Rebellion.

By this time, a concerted movement was under way to bypass the prescribed method for amending the Articles and to create a stronger government through constitutionally questionable means. The movement was initiated by a small group of national-minded men, particularly George Washington and James Madison in Virginia and Alexander Hamilton in New York. Washington shared the fears of anarchy held by other men of the upper classes, but his nationalism was more than a class prejudice. His views reflected his position as the preeminent personal symbol of American nationality, and he cared deeply about the strength, dignity, and perpetuity of the nation he had done so much to bring to birth.

Hamilton and Madison were younger men. After serving as Washington's aide-de-camp during the Revolution, Hamilton had become a highly successful lawyer in New York, where he had married into one of the leading families and had proved himself a staunch defender of property rights. But Hamilton was not primarily a servant of propertied interests. Instead he was obsessed with the need for vigor and strength in government and sought to ally wealth with government in the interest of strong government rather than wealth.

Madison was a nationalist on more theoretical grounds. A close friend of Jefferson and, like him, a member of the liberal wing of Virginia's planting gentry, Madison had combined study of ancient and modern governments with a quiet but increasingly influential role in Virginia politics. His nationalism was a matter of intellectual conviction, stimulated by his association with Washington and buttressed by his wide reading and disinterested reflection on political problems. Although, until his death in 1836, he generously and accurately protested that the Constitution was not "the offspring of a single brain" but "the work of many heads and many hands," he, more than any other framer, was the father of that document.

In 1785, on Madison's initiative, a conference of commissioners from Virginia and Maryland met at Mount Vernon and Alexandria to consider improving navigation of the Potomac. Madison and Washington persuaded the commissioners that other states should be brought into the consultation, and the Virginia legislature invited all the states to send delegates to a convention at Annapolis in 1786 to deliberate on "a uniform system in their commercial regulations." When delegates from only five states appeared at Annapolis, Hamilton, a delegate from New York, persuaded the convention to send out a call for another convention in Philadelphia in May, 1787, to "devise such further provisions as shall appear . . . necessary as to render the constitution of the federal government adequate to the exigencies of the union."

The call for the Philadelphia convention was grudgingly endorsed by the Confederation Congress with the explicit stipulation that any amendments it proposed must be endorsed by all the states as the Articles required. During the spring, delegates were selected by the legislatures of every state save debtor-dominated Rhode Island. With only a few exceptions, those who were satisfied with the Articles as they stood refused to serve as delegates, thus permitting men who were inclined to a stronger government to represent even those states where they were in a minority. The legislature of Hamilton's New York, dominated by his opponents, permitted him to be a delegate only as a member of a three-man delegation controlled by two staunch opponents of change.

THE CONSTITUTIONAL CONVENTION

Except for the two New Yorkers, and a few scattered delegates from other states, the convention was composed of men from the national-minded side of the political spectrum. Predominantly lawyers, merchants, and planters, the delegates were drawn heavily from urban and seaboard areas and from the upper classes. Collectively they presented an impressive showing of youth, education, ability, and disinterested patriotism. From the circumstances of their selection, the crucial political decision that faced the convention—whether the government should continue to be a weak "confederated" government with some additional powers to raise revenue and regulate commerce or whether it should become a "national" government acting directly on the citizens of the states—was settled before the delegates ever met.

Had this not been the case, Madison could never have scored such a resounding victory for a national plan at the very outset of the convention. The Virginia delegation arrived in Philadelphia some days before the convention opened, and Madison had his fellow Virginians hard at work on a "Virginia Plan" that became the basis for the convention's early deliberations. By accepting the Virginia Plan as its basis for deliberation, the convention made the momentous decision that it would propose not simply amendments to the Articles but an entirely new frame of government. It also indicated that it favored a government radically different from the Confederation.

The two principal features of the Virginia Plan were its grant of sweeping powers to the central government and its requirement that representation in the national legislative body be in proportion to population. It was the second feature that raised the only fundamental disagreement in the convention's proceedings, for delegates from the small states rightly feared that basing representation on population would allow the large states to control the new government. Consequently the small-state delegates presented a "New Jersey Plan" to amend the Articles rather than draft an entirely new constitution. The heart of the New Jersey Plan was the continuance of a one-house Congress in which each state would have one vote. By adhering to the form of the Articles, the small-state men were also proposing a confederated government of limited powers, though their plan did give Congress the power to levy import duties, regulate commerce, and admit new states. Yet it was the matter of representation rather than the question of nationalism that was at the bottom of the disagreement, and a compromise was finally effected by proposing a two-house Congress where representation in the lower house was apportioned by population and where the influence of the small states was safeguarded in an upper house composed of two senators from each state. Once the small states won this concession, their delegates showed less zeal in defending a confederated structure. From this point on, the convention was able to work out the detailed powers and structure of the new government without serious disagreement.

Though the delegates were predominantly nationalists and though many of them feared the influence of popular majorities, they were also political realists who recognized that whatever they proposed would have to be accepted by a society that was considerably more confederationist and democratic than the convention itself. Consequently, and to Hamilton's discomfort, the document that resulted from their deliberations was a compromise between the two poles of political thought. Its basic feature was the creation of a "federal" system in which powers and responsibilities were distributed between the state and national governments. While the powers given Congress were specified with the implication that only these powers could be exercised, the specified powers were quite ample. The new government was to have virtually unlimited authority to levy taxes, borrow money, regulate domestic and foreign commerce, conduct foreign relations, and maintain an army and navy. Moreover the states were specifically forbidden to engage in diplomatic negotiations, maintain armies, or—closing the door on debtor legislation and paper money—"emit Bills of Credit, make any Thing but gold and silver Coin a Tender in Payment of Debts; pass any . . . Law impairing the Obligation of Contracts. . . ." Finally, and most important, the new national government was to operate directly upon the citizens rather than upon the states, and the proposed national constitution and laws and treaties made in pursuance of it were declared to be "the supreme Law of the Land."

Following the eighteenth-century doctrine of separation of powers and fearful of a concentration of power anywhere in government, the convention was at pains to create, in addition to Congress, a strong and independent executive and judiciary so that the three branches would act as "checks and balances" on each other. The vesting of the executive function in a single president with ample authority was a particularly important departure from existing practices in the states and the Confederation. The president was given a veto over congressional legislation (unless repassed by two thirds of both houses), he was to appoint judges and other officers (with consent of the Senate), he was given primary responsibility for foreign relations and the making of treaties (with the advice and consent of two thirds of the Senate), and he was to be commander in chief of the armed forces.

The convention spent much of its time working out the methods for choosing the personnel of the legislative, executive, and judicial branches. Nearly all the delegates recognized that popular majorities must have a voice somewhere in the governmental structure they were planning, but they were equally anxious to erect ample safeguards against the workings of popular passions and temporary enthusiasms. Popular majorities were allowed direct sway in the House of Representatives, whose members were to be elected every two years by those who were qualified to vote for the popular branches of the legislatures in the respective states. But laws passed by the House of Representatives also had to be approved by the Senate, and the Senators were to be chosen for six-year terms by the state legislatures. Even after passage by both houses of Congress, laws still needed the approval of the president, and the convention worked long and hard before devising a method of selecting the president that would leave him independer ' ot state legislatures, Congress, and popular majorities. The result was that famous invention, the electoral college. Each state was to appoint, as its legislature directed, as many electors as it had members of Congress, and the electors were then to elect a president who was to serve for four years. Finally, the members of the judiciary were to be appointed by the president for life.

The system as a whole seemed admirably contrived to frustrate direct popular control of all branches of the government at any one time and to ensure that the various branches would pull in such different directions as to hobble effective government. The convention did not foresee that the rise of political parties would quickly subvert its intentions in both respects, and indeed the government under the Constitution would probably have proved unworkable if it had operated exactly as its architects intended that it should.

RATIFICATION

It was September, 1787, before the convention lifted the veil of secrecy with which it had covered its debates and presented its handiwork to the country. Only then did men outside the convention discover that the delegates had exceeded their authority by not only drafting an entirely new Constitution, but also by providing that it should go into effect when approved by special ratifying conventions in only nine of the thirteen states.

The supporters of the Constitution, calling themselves Federalists, won quick and decisive ratifications in the small states of Delaware, New Jersey, and Connecticut, whose powerful neighboring states had taken advantage of them under the Confederation, and in the small and exposed frontier state of Georgia. Two states, Rhode Island and North Carolina, were so well satisfied with the virtually independent course they had been pursuing that they refused even to consider ratification until after the new government was in full operation.

The crucial struggles occurred in the great states of Pennsylvania, Massachusetts, Virginia, and New York, which had been able to take care of themselves under the confederated system. Anti-Federalist delegates were probably in a majority when the ratifying conventions of several of these states opened—certainly overwhelmingly so in New York—but ratification finally carried in all of them. Federalist superiority in initiative, organization, and debate counted heavily in these close contests as did the strategy of agreeing to recommend whatever amendments the anti-Federalist delegates wished to propose. Thus not only was the Constitution adopted by extraconstitutional means, but the Federalists' tactical advantages may well have given them victory over a potentially opposed but ineffectively organized majority of the country.

Allowing for the multitude of particular interests affecting men's attitudes toward the Constitution, there seems to have been a general pattern of division. The urban and seaboard areas were almost solidly in favor of the document, not just because particular interests were stronger here, but because in these wealthier, more commercial, more cosmopolitan areas, general commercial-mindedness and elite-mindedness were more prevalent. Conversely, the Constitution tended to be strongly opposed in the more provincial backcountry areas of small farms because of the greater prevalence of agrarian- and democratic-mindedness. The numerically predominant small farmers were well satisfied with things as they stood and saw little need for stronger government.

While the agrarian-minded majority might have defeated the Constitution had it been effectively mobilized, the very fact that it was not should warn us against assuming that the opposition was terribly intense. Politics beyond the local and state level was still a matter of indifference to most farmers. Only a small proportion of the eligible voters bothered to vote at all for delegates to the ratifying conventions, and when the Constitution went into effect, it was readily accepted by all elements of the population. Within little more than a decade, under a Constitution whose operations had been transformed by political parties that the framers did not envisage, the hitherto apathetic agrarian- and democratic-minded majority would come into its own.

CONFLICTING HISTORICAL VIEWPOINTS

2. How Democratic Was the Constitution?

Thomas Jefferson believed that the Constitution was the work of an "assembly of demi-gods," and most early scholars agreed. In fact, there was no article of American faith more sacred to nineteenth-century nationalist historians than the document of 1787. In his History of the Formation of the Constitution *(2 vols., 1882), pious, patriotic George Bancroft concluded that the nation's fundamental law fulfilled the promise of the Revolution. It was inspired by the scriptures, he believed, and drafted with providential blessings. Much the same conclusion was reached by John Fiske, who portrayed the document as one of the supreme achievements of human intelligence. In full agreement with Bancroft, his older contemporary, Fiske viewed the Articles of Confederation as an unfit instrument for national government. In his* The Critical Period of American History *(1893), he described the half dozen years following the Revolutionary War as "the most critical moment in all of the history of the American people." The*

*period of national crisis passed, he believed, only upon the creation of a
strong central government. To both Bancroft and Fiske, the Founding
Fathers were men of noble purpose and unquestioned devotion to the
national welfare.*

*A later generation of scholars, however, was more critical of both the
Constitution and its framers. In his path-breaking study,* An Economic
Interpretation of the Constitution *(1913), the progressive historian Charles
Beard offered the then shocking argument that the Founding Fathers were
not selfless patriots but self-serving plutocrats: "men whose property interests were immediately at stake." The product of their labor represented
not the culmination of the democratic revolutionary spirit of 1776, but a
counterrevolution. Thus, through the instrument of the Constitution,
Beard averred, a few conservative men of property effected a "coup
d'etat" to protect their economic self-interest and check the growth of
popular democracy.*

*Although Beard confessed that his work was "fragmentary" and his
conclusions "tentative," his interpretation won prompt and almost universal acceptance. Among the many latter-day Beardians, none did more to
fill out and document the Columbia University scholar's interpretation
than Merrill Jensen. In* The Articles of Confederation *(1940) and* The New
Nation *(1950), Jensen carefully supported Beard's contention that the
Confederation government was not one of "stagnation, ineptitude, bankruptcy, corruption, and disintegration." In his view, the democratic radicalism that waxed with the Declaration of Independence, waned with the
Constitution. The framers engineered a "conservative counter-revolution"
that served to "thwart the will of 'the people'."*

*More recently, Beard's critics have all but discredited his economic
interpretations. Robert E. Brown* (Charles A. Beard and the Constitution
[1955]) and Forrest McDonald (We the People *[1958]), for example, have
questioned Beard's use of the evidence and nearly all of his conclusions.
Neither scholar accepted his class-conflict theories and Brown argued
cogently that the Constitution was an essentially middle-class democratic
document ideally suited for essentially middle-class democratic America.
Other scholars have offered different conclusions, and both Jackson
Turner Main* (The Antifederalists *[1961]) and Lee Benson* (Turner and
Beard *[1960]) have found elements of Beardian conflict in the alignment
of mercantile capitalists versus agrarians during the period of struggle over
the Constitution. Yet most historians of the present generation (Main and
Benson included) agree that Beard's thesis is seriously deficient. As the
intellectual historian Gordon Wood writes in his important* Creation of the
Republic *(1969), the notion that the ideas and behavior of the Founders
were determined by material consideration is "so crude that no further
time should be spent on it." Wood does not reject the progressive view
of the Constitution as an "intrinsically" aristocratic document designed to*

curb the democratic "excesses" of the Revolution. But he does suggest that the struggle between Federalist and Antifederalist was actually a struggle over what kind of democracy America would have—an elitist, nationally-oriented democracy or a popular, locally-based democracy.

The Founders, then, may not have been Jefferson's "demi-gods" nor Bancroft's agents of Providential will. But most modern scholars agree that the product of their labors was basically democratic and that they themselves were men of great stature and vision whose devotion to nation transcended pocketbook concerns.

FOR FURTHER READING:

An excellent beginning point for any study of the political and constitutional significance of the American Revolution is R. R. Palmer's *Age of the Democratic Revolution* (1959). The classic interpretation of the Constitution itself is found, of course, in *The Federalist* (many editions), essays by Hamilton, Madison, and Jay. But several modern-day studies—Clinton Rossiter, *1787: The Grand Convention* (1966); Catherine Drinker Bowen, *Miracle at Philadelphia* (1966); and especially Charles Warren, *The Making of the Constitution* (1947)—may prove more useful to the student. The second and third volumes of Irving Brant's biography of *James Madison* (6 vols., 1941–1961) give an excellent detailed view of both the Confederation period and the Constitutional convention. David B. Davis's *The Problem of Slavery in an Age of Revolution* (1975) and Staughton Lynd's *Class Conflict, Slavery and the United States Constitution* (1968) offer differing perspectives on a common problem. Both E. James Ferguson, *The Power of the Purse* (1961) and Forrest McDonald, *E Pluribus Unum* (1965) develop the financial dimensions of union; while Paul C. Nagel, *One Nation Indivisible* (1964), explores the concept of union in American thought.

PRESIDENTIAL ELECTIONS AND MAJOR EVENTS, 1789–1800

1789   **George Washington** elected without opposition.

1790–1791   Hamiltonian program enacted.

Funding the national debt.

Assumption of state debts. Bargain involving location of the national capital.

First Bank of the United States.

Excise taxes. Whiskey Rebellion, 1794.

1792   **George Washington** reelected without opposition.

1793   Wars of the French Revolution begin. Neutrality Proclamation.

1795   Jay's Treaty with Great Britain.

1796   Pinckney's Treaty with Spain.

John Adams (Federalist) elected over Thomas Jefferson (Republican).

1797–1798   American commissioners to France insulted.

1798   Undeclared naval war with France begins.

Alien and Sedition Acts.

1798–1799   Virginia and Kentucky Resolutions.

1800   Convention of 1800 resolves differences with France.

Thomas Jefferson (Republican) elected over John Adams (Federalist).

Federalists and Republicans
1789–1800

7

The new Constitution as written and ratified was merely a grand outline of government. An actual government was created only as the Constitution was put into practice, through adaptation and conflict, in the 1790s. During this stormy decade there were three major developments that lastingly affected the nature of the federal government. First, precedents were set with regard to the composition and functioning of the various branches of government. Second, the real and potential scope and authority of the new government were enormously broadened by Alexander Hamilton's vigorous program of exercising to the limit every power granted or even implied by the Constitution. Finally and most important, Hamilton's policies provoked a growing opposition around which a political party formed; and by the end of the decade a two-party system was well established, with the most profound influence on the way the new government operated.

LAUNCHING THE NEW GOVERNMENT

It was only natural that friends of the Constitution should be chosen to put it into effect. To no one's surprise, the first electoral college agreed unanimously on Virginia's George Washington for president. To provide geographical balance while avoiding the suspect Samuel Adams and John Hancock, the electors turned for vice president to that sturdy patriot and nationalist, Massachusetts' John Adams. When the first Congress tardily assembled in New York's City Hall in April, 1789, both houses were dominated by Federalists.

While the Senators squabbled behind closed doors about titles and ceremonial procedures, James Madison was pushing through the House of Representatives a series of laws that would put the new government into practical operation. Income was provided by a tariff act levying import duties at a moderate rate designed for revenue purposes only. An organization for the executive branch was provided by the creation of departments of state, treasury, and war. The Judiciary Act of 1789 specified that the Supreme Court should consist of six justices, that there should be a district court for each state, and that two Supreme Court justices sitting with a district judge should constitute an intermediate court of appeals. The Act also provided for an Attorney General and explicitly specified that any decision in the state courts that questioned federal as opposed to state powers could be appealed to the Supreme Court, thus authorizing the Supreme Court to pass on the constitutionality of state laws.

Finally, this first Congress considered the seventy-eight amendments to the Constitution that had been proposed by the state ratifying conventions. Somewhat reluctantly, the House approved seventeen of these, the Senate approved twelve of the seventeen, and by 1791, a sufficient number of states had ratified ten of the twelve. These first ten amendments, now known as the Bill of Rights, guaranteed citizens that the federal government would not invade such rights as trial by jury and freedom of religion, speech, and the press. All proposed amendments that substantially modified the powers of the federal government had been carefully omitted from the approved list, and disgruntled anti-Federalists could take only small comfort from the Tenth Amendment, which "reserved to the States respectively, or to the people" all powers not mentioned by the Constitution.

Meanwhile President Washington was enhancing the dignity of the new government through formal and ceremonial behavior that some critics thought too high toned for a republic. Also, during the first years of his administration, he contributed to the popularity of the new regime by taking exhausting tours through all parts of the country. The President influenced the course of events most by his appointments, especially of Alexander Hamilton as Secretary of the Treasury and Thomas Jefferson as Secretary of State. Washington consulted with them regularly, along with his Secretary of War and Attorney General, and soon the Cabinet, nowhere mentioned in the Constitution, emerged as a major governmental institution.

THE HAMILTONIAN PROGRAM

Alexander Hamilton had no sooner taken office than he became the master spirit of the administration; indeed he thought of himself as Washington's prime minister. This remarkable man burned with a vision of national greatness. Aiming at a powerful, unified nation, he detested the localistic tendencies of the states. Convinced that vigorous leadership, especially in the executive branch of the government, by the able few, was the only way to build a powerful nation, he feared the turbulence and irresponsibility of the democratic masses. Astutely aware of the relationship between political power and economic power, he was determined to promote the rapid economic growth of the country and to forge firm ties, political and economic, between the government and the wealthy.

Hamilton was far from satisfied with the Constitution as an instrument for national power and economic growth. Yet he recognized that it was the best that could be secured, and he came into office resolved to strengthen it by stretching its provisions and by vigorous administration. Seizing from Congress the initiative for public policy, he outlined in a series of four reports a brilliant, tightly integrated program for the achievement of his objectives.

Hamilton first proposed that the long unpaid Continental debt, having a face value of over $50 million, be funded at par—that is, that the old and greatly depreciated securities be called in and exchanged for new federal bonds on which interest would be regularly paid and which at maturity would be redeemed at full value. This would not only dramatically restore American public credit, but would at the same time bolster the private credit of American entrepreneurs and make it easier for them to obtain the European capital needed for a rapidly growing economy. Gilt-edged federal bonds could form the basis for investment capital. Moreover, the whole class of wealthy investors (or speculators) in Continental securities would be greatly enriched, for many of them had obtained their securities from the original holders for as little as twenty or twenty-five cents on the dollar. On all these grounds, funding would have the political effect of attaching the wealthy to the idea of a strong federal government.

Hamilton next proposed that the federal government assume, in similar fashion, over $20 million in unpaid debts incurred by the various states during the Revolution. This would have the advantage of attaching the large class of state creditors to the federal government rather than to the states, thus strengthening the prestige of the former at the expense of the latter.

Funding and assumption of debts required additional revenue, and Hamilton recommended that this be raised by increasing tariff duties and by levying a direct excise tax on spirituous liquors. He frankly advocated the latter tax both as a means of increasing the government's power to collect a tax and of demonstrating that power to the fiercely independent whiskey-making farmers of the interior.

The capstone of Hamilton's financial system was his proposal for a national bank. The bank was to be chartered for twenty years as a mixed public-private corporation controlled by private investors who were to purchase four-fifths of the $10 million worth of capital stock. Investors could pay three-fourths of their stock subscriptions in the form of federal bonds and one-fourth in gold or silver coin (specie). On the basis of this capital the bank was to issue specie-redeemable bank notes for loan to borrowers. The fact that these notes were to be receivable for all dues to the government would tend to keep up their value. Such an institution, Hamilton argued, would provide an ample and uniform circulating medium, a source of credit for businessmen, and a profitable investment for capitalists. More particularly it would convert into fluid and expandable capital the funded Continental and state securities. In all these ways, it would be another instrument for binding the wealthy to the federal government. A final advantage of the bank, Hamilton believed, was that it was nowhere authorized in the Constitution; it could be chartered only under a "broad construction" of that instrument and would help to establish a doctrine of "implied powers."

One major element in Hamilton's economic vision remains to be mentioned. As a pioneer student of what today would be called the economic growth of underdeveloped countries, he was far ahead of his time in recognizing the importance of promoting manufacturing, and a major factor in his financial proposals was the desire to provide capital for industrial development. The last of his four great reports was devoted wholly to this subject, calling for tariff rates that would give "infant industries" a competitive advantage in the domestic market until they could become well established.

To win congressional support for these proposals Hamilton fought with every political weapon at his command. The more agrarian-minded sections of the country had taken immediate alarm, and the first battle came over funding the Confederation debt. Critics objected particularly to the windfall profits of speculators who had acquired Continental securities at greatly depreciated rates. Indeed the opposition was so strong in Virginia that Madison parted with Hamilton, proposing that current holders be paid at only the depreciated rate with the remainder going to the original holders. Nevertheless, Hamilton's will prevailed. The commercial-minded Federalists in the first Congress passed the measure as originally proposed.

Assumption of state debts aroused even stronger opposition, especially from states like Virginia that had already paid off many of their own debts, and again Madison was in opposition. This time the measure was stalled, until Hamilton adroitly connected it with the simultaneous controversy among New York, Pennsylvania, and the southern states over the permanent location of the national capital. At a dinner with Hamilton, Jefferson agreed that he and Madison would draw off some of the opposition to assumption and that in return the national capital would be moved for ten years to Philadelphia and then permanently to a ten-mile-square tract to be selected by Washington on the Potomac River between Virginia and Maryland.

Hamilton's revenue proposals met their strongest opposition not in Congress but among backcountry farmers who violently resisted the tax on whiskey, their only easily transported and salable product. By 1794 this resistance culminated, in Pennsylvania, in a Whiskey Rebellion, and only when Washington sent an army of some thousands into the disaffected area were the armed mobs dispersed and order restored.

The serious constitutional objections to the national bank gave even Washington pause, and before signing the bill he requested written opinions from members of his Cabinet. Arguing the doctrine of implied powers,

Hamilton pointed out that the Constitution authorized Congress to "make all laws which shall be necessary and proper for carrying into Execution" the specifically enumerated powers. "Necessary" should be construed, he thought, as meaning *"needful, requisite, incidental, useful,* or *conducive to,"* and he argued that powers "ought to be construed liberally in advancement of the public good." Jefferson, a strict constructionist, on the other hand, contended that all powers not expressly granted (restricting "necessary" to the narrowest sense) were reserved by the Tenth Amendment to the states or the people, and hence he believed the bank was unconstitutional. Washington finally followed the opinion of Hamilton and signed the bank bill.

Hamilton's proposals for encouraging manufacturing were the only part of his program that failed in Congress. Manufacturing was still in an infant state in the country, most of it carried on by independent artisans and in people's homes, and there was no strong interest group to back Hamilton's plans. Indeed, the wealthy mercantile capitalists who were his strongest supporters on other measures were opposed to tariff barriers that would impede the flow of international trade.

On the whole Hamilton had been brilliantly successful, and his policies gave to the new government a vigor and direction that profoundly affected its future development. At the same time, however, the forceful financier had provoked a rising opposition from agrarian-minded men. By 1791, there was a recognizable group in Congress opposed to the Hamiltonian policies, and Madison and Jefferson were beginning to work together to organize resistance to the New Yorker's influence. Already men spoke of a Republican or anti-Federalist "interest" as opposed to the Federalist "interest" of Hamilton and his followers. At the time of Washington's reelection in 1792, this nascent Republican party was strong enough to garner fifty electoral votes for New York's George Clinton for vice president, against John Adams' seventy-seven.

THE WARS OF THE FRENCH REVOLUTION

The outbreak of the French Revolution in 1789 was greeted with enthusiasm by most Americans for it confirmed their faith that their own Revolution had blazed a trail to liberty that all mankind would eventually follow. But widespread "Bastille fever" lasted only so long as the revolution in France remained relatively moderate. As the great upheaval moved into a new and more somber phase, American ardor cooled and public opinion divided sharply. The people who tended toward Federalism in domestic politics were shocked by the execution of Louis XVI and the wholesale guillotining of political opponents. When the revolutionary agitation spread to other countries, followed by French revolutionary armies, conservative Americans were driven into hysterical fears of mob rule, atheism, and Jacobinism at home. On the other hand, more democratic-minded Americans, those who tended toward Republicanism in domestic politics, although often deploring the worst excesses of the "reign of terror," remained steadfast in their support of the goals of the French Revolution. Jefferson, for one, did not applaud the beheadings, but he believed that "the liberty of the whole earth" depended on the triumph of *liberté, égalité* and *fraternité* in France. To Jefferson and his followers, the conservative reaction was proof that their Federalist opponents were really monarchists.

The French Revolution precipitated a great European war, lasting with brief interruptions from 1793 until 1815 and pitting France against a series of European coalitions headed by Great Britain. American leaders of all persuasions agreed that their infant nation should avoid becoming directly involved on either side, but there were sharp differences in sympathies. The Hamiltonians favored the British, partly out of a preference for British conservatism as opposed to French radicalism and partly because the large trade with Great Britain enriched the merchant class and provided 90 percent of the tariff revenues essential to Hamiltonian financial policies. Jefferson and his friends, more sympathetic to French aims, argued that the country owed its independence to the Franco-American alliance of 1778, which was still in force, and urged a neutrality that would be benevolent toward France.

Actually France did not want to invoke the alliance to bring the United States into the war as a belligerent. The powerful British navy was sweeping French merchant ships from the seas, and the French hoped that if the United States remained neutral, American merchantmen could supply her with foodstuffs and raw materials. Britain, too, as she devoted more of her resources to war, relied increasingly on American shipping. As a result, commercial interests and producers of exports in the United States entered upon a period of unparalleled prosperity.

Washington's proclamation of American neutrality in 1793 made considerable sense economically, but it did not begin to solve all the problems created by the European war. Existing American grievances against Great Britain over the northwest posts, incitement of the northwestern Indians, and discrimination against American trade were compounded in 1794 when Great Britain moved to cripple the newly flourishing American commerce on the high seas. Determined to starve France into submission, the British navy suddenly seized some three hundred American ships under newly promulgated rules that forbade neutrals to carry grain or flour to France, to carry any French-owned goods whatever, or to engage in trade with the French West Indies. Adding insult to injury, British naval commanders began stopping American merchantmen and forcibly taking off seamen thought to have deserted from the British navy, including some who were American citizens.

Despite a storm of indignation, Hamilton was determined to avoid a break with Great Britain at all costs. Jefferson had already resigned in disgust at Hamilton's domination of the administration and interference in the affairs of the State Department, leaving no one in the Cabinet strong enough to oppose the iron-willed Treasury Secretary. The only diplomatic weapon against the British the United States had was the threat to join the Armed Neutrality of smaller European trading nations that was forming to resist British restrictions on international trade. Chief Justice John Jay was sent to London to negotiate, but Hamilton undercut his mission by assuring the British minister that the United States would not join the Armed Neutrality.

As a result Jay had to accept whatever terms the British offered. The British did agree to pay indemnities for seized American shipping and to withdraw by 1796 from their posts within the northwestern boundary of the United States. In return, Jay had to agree that the United States pay old claims of British merchants against American citizens and tacitly accept the restrictive British definitions of the rights of neutrals in international trade. Not a word was said about British impressment of American seamen, British interference with the northwestern Indians, or indemnity for the slaves carried away by British armies.

Hamilton's outraged opponents charged that these terms were a humiliating surrender to British power; and in the violent debate over Jay's treaty during 1795, the emerging line of division between Federalists and Republicans finally crystallized. The only alternative to accepting the treaty, argued the Hamiltonians, was war with England. And ratification of the treaty by the Senate guaranteed a return of commercial prosperity and gave the young nation a further period of freedom from European embroilments during which it could further strengthen its independence and institutions.

In another area of diplomacy, the Washington administration was able to capitalize on Spain's involvement in the European wars to achieve a brilliant diplomatic triumph. When Spain shifted in 1795 from the British to the French side and when the Jay Treaty appeared to align the United States with Great Britain, the Spanish authorities recognized that their possessions on the southwestern border of the United States had become exceedingly vulnerable. Consequently, the American minister Thomas Pinckney had little difficulty negotiating a treaty, ratified in 1796, that granted all the American demands: fixing of the Florida boundary at the thirty-first parallel, free navigation of the Mississippi and a right of "deposit" (the right to bring goods down the Mississippi and land them while awaiting oceangoing ships) at New Orleans for American citizens, and a Spanish promise to restrain the Indians along the frontier.

Thus by the end of Washington's second term, the Jay and Pinckney treaties had eased America's difficulties with two of the three European powers with which the United States was dangerously involved. Washington's policy of preserving American neutrality had strengthened the nation's independence and yet afforded it opportunities to capitalize on the involvements of European nations. Whether this policy could be pursued in the face of difficulties with a third European power, France, was the major problem facing Washington's successor, John Adams.

THE TRIALS OF JOHN ADAMS

Washington's determination to retire at the end of two terms inopportunely deprived the Federalists of their greatest political asset just as the Jay Treaty controversy unfolded. Consequently the election of 1796 was the first hard fought and closely contested presidential election. Hamilton had made too many bitter enemies to be a successful candidate, and moreover his ultra-commercial and elitist views were too extreme even for many Federalist voters. Vice President John Adams, to whom the party leaders now turned, represented a more moderate federalism. The Republican opposition almost without discussion accepted Jefferson as their candidate. After a vituperative campaign, Adams barely edged Jefferson, seventy-one electoral votes to sixty-eight; Jefferson became vice president.

At the time of Adams' election, the French were enraged by the Jay Treaty. Truculently they ordered seizure of American ships carrying British goods, and this time it was the Hamiltonians who beat the drums for war. Resisting Hamiltonian pressure, however, Adams sent a special three-man commission to France to try to settle the difficulties. When the French treated the commissioners insultingly and made impossible demands, including bribes, the war spirit again flamed high in the United States. By the spring of 1798, the President and Congress were making preparations for war, and an undeclared naval war broke out between French and American vessels on the high seas. Yet Adams was never quite swept away by the war fever, and in early 1799, against bitter Hamiltonian opposition, he resolved to make one last effort for peace. Another three-man commission was sent to France and this time an agreement was reached that recognized American principles of neutral rights and abrogated amicably the Franco-American alliance of 1778.

John Adams must be credited with courage and disinterestedness for single-handedly resisting the war hysteria at the cost of his own popularity and the political success of his party, but there was one respect in which he went along with the Hamiltonian extremists. As in other periods of national crisis, the popular mood was highly suspicious of dissenters and foreigners, and the Federalists were all too ready to regard the Republicans as traitorous sympathizers with the nation's enemies. Indeed the ideas of free speech, a free press, and the legitimacy of partisan opposition were not yet firmly established. Under the circumstances, the Federalists, including President

Adams, capitalized on the war hysteria to push through Congress in 1798 four measures known as the Alien and Sedition Acts. Three of these laws lengthened the minimum residence requirements for new American citizens from five to fourteen years and authorized the president to deport any alien he thought dangerous and to imprison dangerous aliens during war. The fourth, the Sedition Act, prescribed fines up to $5,000 and imprisonment up to five years for persons who conspired to oppose measures of the government, who promoted riots or unlawful assemblies, or who published "any false, scandalous, and malicious writing" against the government or its officials.

No aliens were deported under the new laws, although many left the country in fear of prosecution. But partisan Federalist district attorneys and judges used the Sedition Act to secure indictments against fifteen Republican editors; ten were convicted, one of them a congressman from Vermont.

No man in the United States was more alarmed by the Alien and Sedition Acts than Thomas Jefferson. Seeking some means of arousing protest, he drafted a set of resolutions and sent them by a friend to Kentucky where the legislature adopted them. Meanwhile Madison had secured adoption of similar resolutions by the Virginia legislature. These Kentucky and Virginia resolutions of 1798 took the position that the Alien and Sedition Acts, being contrary to the Constitution, were null and void. These resolutions called on the other states to join in asking Congress to repeal them.

THE REVOLUTION OF 1800

The Kentucky and Virginia resolutions opened the campaign for the return match between Adams and Jefferson in the presidential election of 1800. Again there was a close, hard-fought contest. The Republicans had been greatly weakened by the charge of Francophilism during the war hysteria, but with the passing of the threat of war, the reaction against the Alien and Sedition Acts gave hope of a Republican comeback. Moreover the Federalists were weakened by mounting friction between the Adams and Hamilton wings of the party and by unpopular taxes levied to support the war-preparedness program. This time Jefferson edged ahead of Adams, seventy-three electoral votes to sixty-five.

This "revolution of 1800" inaugurated no revolutionary change in public policy nor even, as yet, a revolutionary shift in the balance of strength between the parties. But the working of the constitutional system had been transformed beyond the intention of the framers by the growth within it of a system of two opposing political parties, representing divergent constituencies, holding divergent ideologies, and proposing divergent policies. The potentially overwhelming majority of the Republicans was not yet fully mobilized for political action in pursuance of its democratic- and agrarian-minded objectives. But already that party had overcome the great initial advantages of its competitor and won a majority. Thus the revolutionary principle of peaceful competition and transfer of power between parties was established. Meanwhile, the Federalists, though often out of tune with the slowly awaking majority, had given the new government a vigorous start, steered it safely through the shoals of international war, and presented it thriving and intact to the party of Thomas Jefferson.

FOR FURTHER READING:

The most influential interpretation of the difference between Federalists and Republicans has been Charles A. Beard, *The Economic Origins of Jeffersonian Democracy* (1915).* Joseph C. Charles has written a series of suggestive essays on partisan divergence in *The Origins of the American Party System* (1956).* John C. Miller's *The Federalist Era* (1960) is a useful and sympathetic overview of the Federalists, while Marcus Cunliffe's *George Washington: Man and Monument* (1958)* and James T. Flexner's *George Washington and the New Nation* (1970) are excellent interpretative studies of the first president. Manning J. Dauer has distinguished between two wings of the Federalist party in *The Adams Federalists* (1953), and Broadus Mitchell's sympathetic *Alexander Hamilton: The National Adventure* (1962) is the best biography of an extraordinary figure. On the Republican side, Eugene P. Link has described those forerunners of the Republican party, the *Democratic-Republican Societies* (1942); Noble E. Cunningham has analyzed the development of the Republican party organization in *The Jeffersonian Republicans: The Formation of Party Organization, 1789–1801* (1957)*; and Alfred F. Young has carefully studied *The Democratic Republicans of New York: The Origins, 1763–1797* (1967). A political scientist, William N. Chambers, has written a suggestive analysis of the role of *Political Parties in a New Nation: The American Experience, 1776–1809* (1963)*; and a sociologist, Seymour M. Lipset, in *The First New Nation* (1963),* has made a suggestive comparison between the problems faced by American leaders in the 1790s and the problems faced by leaders of the new nations of the twentieth century. Both James M. Smith, *Freedom's Fetters* (1956)*, and Leonard Levy, *Legacy of Suppression* (1960), focus on the Alien and Sedition Acts; Charles R. Ritcheson's *Aftermath of Revolution* (1969) offers a bold new interpretation of early British policy toward the United States; and Samuel Bemis's *Jay's Treaty* (1923) is still unsurpassed.

---

*Available in paperback edition.

PRESIDENTIAL ELECTIONS AND MAJOR EVENTS, 1800–1823

1800   **Thomas Jefferson** (Republican) elected over John Adams (Federalist).

1803   Marbury *vs.* Madison. John Marshall's Supreme Court declares a law of Congress unconstitutional.
Louisiana Purchase.

1804   **Thomas Jefferson** (Republican) reelected over Charles C. Pinckney (Federalist).

1804–1806   Lewis and Clark expedition.

1805–1807   Mounting seizures of American shipping under British Orders in Council and Napoleon's Decrees.

1807   Chesapeake-Leopard affair.
Embargo Act.

1808   **James Madison** (Republican) elected over Charles C. Pinckney (Federalist).

1809   Nonintercourse Act replaces Embargo Act.

1810   Macon's Bill No. 2 replaces Nonintercourse Act.

1811   Recharter of First Bank of the United States defeated.
Power of northwestern Indians broken at Tippecanoe.

1812   **James Madison** (Caucus Republican) reelected over DeWitt Clinton (Independent Republican).

1812–1815   War of 1812.

1814–1815   Treaty of Ghent.

1816   **James Monroe** (Republican) elected over Rufus King (Federalist).

1817   Rush-Bagot Agreement with Great Britain demilitarizes the Great Lakes.
Andrew Jackson invades Spanish Florida.

1818   Convention of 1818 settles outstanding differences with Great Britain.

1819–1821   Transcontinental Treaty with Spain acquires Florida.

1820   **James Monroe** (Republican) reelected without opposition.

1823   Monroe Doctrine enunciated.

The Jeffersonian Republic in a Threatening World 1800–1823

8

Thomas Jefferson wisely recognized the political foolhardiness, if not the practical impossibility, of trying to erase the legacy of Hamiltonian measures that he inherited. The national bank was allowed to run its course undisturbed until its twenty-year charter expired in 1811, and the funded federal debt continued to be honored. Yet there was a significant shift in the tone and direction of public policy. The government had just moved to the new Washington City. In sharp reaction to the formality and ceremony that his more aristocratic predecessors had cultivated, Jefferson invested the muddy little capital on the Potomac with an almost ostentatious simplicity. This lack of pretension symbolized his deliberately negative policy: to avoid ambitious measures, to keep the federal establishment as plain and simple as possible, to practice the most rigorous economy, and, thus, to pay off as rapidly as possible the federal debt that Hamilton had designed as semipermanent.

In taking this line, Jefferson was not only following his own agrarian and democratic preconceptions, but also proving himself a shrewd reader of the mood of the country. The Hamiltonian system, for all its brilliant success, had been premature, resting on the transitory and fortuitous ascendancy of a commercial-minded minority that was out of tune with the bulk of the population. Even in the Federalist stronghold of New England, religious and sectional considerations had contributed more to that party's strength than commercial-mindedness, and the Adams brand of Federalism was more popular than the Hamilton brand. Despite a flourishing overseas commerce that was gradually pulling more farmers and planters into producing staples for market, the country as a whole remained wedded to the vision of a simple, unprogressive, democratic utopia, dominated by self-sufficient and, therefore, independent and virtuous farmers. Jefferson's reasonable behavior in office and the eloquence of his statements and policies in behalf of the agrarian, democratic ideal won him overwhelming political strength, even in New England.

During these Jeffersonian years Americans appeared to believe that their utopian republican order might endure without change forever. They failed to realize that history will not leave societies, much less utopias, alone. The only problems that most of them saw were those arising out of the continuing international conflict. These were indeed to be severe problems for Jefferson and his successor Madison and would lead ultimately to war. Yet it was not war that was to undermine the republican utopia, but the unsuspected forces of westward expansion and economic change that were already gaining momentum.

VESTIGES OF FEDERALISM

Jefferson's disciplined majorities in Congress had moved promptly to repeal the whiskey tax, the unpopular war-preparedness taxes, and the parts of the Alien and Sedition Acts that had not already expired. The only serious battle over remnants of Federalism arose in connection with the judiciary.

The federal courts were staffed entirely by Federalists serving for life, and some of the judges had conducted themselves with flagrant partisanship. In the last days of the Adams administration, the Federalists had sought to strengthen their judicial bastion with an act establishing a series of new courts, and President Adams had spent his last hours in office signing commissions for the "midnight judges" and other officials who were to staff the new courts. Adams had made his most important contribution to perpetuating Federalist principles a month earlier by appointing as Chief Justice of the Supreme Court John Marshall, a Virginian of the Washington rather than the Jefferson-Madison stamp, whose nationalistic ideas were to dominate the Court from 1801 until 1835.

The Republicans had no sooner assumed power than they repealed the act establishing the new courts, and Jefferson ordered his Secretary of State, James Madison, to withhold the commissions of Adams's "midnight" appointees. The stage was set for a showdown when one of these appointees applied to the Supreme Court for a writ of mandamus ordering Madison to deliver his commission. Chief Justice Marshall's famous decision in the case of Marbury vs. Madison was handed down in 1803. Marshall knew that he had no means of forcing Madison to deliver the commission so he skillfully sidestepped a direct confrontation with the administration while he gained an advantage in another quarter. Declaring that the petitioner was entitled to his commission, he contended nevertheless that the Supreme Court was not empowered to act in this kind of case. It had been given such jurisdiction by the Judiciary Act of 1789, but Marshall argued that in this respect the Judiciary Act contradicted the constitutional definition of the Court's jurisdiction. Therefore, said Marshall, this section of the Judiciary Act was unconstitutional and consequently void. The Court for the first time asserted the power, nowhere explicitly given it, to invalidate an act of Congress on constitutional grounds.

Even before Marshall's decision, the Republicans had begun a campaign to neutralize the Federalism of the judiciary. Incensed by the prosecutions under the Sedition Act and fearful of keeping any branch of the government from popular control, Jefferson favored making the judiciary amenable to political influence. This he thought might be accomplished by congressional impeachment of the more notorious judges. The Republicans had little difficulty getting one drunken and incompetent district judge removed from office. In a key case, however, they failed to get enough votes to impeach Supreme Court Justice Samuel Chase. This failure preserved the principle of an independent judiciary and left Chief Justice Marshall free to develop the Supreme Court into a fortress of nationalistic and anti-Jeffersonian influence.

AN EMPIRE FOR LIBERTY

Early in Jefferson's administration, the exigencies of international war again presented the United States with a splendid diplomatic opportunity. Napoleon had just forced Spain to return Louisiana (in Spanish hands since 1763) to France, hoping to use it as the granary for a growing French empire in the western hemisphere. Under Spanish control, Louisiana had been no great threat to the United States, but the prospect of having Napoleonic France astride the Mississippi with an economic stranglehold on the whole interior of the country was another matter. Promptly, Jefferson sent James Monroe to aid the American minister in Paris, Robert R. Livingston, in securing American interests at the mouth of the Mississippi. If possible, they were to purchase the isle of New Orleans, that small portion of Louisiana that lay east of the lower Mississippi.

By the time the negotiations opened, in 1803, the collapse of the French expeditionary force in the West Indies and the resumption of the European war after a brief truce had caused Napoleon to abandon his plans for a French empire in America. To the astonishment of the American negotiators, the French offered to sell not only New Orleans but the whole of Louisiana, the entire western watershed of the Mississippi. A price of $15 million was quickly agreed upon, although the Americans were exceeding their instructions. When the news reached Washington, Jefferson, the strict constructionist, worried briefly about the lack of specific constitutional authorization for such purchases of territory, but his doubts were easily dissipated in his enthusiasm for so vast an extension of his agrarian "empire for liberty." Advising Congress to ratify quickly, lest Napoleon change his mind, he seemed to embrace the Hamiltonian doctrine of implied powers.

Even before the Louisiana Purchase was consummated, Jefferson had evinced his interest in the western country by beginning preparations for the exploration led by Meriwether Lewis and William Clark. Between 1804 and 1806, Lewis and Clark's party ascended the Missouri River to its sources, crossed the Rocky Mountains, and descended the Columbia River to the Pacific, returning with a wealth of information about the vast domain the United States had acquired.

During these years, a strong tide of migration was running westward out of the original states; the line of regular settlement had not yet reached the Mississippi River. The first of the new states (Vermont, 1791, Kentucky, 1792, Tennessee, 1796, and Ohio, 1803) were becoming populous commonwealths, while the French-Spanish settlements around New Orleans were attracting sufficient immigrants from the older states to enter the union as the state of Louisiana in 1812.

Thomas Jefferson and his party showed a special solicitude for the agrarian, democratic West. One demonstration of this was the provision made that a percentage of the public land proceeds from the new state of Ohio would be used to construct a great National Road from Cumberland, Maryland, on the Potomac River across the mountains to Wheeling, Virginia, on the Ohio. From there, the National Road was eventually extended through Ohio and Indiana and surveyed as far as St. Louis.

The new western states returned Jefferson's solicitude with overwhelming support for the Republican party. And so, increasingly, did the other states. In 1804, Jefferson was elected to a second term by a resounding victory over Charles Cotesworth Pinckney, with 162 electoral votes to 14.

THE PERILS OF NEUTRALITY

During Jefferson's second administration the European war entered a more desperate phase. Napoleon's authority was extending over the whole of continental Europe, while the British were achieving unchallenged supremacy on the high seas. As the great land power and the great naval power moved into their final mortal struggle, each increasingly sought to cripple the other through economic warfare, and Americans, the leading neutral traders, were caught in the middle.

Out of self-interest and principle the United States had asserted an advanced doctrine of neutral rights, claiming the right to trade unmolested with all belligerents. This doctrine had been tenable in connection with the limited warfare of the sixteenth and seventeenth centuries, and it was supported by the code of international law that won considerable acceptance during that period. But the wars of the French Revolution brought a new kind of general warfare, precursor of the total war of the twentieth century, ranging populations against populations. This new warfare was waged by mass armies with sweeping ideological and nationalistic objectives, in place of the earlier small professional armies seeking limited national goals.

Under these circumstances, it was not realistic to expect belligerents to respect the doctrines of neutral rights that the United States sought to maintain. The Federalists had earlier recognized the realities of the world power situation in accepting Jay's Treaty as an alternative to war. Faced with these same realities, Jefferson was just as anxious as the Federalists had been to avoid American involvement in the war but more reluctant to compromise American principles of neutral rights. Believing that the belligerents needed American trade too much to risk war with the United States, he embarked on the difficult task of using American commerce (the strength of which he overestimated) as a weapon to coerce the belligerents into respecting neutral rights.

During Jefferson's first administration, American shippers had been able to pile up such tremendous profits as to more than offset their losses from seizures under the temporarily relaxed British and French restrictions. But in 1805, in the *Essex* case, the British admiralty courts outlawed the most lucrative part of this trade, involving goods shipped from the French West Indies to France by way of the United States. This was but the first in a series of British decisions blockading the Continent to stem the flow of commodities useful to the French war effort. As a result, seizures of American shipping mounted alarmingly. Even more intolerable to American pride was an increase in British impressments of seamen from American ships.

Congress responded in 1805 by barring certain British goods from American ports, and the Jefferson administration sought to use this Nonimportation Act as a counter in negotiations in London. The British were willing to relax their restrictions on the French West Indian trade, but since they refused to renounce altogether the right of impressment, Jefferson would not submit the resulting treaty to the Senate for ratification. British indignities culminated in 1807 when the British naval vessel *Leopard* opened fire on the unsuspecting American naval vessel *Chesapeake,* stopped her, and impressed at cannon's mouth four seamen.

Like Adams before him, Jefferson had to resist the clamor for war, meanwhile pushing through Congress the Embargo Act of 1807. This extreme measure of economic coercion forbade American ships to sail for Europe. Jefferson hoped, of course, to force the British to terms by denying them desperately needed American goods and shipping. Unfortunately the effects of the Embargo were felt more severely by American commercial and exporting interests than they were by the British. New England, its economy prostrate and its people bitter, moved back into the Federalist orbit. Finally even Jefferson concluded, just before he left office in the spring of 1809, that the Embargo could no longer be sustained. Congress repealed the Act, and it was left to James Madison to seek some better solution to the prickly problem of neutral rights.

115°

105°

BRITIS

49°—Convention of 1818

45°

Columbia

OREGON
(Joint occupation with
Great Britain, 1818-46)

Missouri

LOUISI

R O C K Y   M O U N T A I N S

Snake

42°—Transcontinental Treaty, 1819-21

SPANISH

35°

POSSESSIONS

Santa Fé

PACIFIC

Rio Grande

OCEAN

25°

WESTWARD MOVEMENT

$\dfrac{\text{OHIO}}{1803}$ New states, with date of admission

115°

105°

POSSESSIONS

85°   75°

L. Superior

NORTHWEST

L. Michigan   L. Huron

L. Ontario

L. Erie

TERRITORY 1787

ME.
1820   45°

VT.
1791

N.H.

N.Y.

MASS.

R.I.
CONN.

s and Clark
804-06

ILL.
1818

IND.
1816

OHIO
1803

PENN.

Pittsburgh
1765

Wheeling

Cincinnati
1789

Marietta
1788

N.J.

MD.

DEL.

St. Louis
1764

Louisville
1778

Lexington 1776

Ohio

KY.
1792

Harrodsburg
1775

MO.
1821

HASE

Nashville
1779

TENN.
1796

Wautauga
1768

VA.

Cumberland MTS.

APPALACHIAN MTS.

N.C.

35°

ATLANTIC OCEAN

Mississippi

Tennessee

S.C.

GA.

MISS.
1817

ALA.
1819

LA.
1812

1810   1813

31°—Pinckney's Treaty, 1796

Mobile 1710

New Orleans
1718

FLORIDA PURCHASE
1819-21

25°

Gulf of Mexico

0   200   400
MILES

85°

75°

© RAND & CO.

MADISON TRIES HIS HAND

By the time of Madison's accession, French depredations on American commerce were becoming as serious as those by the British. Napoleon had responded to the British blockade of the Continent with a series of decrees declaring the British Isles blockaded. Though he did not have the naval power to enforce a blockade, he could and did order the seizure of American ships reaching French ports after having submitted to British regulations. Such seizures reached wholesale proportions early in the Madison administration.

Shifting from one expedient of economic coercion to another, Madison and his congressional followers tried supplanting the Embargo with a Nonintercourse Act (1809), freeing American shippers to trade with all nations except France and England and promising to resume trade with whichever of these nations would first remove its restrictions. Profits of trade were so high, however, that American shippers preferred to take their chances on the British and French trade even under the restrictions, and in 1810 Congress supplanted the Nonintercourse Act with a measure known as Macon's Bill No. 2. This overingenious measure reopened the whole world to American trade, but declared that whenever either of the major belligerents rescinded its restrictions on neutral shipping, nonintercourse would be reinvoked against the other.

American embarrassment was compounded by the pathetic eagerness of the Madison administration to seize upon any indication that its policy of economic coercion was working. Under the Nonintercourse Act, the President used favorable negotiation with a too pliable British minister as a pretext for announcing resumption of trade with Great Britain, only to have to eat his words when the British minister's work was disavowed in London. Napoleon exploited Macon's Bill No. 2 with even greater cynicism. A carefully ambiguous French promise to rescind the obnoxious decrees against neutral shipping hoodwinked Madison into reinvoking nonintercourse against Great Britain, whereupon the French resumed seizing American ships.

Thus by 1811, the pacific, agrarian-minded diplomacy of economic coercion had been tried in every way that could be imagined, all to no avail. The nation had never seemed so powerless to avert indignities, and the only alternatives seemed to be humiliating submission or war.

THE WAR OF 1812

Submission was utterly unacceptable to a remarkable group of vigorous young men who were elected to the Congress that convened in December, 1811, and who came to be known as the War Hawks. Led by the captivating Henry Clay of Kentucky and the intellectually impressive John C. Calhoun of South Carolina, the War Hawks represented a new generation of Republican politicans who were eager to wrest leadership from the tired hands of Madison and his dispirited companions of the Revolutionary generation.

These new Republicans were nationalistic, not only in their patriotic love of country but also in their freedom from the agrarian localism that animated the companions of Jefferson. This was especially true of Clay, whose Kentucky Bluegrass constituency had been drawn into flourishing hemp production for the international market by way of New Orleans, and Calhoun, whose South Carolina upcountry was undergoing a heady transformation into a land of cotton plantations. Such areas of recent economic boom shared the cosmopolitanism, progressivism, and nationalism of the older commercial-minded areas and might be characterized as agrarian-commercial in spirit. From such areas was beginning to emanate a new-style Republican nationalism whose spokesmen par excellence were Clay and Calhoun.

It was no accident that the spokesmen for the agrarian-commercial areas were War Hawks in 1811 and 1812. In the older, strictly commercial areas of the Northeast, merchants and shipowners could run the risk of British and French seizures and still make great profits; they opposed both the Republican measures of economic coercion and the talk of war. But in the agrarian-commercial enclaves of the South and West, exhilarating booms had been stalled by the disorganization of international trade. As loyal Republicans, men in these areas had been willing to give the policies of economic coercion a trial, but now their patience had run out. Only war could save the national honor and enable the march of progress and prosperity to resume.

Embarrassingly, Great Britain and France had been equally obnoxious, and the United States could hardly take on both. There were special reasons for hostility to Great Britain. The British officials in Canada were thought to have encouraged Indian unrest in the Old Northwest and the organization of an ominous Indian confederacy, headed by Tecumseh and his brother the Prophet, to oppose the advance of American settlement. Though a frontier army destroyed Tecumseh's power at Tippecanoe in 1811, the bumptious Republicans of the Ohio Valley clamored for the conquest of Canada.

Similarly the Southwest was calling for the conquest of Spanish Florida, and Spain was again allied with Great Britain in the European war. Through Spanish Florida ran the rivers on which the men of the Georgia, Alabama, and Mississippi country depended for trade. The Spanish authorities were also suspected of encouraging Indian hostility, and their territory was a haven for the runaway slaves of the Americans. The United States asserted a doubtful claim under the Louisiana Purchase to West Florida, roughly the territory between Mobile Bay and New Orleans. Already by 1810, the Madison administration had taken advantage of a "revolution" by immigrants from the United States to annex part of this area. War with Great Britain would provide an opportunity to complete the conquest of Florida.

Thus the stalling of economic booms in several agrarian-commercial areas, resentment of British tampering with the Indians, and a desire for Canada and Florida made the war fever especially intense in a great arc running along the frontier from northern New England out through Kentucky and Tennessee to South Carolina and Georgia. Yet more important than any of these specific grounds for war was the widespread desire, especially among younger Republicans of the War Hawk stripe, to avenge the national honor and dignity. The callous impressments of American seamen made Great Britain the inevitable enemy.

By the spring of 1812, the Madison administration, not knowing what else to do, was ready to go along with the agitation for war. In June, on the President's recommendation, a declaration of war was pushed through a seriously divided Congress. Two days before the declaration, the British government in London decided to repeal all its restrictions on neutral trade. The Republican diplomacy of economic coercion had finally accomplished its purpose, barely too late to save the country from a disgraceful war.

The War of 1812 was a military debacle. But for British preoccupation with Napoleon, it would have been an utter disaster. Feeble administration in Washington and feebler generalship in the field brought defeat after defeat. Grandiose western boasts about the easy conquest of Canada eventuated in the disgraceful surrender of the American army at Detroit. In 1814, the defeat of Napoleon enabled the British to pay serious attention to the American war. One invading army easily captured Washington and burned the public buildings. Another, marching down from Canada to cut the country in two along the line of the Hudson, would have succeeded if its timid general had not been unduly discouraged by the success of a small American flotilla in maintaining naval control of Lake Champlain along his line of march. A final formidable force, fresh from victories over Napoleon, was sent to seize New Orleans with the aim of wresting much of the West from the United States. This seasoned army was annihilated by Andrew Jackson and his western militiamen in the only significant American triumph of the war. Americans were able to take pride in the naval victories of individual ships, but these could not prevent the mighty British navy from establishing unquestioned control of the seas along the American coasts.

Much of the American weakness arose from internal dissension. Southerners had little enthusiasm for the conquest of Canada, and Northerners had little for the conquest of Florida. The whole war was bitterly opposed in commercial areas, especially New England. New England banks and capitalists would not lend money to rescue the bankrupt federal treasury, the New England governors refused to supply troops, and in December, 1814, a convention of the New England states met at Hartford to seek redress against the tyranny of the federal government. Some participants advocated the secession of New England, but the more moderate majority contented itself with proposing constitutional amendments that would protect the interests of their section.

The unfortunate war had hardly started when the Madison administration began efforts to end it, but it was 1814 before a group of British and American commissioners got down to negotiating in earnest at Ghent in Belgium. The treaty they finally agreed on in December simply restored the state of things existing at the beginning of the war without mention of neutral rights, impressment, or any of the other questions that had been in dispute between the two countries. The United States escaped without loss of territory only because the British were too war weary at the end of their long struggle with Napoleon to go on fighting. Indeed, had the British defeated Jackson as expected at New Orleans in January, 1815, two weeks after the peace terms were agreed upon at Ghent, they would probably have insisted on territorial concessions before ratifying the treaty.

THE CENTURY OF SECURITY

However ignominious the War of 1812 seemed at the time, the independence of the United States was not really secure until it had been fought and, by great good luck, survived. It also began a century such as no other western nation has ever had the good fortune to enjoy, a century in which to develop free from any external threat.

This marvelous security was guaranteed primarily by British domination of the seas. By the end of the War of 1812, Great Britain was ready to accept the permanence of the United States and to look for advantage in encouraging trade between the two countries. Seeing great commercial opportunities throughout the Americas, British ministries observed with satisfaction the crumbling of the Spanish Empire, the last great colonial empire in the New World, and resisted any efforts by other European powers to extend their influence across the Atlantic.

This happy turn in British-American relations was signaled by the amicable settlement of the outstanding questions between the two countries shortly after the War of 1812. The Rush-Bagot Agreement of 1817 provided for demilitarization of the Great Lakes, and in the Convention of 1818, American fishing rights in Canadian waters were specified, the northern boundary of the United States was set at the forty-ninth parallel from the head of the Mississippi to the Rocky Mountains, and the two countries agreed to joint occupation of the Oregon country beyond the Rockies for a period of ten years. In 1827 the joint occupation agreement was extended indefinitely until such time as either nation should give a year's notice for terminating the arrangement.

The Anglo-American rapprochement facilitated another diplomatic achievement of this period: the liquidation of American difficulties with Spain through the acquisition of Florida. After acquiring West Florida as far east as the Pearl River (the area now a part of the state of Louisiana) through "revolution" in 1810, the Madison administration took advantage of the war to annex, in 1813, another chunk extending beyond Mobile Bay east to the Perdido River (the coastal areas of the present states of Mississippi and Alabama). Following the war, Spain was wracked by political turmoil at home and revolution in her South American colonies. Forays on American territory by Florida Indians intensified southwestern demands for annexation and furnished the pretext that Spain was not living up to her obligations under Pinckney's Treaty. When Andrew Jackson was sent to pacify the Indians along the Florida border in 1817, he moved on into Florida and seized the whole northern Gulf Coast area.

The administration in Washington could not sanction this rash and unauthorized occupation, but Secretary of State John Quincy Adams finally persuaded his Cabinet colleagues that Jackson should not be censured. Instead Adams told the Spaniards that the incident revealed their inability to maintain their treaty obligations along the Florida boundary, indicating the propriety of ceding Florida to the United States. Under this implied threat of forcible seizure, Spain yielded. By a treaty signed in 1819 but not ratified until 1821, Florida was ceded to the United States in exchange for the sum of $5 million. In the process, the Americans won undisputed control of the territory to the Rocky Mountains as well as a window on the Pacific. Sometimes called the Transcontinental Treaty, this remarkable agreement defined the boundary between the United States and the Spanish possessions to the southwest as running from the Gulf of Mexico up the Sabine River (the western boundary of the state of Louisiana), then west and north of the Rockies, then west along the forty-second parallel to the coast.

The Florida treaty was consummated during the administration of James Monroe, who had succeeded Madison in 1817 and who was to provide the classic definition of america's diplomatic position in the Century of Security. The Monroe Doctrine was enunciated in the President's annual message to Congress in December, 1823, and contained two principal parts. The first was the assertion that the American continents were no longer open to colonization by European powers. The second was a warning against any interference by European powers with the revolutionary new nations of Latin America or any extension of the political systems of Europe to the Americas.

The noncolonization declaration was prompted by an expansion of the sphere of Russian activity down the northwest American coast from Alaska, and in 1824, the Russians agreed to limit their interests to the area north of 54°40', leaving the United States and Great Britain as the only claimants of the Oregon country between that line and the Spanish-Mexican boundary at 42°.

The other part of the Monroe Doctrine was prompted by the fear that the major continental powers might unite in an effort to subdue Spain's rebellious American colonies. The British foreign secretary had suggested that the United States join his country in opposing any such action, but Secretary of State Adams and President Monroe decided that it would be better for the United States to make a unilateral statement, knowing that British seapower would back up the policy. The European powers had no enthusiasm anyhow for the reconquest of Spanish America against British opposition so the Doctrine had little effect on the immediate situation. But it did clarify, for Americans and for others, the idea of the proper relation between the Old World and the New that was to be the basis for American diplomacy during the Century of Security.

CONFLICTING HISTORICAL VIEWPOINTS

3. What Caused the War of 1812?

The American war cry of 1812, "free trade and sailors rights," moved the eccentric Virginian, John Randolph, to quip: "men shall not live by bread alone, but mostly by catch phrases." Catchy or otherwise, the phrase appealed to the men of Randolph's generation, who believed that the second Anglo-American war was fought for national honor and neutral maritime rights. With their president, James Madison, they traced the origins of conflict to "the continued British practice of violating the American flag on the great highway of nations, and of carrying off persons sailing under it." Actually, in his war message to Congress, Madison had mentioned other causes as well, but the maritime interpretation captured the American imagination. And throughout the century, laymen and scholars alike believed that British commercial interference lay at the heart of the conflict. Historians as diverse as John Bach McMaster (History of the People of the United States *[8 vols. 1883–1913])* and Alfred T. Mahan *(Sea Power in Its Relations to the War of 1812 [1905]) stressed impressment of seamen, the interruption of trade, and the Royal Navy's blockade. Even Henry Adams* (History of the United States *[9 vols. 1889–1891]), who found the exclusive emphasis on maritime matters oversimple, offered only a slightly modified version of the standard interpretation.*

Following World War I, however, a generation of scholars, disillusioned by the failures of American wartime idealism, looked for causes less lofty than patriotism and principle. For example, Louis Hacker (Mississippi Valley Historical Review *[March, 1924]), then an economic determinist, identified conflict in the "war hawk's" lust for Canadian land. Julius Pratt* (The Expansionists of 1812 *[1925]), on the other hand, emphasized southern yearnings for the Floridas and a western desire to drive Britain from Canada as a solution to the Indian problem. A third scholar, George Taylor* (Journal of Political Economy *[1931]) linked westerners to seaboard grievances by noting that the farmers of the interior, hardly less than New England merchants, were economically dependent on foreign trade.*

More recently, pocketbook and sectional considerations have fallen from favor. Since World War II, a growing number of scholars have returned to arguments of national honor and free seas. Bradford Perkins (Prologue to War [1961]), *Reginald Horsman* (The Causes of the War of 1812, [1962]), *and Norman Risjord* (William and Mary Quarterly [April, 1961]), *with varying degrees of emphasis, have led us back to the maritime causes stressed by nineteenth century historians. Indeed, most historians today agree that England's policies of impressment and commercial restriction left its former colonies with but two alternatives: submission or war. As Risjord put it, "war was the only alternative to national humiliation and disgrace."*

FOR FURTHER READING:

Henry Adams's *History of the United States during the Administrations of Jefferson and Madison* (9 vols., 1889–1891) is a classic of American historical writing. Much material that has come to light since Adams wrote is utilized in two distinguished multi-volume biographies: Irving Brant, *James Madison* (6 vols., 1941–1961); and Dumas Malone, *Jefferson and His Time* (4 vols. so far, 1948–   ). Merrill D. Peterson's *Thomas Jefferson and the New Nation* (1970) is an excellent one-volume biography; Marshall Smelser's *The Democratic Republic* (1968) views Jefferson as a "Whiggish moderate"; and Leonard Levy's *Jefferson and Civil Liberties* (1963) savagely explores "the darker side" of the Sage's life. Noble Cunningham has written a study of *The Jeffersonian Republicans in Power* (1963)*; and Richard E. Ellis's *The Jeffersonian Crisis* (1971) carefully analyzes judicial politics and reform in the young republic. David H. Fischer's *The Revolution of American Conservatism* (1965) examines Federalist efforts to adapt to a more popular style of politics, and Linda K. Kerber's *Federalist in Dissent* (1970) assesses Federalist ideology in the period of Republican ascendancy. For the Lewis and Clark expedition and western development during the Jeffersonian era, see Bernard De Voto's *Course of Empire* (1952)* and his edition of *The Journals of Lewis and Clark* (1953)* and Paul R. Cutright, *Lewis and Clark: Pioneering Naturalists* (1969). On the coming of the War of 1812, A. L. Burt, *The United States, Great Britain, and British North America* (1940) offers a spirited defense of the maritime thesis; and Harry L. Coles, *The War of 1812* (1965) is a good history of the military aspects of the conflict. Much about the period can be learned from Bernard Mayo's account of the earlier career of one of the leading War Hawks in *Henry Clay,*

---

*Available in paperback edition.

Spokesman of the New West (1949). The Treaty of Ghent and postwar diplomacy are splendidly delineated in Samuel Flagg Bemis, *John Quincy Adams and the Foundations of American Foreign Policy* (1949) while Dexter Perkins, *Hands Off: A History of the Monroe Doctrine* (1941),* is the standard account of that subject.

THE TRANSPORTATION REVOLUTION
to 1860

~~ Important roads	Principal railroads
	┤┼┼├ completed by 1840
•—•—•— Principal canals	——— completed by 1860

The Market versus
the Agrarian Republic

9

The Century of Security into which the Republican statesmen ushered the country was also a century of exceptional growth and development in the United States. Freedom from all entanglements with the Old World, except a free and peaceful trade, was deemed essential to the simple, and therefore virtuous, republic that Jefferson and his colleagues sought to perfect. Yet this freedom and security helped to foster a spirit of enterprise and rapid change that undermined the agrarian ideal.

The spirit and direction of American life became so strikingly different after the War of 1812 that the period around 1815 must be regarded as one of the major turning points in American history. The change was not quite so abrupt as it may appear—war has a way of temporarily damming up latent tendencies in a society and accelerating others so that they all seem to burst forth at the end of the conflict and as a result of it. In this case, economic changes were primary.

THE MARKET REVOLUTION

The American economy has developed through three main stages. The economy of the colonial period was a *staple-exporting economy,* in which people either concentrated on producing tobacco, grain, and other staples for overseas markets or on the carrying trade or were largely self-sufficing in their economic activities. About the middle of the eighteenth century, population flowed heavily into the interior where poor transportation prevented staple production, and the self-sufficing sector of the economy began to grow relative to the staple-exporting and, therefore, commercial sector. It was this development that set the stage for the struggle between commercial-mindedness and agrarian-mindedness in the last quarter of the century.

From the point of view of economic development, the important thing about the staple-exporting economy was its static quality, its lack of any tendency to self-acceleration or change. The overseas markets for American staples were seriously disturbed by the Revolution, and with the steady growth of the self-sufficing sector toward the end of the century, the economy was becoming, if anything, more set in its ways. This unprogressive, staple-exporting economy, with its sizeable self-sufficing sector, supported the stable agrarian utopia of Thomas Jefferson.

How, then, did this economy become a dynamic *industrial economy?* the "industrial revolution' that brought factories, large-scale enterprises, and rapid technological change did not really gain full momentum in the United States until after the Civil War. But the critical shift in the pace, direction, and spirit of the economy had occurred decades before as a result of the "market revolution," which brought most American economic activity into the orbit of an intricately intermeshed national market system. Beteween the *staple-exporting economy* of the eighteenth century and the *industrial economy* of late nineteenth century there intervened a *national market economy,* which did not until the 1850s begin to become significantly industrial.

The essence of the market revolution was a vast extension of the division of labor or, in other words, specialization of economic activities. Areas and individuals that formerly had been self-sufficing or that had engaged in mixed enterprises began to concentrate on the one product or service they could produce most efficiently, selling it for money and then buying with that money the other goods and services they needed. Areas and individuals that had formerly engaged in only barter or limited local trade were inexorably drawn into a national and international market system linked together by the mysterious mechanisms of money and credit. It was the resulting gains in efficiency and productivity that overnight jolted the formerly static economy into rapid growth. And it was in this atmosphere of rapid growth and ready profits that an economically conservative population became deeply infected with the spirit of enterprise, progress, and economic individualism.

The market revolution seemed to spring full blown from the War of 1812. With a staple-starved Europe paying high prices for American products, a long dammed-up flood of European imports pouring into American harbors, and settlers swarming over the newly opened lands of the West, the country was swept into an unprecedented four-year boom (1815–1818). Lured by high profits and easy credit into venturing their all on enterprises ranging from farms to steamboats, countless Americans were drawn for the first time into the money-market nexus. This spectacular boom ended in the even more spectacular bust of 1819 and the depression of the 1820s, to be followed by another boom-bust cycle in the 1830s.

The short-term boom-bust cycle of 1815–1819 arose immediately out of war and peace, but it had roots in the market revolution and in the greater interdependence of the economy that the market revolution produced. The market revolution itself was rooted in certain long-term developments that began before and continued long after the War of 1812. One of these was the accumulation of investment capital from the high profits of the American carrying trade during the Napoleonic Wars. Others will be discussed in the following sections.

THE ADVANCE TO THE MISSISSIPPI

A major stimulus to the growth of the American economy after 1815 was the rapid settlement and economic development of the West up to and across the Mississippi River. Much of this area was not open to settlement until William Henry Harrison destroyed the Indian power in the Northwest and Andrew Jackson crushed the Creeks and Cherokees of the Southwest during the War of 1812. Following the war, the broken tribes yielded to repeated demands for additional cessions of territory. In the 1820s, John C. Calhoun, Monroe's Secretary of War, inaugurated a policy of resettling the remaining Indians beyond the Missouri River, and by the middle 1830s, this objective had been substantially accomplished.

With the return of peace in 1815, a flood of settlers poured west to take up rich lands under the liberal Harrison Land Act of 1800. A tract of as little as 160 acres could be bought for a minimum down payment of fifty cents an acre with four years to make the remaining payments of $1.50. Overnight great plantations appeared on the fertile river lands of Alabama and Mississippi as planters from the worn soils of eastern Virginia, the Carolinas, and Georgia moved west with slaves, stock, and plantation gear. Along the line of the Mohawk Valley and the Great Lakes came a torrent of refugees from the stony hill farms of northern and western New England, blanketing the productive plains of nothern Ohio, Indiana, and Illinois with townships, churches, and school houses on the New England pattern. The older western states of Kentucky and Tennessee became thickly settled, and from them and from farther south and east a stream of immigrants moved into southern Ohio, Indiana, and Illinois, establishing a pattern of life that differed from the New England-based style in the northern sections of those states.

During the boom years, this great migration attained staggering proprotions. Federal land sales, which had risen from 67,800 acres in 1800, to over 500,000 acres in 1813, abruptly shot to 1,306,400 acres in 1815, and reached a peak of 3,491,000 acres in 1818. Even during the depressed twenties, the tide continued to run strongly. The population of the country beyond the Appalachians doubled between 1810 and 1820 and again between 1820 and 1830. In quick succession, five new states were produced: Indiana (1816), Mississippi (1817), Illinois (1818), Alabama (1819), and Missouri (1821).

The typical western migrant was no solitude-loving Daniel Boone, but a man of enterprise, bent on bettering himself through shrewd investment, hard work, and a ride on a rising market. The market revolution in its early stages fostered the western boom that stimulated migration, and the great migration in turn accelerated the market revolution. The great migration cannot be understood, therefore, apart from other major factors in the market revolution.

COMMERCIAL AGRICULTURE

The most important feature of the market revolution was the spectacular expansion of commercial agricultural production with cotton leading the way. The development in England during the latter part of the eighteenth century of machinery that could manufacture cotton cloth cheaply had created a heavy demand for cotton. Cotton production was restricted for a time by the difficulty of separating the fibers from the seeds, but after Eli Whitney perfected in 1793 a gin that performed this task, cotton plantations mushroomed across the interior of Georgia and South Carolina. Checked for a time by the Embargo and the War of 1812, the cotton boom roared ahead with the return of peace and the opening of the rich southwestern lands to cultivation. Production rose from 146,000 bales in 1814 to 209,000 bales in 1815 and 349,000 bales in 1819. Within a few years after 1815, a wide belt extending from North Carolina around to Louisiana had been converted into the world's largest cotton-producing area, and cotton was the country's leading export.

Unlike the staple-exporting sector of the colonial economy, the new cotton sector was intimately tied to the national as well as the international market system. While the bulk of the cotton shipped from New Orleans, Mobile, and Charleston went to Europe, much of it went by way of northeastern ports, especially New York. The proceeds of the crop paid for imports from Europe that found their way back to all parts of the United States through northeastern mercantile houses. Importations from Europe were financed to a great extent through the services of merchants in the Northeast in shipping and selling the South's cotton crop, through the South's purchases of northeastern manufactures, and through the foodstuffs and livestock shipped by the farmers in the Northwest to southern cotton planters. For some decades after 1815, the ever-mounting cotton exports were the most important factor in the growth of the economy.

Cotton production was merely the biggest segment of an expanding commercial agriculture. Tobacco cultivation in the old tidewater area of Virginia and Maryland, never recovered from its post-Revolutionary slump, but new tobacco belts developed along the North Carolina-Virginia border and in sections of Kentucky, Tennessee, and Missouri. Not until the 1840s, however, did tobacco production flourish and become highly profitable. Rice culture benefited from improved seed selection and methods of cultivation, but did not expand beyond its long-established locale in the coastal region of South Carolina and Georgia. The development of an improved variety of ribbon cane fostered a booming sugar plantation economy in Louisiana following the War of 1812, and hemp, used especially for baling cotton, similarly afforded a profitable commercial crop for areas in Kentucky and Missouri.

While the great export staples were concentrated in the South, other sections were not lacking in an extensive commercial agriculture produced at first for the national market. Areas of commercial wheat production expanded steadily west from Pennsylvania's Susquehanna Valley to New York's Mohawk and Genesee valleys to Ohio, Indiana, and Illinois. In the decade after 1815 a mounting stream of wheat, flour, corn, pork, beef, and livestock began pouring from the Old Northwest into the East and South. Cincinnati became the country's leading center of flour milling and meat packing, and by the 1840s, the flood of cheap wheat and flour from the fertile Northwest was becoming a major item in American exports to Europe.

Farmers on the less productive soils of the Northeast, forced out of cereal and meat production by the cheap western products, turned to producing perishables—fruits, vegetables, poultry, and dairy products—for the growing eastern cities. Improved breeds of wool-bearing sheep and increased demand from an expanding woolens industry made wool production a profitable enterprise in many parts of the Northeast as well as the Northwest.

Thus within a brief space of time, mainly following the War of 1812, countless self-sufficing or general farmers had responded to the lure of cash returns held out by a mushrooming national and international market system and were concentrating on those staples that they could produce most efficiently. Little of this would have occurred however, had it not become possible to transport bulky products cheaply from one part of the country to another.

THE CONQUEST OF DISTANCE

So important were the dramatic improvements in transportation facilities in the early nineteenth century that some historians have called the market revolution a transportation revolution. Like the great westward migration, the transportation revolution was part cause and part effect of the broader market revolution.

During the colonial period, production for market had been confined to areas along navigable waterways, and at the beginning of the nineteenth century, almost the only other transportation was by wagon or pack team over primitive dirt roads. As late as 1816, a ton of goods could be shipped three thousand miles from England for what it cost to transport the same goods thirty miles overland in America. The cost of moving a bushel of wheat from Buffalo to New York City in 1817 was three times the market value, it was six times the market value for corn, and for oats, twelve times the market value. Cheaper transportation was an obvious prerequisite to a national market economy.

The first attempts to solve the problem were through improved roads. In 1794, a company chartered by the Pennsylvania legislature opened between Lancaster and Philadelphia the first major turnpike, or graded and paved road on which tolls were charged. So dramatically dit it lower wagoning rates and stimulate commercial development and so profitable did it prove, that a wave of turnpike construction followed. By the War of 1812, most of the major cities in the Northeast were connected by turnpikes; but not until after the war did the turnpike craze reach its peak and spread into the West. One major turnpike led west from Baltimore to Cumberland, Maryland; from here, the federal government began constructing the National Road. By 1818, this great highway had reached Wheeling, Virginia, on the Ohio River, and by 1833, it extended to Columbus, Ohio. The National Road quickly became a major artery of east-west trade, while elsewhere the turnpikes reduced transportation costs and brought previously isolated areas into the market.

More important than better roads, especially in the West, was the introduction of the steamboat. Flatboating down the Ohio and Mississippi rivers to New Orleans had transported some production for market from the early days of settlement, but this mode of transportation was extremely slow even downriver while upriver shipping by oar-driven keelboat was so slow, backbreaking, and expensive as to inhibit any extensive commerce. A new era was predicted when Robert Fulton operated the first commercially successful steamboat, the *Clermont,* on the Hudson River in 1807. By 1812, a few forerunners of the classic shallow-draft sternwheeler had appeared on the Mississippi. The development of western steamboating came with a rush at the end of the war, and by 1820 there were sixty steamboats on the Mississippi-Ohio system (by 1860 there would be more than a thousand) and others on the river systems of Alabama and Mississippi. Steamboat freight rates were only 5 to 10 percent of what keelboats had charged to haul goods upriver and only 25 to 30 percent of what it had cost to flatboat goods down the river, and there were proportionate gains in speed of shipment. Able to operate far up the network of tributaries that laced the West, the shallow-draft sternwheeler made possible the production of cotton, wheat, and other bulky commercial commodities in widespread areas that could not otherwise have entered the national market.

While the steamboat was accelerating the market's conquest of the West, another transportation development was providing a direct water link between East and West. In 1817, the New York legislature, prodded by

Governor DeWitt Clinton, authorized the construction of a canal from Albany on the Hudson River west along the Mohawk Valley to Buffalo on Lake Erie, and by 1825 the 364-mile Erie Canal was completed. Traffic on the new canal was so heavy that tolls equaled the cost of construction within nine years. Given cheap water communication with New York City and Europe, a flood of commodities from the whole Great Lakes region soon flowed eastward along the canal, meeting a return flow of eastern and European manufactured and other goods destined for the entire West.

The success of the Erie Canal prompted Pennsylvania to build a competing system linking Philadelphia with Pittsburgh on the Ohio, and in the 1830s and 1840s the states of the Old Northwest completed a series of canals connecting the Great Lakes with the Ohio and the Mississippi.

The development of a railroad network in the 1840s and 1850s gave added efficiency to a transportation system that had already succeeded in bringing most parts of the country within the orbit of the irresistible market. Baltimore began constructing its railroad west toward the Ohio in 1828, and in the next decade several thousand miles of short lines were built. Not until the 1850s, however, did the railroad boom reach its height. It was in this decade that the great trunk lines connecting East and West were completed, and by 1860 the country had more than thirty thousand miles of railroad.

In 1815, the shipment of goods from Cincinnati to New York by keelboat and wagon had required over fifty days. In 1850, they could be sent by steamboat to New Orleans and thence by packet to New York in twenty-eight days, by the Ohio and Erie canals and the Hudson River in eighteen days, and by railroad in six to eight days. In 1815, overland freight rates by wagon had ranged from thirty to seventy cents per ton per mile. By the 1850s, the railroads were charging two to nine cents per ton-mile and the canals around one cent per ton-mile. Behind these simple figures lay a revolutionary transformation of American life.

ENTERPRISE AND PUBLIC POLICY

The transportation revolution and the market revolution would have come much more slowly if the men of the early republic had followed the *laissez-faire* notions of political economy that are often mistakenly ascribed to them. Instead, as the market advanced and the spirit of enterprise quickened, Americans demanded that their governments ally themselves with private enterprise to speed the march of progress.

The most notable alliance of public and private enterprise at the state and local level was in the field of transportation, where progress demanded undertakings too vast for individuals or even groups of individuals. The early turnpike companies raised much of their capital from stock subscriptions by states and towns throughout which they ran. The great canals were built directly by states, while other states spent large sums on improving navigable rivers. Governmental aid to transportation reached its peak in the construction of railroads. No one has yet calculated how many millions of dollars towns, cities, and states expended for all these purposes, but it is certain that the revolutionizing transportation network could not have gotten far without this governmental aid.

The turnpike, steamboat, and railroad companies were the forerunners of the modern corporation. These early corporations were born out of the theory of "mixed enterprise," the idea that government should ally itself with private enterprise to accomplish ends beneficial to the public. In the simple days of the staple-exporting economy, all enterprise had been carried on by individuals or partnerships. Economic combinations of many individuals or their capital in large enterprises were thought to be dangerous to the public interest and were frowned upon by the law. Only where some great public purpose was to be accomplished were they thought justified, and then only when chartered by special act of the legislature.

Such corporate charters usually facilitated the raising of capital by granting the privilege of "limited liability," making stockholders in the corporation (unlike members of partnerships) liable for debts of the corporation only to the extent of the stock they held. Charters also usually granted, either explicitly or implicitly, monopolies or semimonopolies, as when a company was given the exclusive right to develop a certain transportation route. Thus the early corporate charter was thought of as a privilege conferred by government in order to enlist private enterprise for the accomplishment of a public purpose.

The corporate device found much of its early use not only in transportation but in banking, and the rapid growth of banking was another of the major factors in the acceleration of economic development. The banking system before the War of 1812 had consisted of the Hamiltonian national bank, chartered by Congress, and a small number of private banks that were called state banks because they were chartered by state legislatures. In theory at least, stockholders bought stock in these banks by paying in gold and silver. On the basis of this "specie" capital, the banks made loans, with the interest they collected from their borrowers providing profits that could be paid back to the stockholders as dividends. What made the banks extremely profitable was the fact that they could safely lend out more than their capital. Instead of lending specie, a bank gave borrowers bank notes, or pieces of paper resembling modern paper money, each bearing a promise that the issuing bank would redeem the note on demand with a specified sum of specie. These bank notes then circulated as money in the vicinity of the bank and, as long as people had confidence in the bank, were not returned for redemption in specie. Thus the bank could safely print, lend, and collect interest on considerably more bank notes than it had specie to cover.

Though at first conservatively managed and restrained by the national bank, the state banks were potentially capable of expanding the supply of credit and investment "capital" almost infinitely and, thus, of stimulating feverish economic activity. This began to happen when the national bank's demise in 1811 and the economic stimulus of the war prompted enterprising politicians and businessmen to secure legislative charters for a large number of new state banks designed to operate on more generous and lucrative principles than their predecessors. The bank mania reached its peak after the war, and the rapid multiplication of banks and bank credit contributed greatly to the boom-and-bust cycle of 1815–1819. Bust was again followed by boom, and the expansion of bank credit reached even greater heights than before in the 1830s. In spite of the violent short-term fluctuations that the banks fostered, they also contributed greatly to the spectacular long-term prosperity of the economy through their active stimulation of its growth.

REPUBLICAN NATIONALISM

The spirit of enterprise was strong in the new generation of Republican leaders who had pushed Madison into war in 1812 and who dominated a transformed Republicanism after the war. Federalism, despite a momentary comeback in Embargo days, was so weakened by the steady swelling of the Republican electorate and so discredited by secession discussion at the Hartford Convention before the war that in 1816 only three states voted for the Federalist presidential candidate. To succeed Madison, the Republicans picked James Monroe, the last prominent Virginian of the Revolutionary generation, and in 1820 Monroe was reelected without opposition.

Monroe himself retained some of Jefferson's agrarian-minded and strict constructionist scruples and rejoiced that the death of Federalism had ushered in an "Era of Good Feelings" when parties should no longer be necessary. In truth, the younger men surrounding the President had moved, in the enterprising atmosphere of the boom years, so far toward the nationalist and commercial-minded views of the Federalists that Federalism had become superfluous. Monroe's State Department was headed by that ardent nationalist John Quincy Adams, who had deserted the party of his father, President John Adams, over the Embargo issue. Monroe's Secretary of the Treasury, William H. Crawford of Georgia, worked for a new national bank. Presiding over the War Department was John C. Calhoun, vigorous champion of a strong army, protective tariffs, and federal road and canal construction. And in Congress, the dominant figure was Speaker of the House Henry Clay, who for a generation would symbolize a broad program of federal action—the "American System" he would call it—to aid enterprise and speed progress.

These men were preaching Hamiltonianism shorn of its elitist overtones. The onrushing market revolution was democratizing business, and the rapid spread of the spirit of enterprise through all levels of society made the new Republican nationalism more dynamic than the old Federalist nationalism of conservative merchants and financiers.

The war was no sooner over than several problems growing out of wartime developments were attacked in the spirit of Republican nationalism. The overexpansion of state banks had led to a financial crisis early in the war. Outside New England, the overextended banks had had to "suspend specie payments" (stop redeeming their bank notes in gold or silver coin on demand), their notes had depreciated, and the resulting financial chaos had contributed greatly to the government's difficulties in carrying on the war. To get the federal government out of its financial troubles and to furnish a sound paper currency and credit system as a basis for orderly business growth, the younger Republicans pushed through Congress in 1816 a charter for a Second Bank of the United States.

This institution, with headquarters in Philadelphia and branches elsewhere, was to have a capital of $35 million as compared with $10 million of Hamilton's national bank. It was to be the depository for all federal funds, and its bank notes were declared receivable for all sums due the government. It was to serve public purposes by making loans to the government and also by regulating the state banks, aiding them to resume specie payments at the earliest possible moment, and thereafter keeping them on a sound basis by sustaining them in periods of financial stringency and restraining them in periods of boom. Its power to do this resulted from its large capital and from the fact that it was constantly receiving large quantities of state bank notes in its role as federal depository. By promptly presenting these notes to the state banks for redemption during booms, it could force them to curtail their issues, while by expanding its own loans and note issues during bust period, it could ease any pressure on the state banks. Yet this was to be essentially a private, profit-making institution with the government subscribing only one fifth of its capital and designating only one fifth of its directors.

Going into operation in 1817, the Second Bank helped secure a general resumption of specie payments, and then succumbed to the boom spirit itself. Inefficient and often dishonest officers so overextended the Bank's own loans and note issues that it lost all power to restrain the expanding state banks. The inevitable reaction, the Panic of 1819, was much more severe than it might otherwise have been because the national Bank suddenly reversed its policy and saved itself by ruthlessly applying pressure against its debtors and the state banks. Not until Nicholas Biddle became the Bank's president in 1823 did it begin to realize its great potential as a balance wheel and regulator for the economy as a whole.

A second problem growing out of the war was the desperate situation of American manufacturers. Most American manufacturing before the War of 1812 had been of the "domestic" variety—spinning, weaving, shoemaking, hatmaking, and countless other enterprises carried on in homes or shops of independent artisans. Large-scale industrial production would develop only in response to the market revolution and the vast national market it created. Yet even before 1812, small cotton textile factories had begun to spring up in New England, iron works were attaining some size in Pennsylvania, and other enterprises in cities like New York and Philadelphia were outgrowing their independent-artisan origins and beginning to employ substantial numbers of journeyman artisans on a wage basis. By cutting off imported European manufactures, the war stimulated a rapid growth in this manufacturing activity. But when the war ended, British manufacturers dumped on the American market their stored-up surplus of products at cut-rate prices, threatening the promising American manufacturing establishment with sudden death.

In the mood of generous nationalism that followed the war, Republican congressmen from all sections of the country responded to the plight of the beleaguered northeastern manufacturers by passing the first tariff act designed primarily to protect American producers from foreign competition. The Tariff of 1816 required foreign imports that competed with such leading American manufactures as cotton and woolen cloth and iron to pay import duties ranging around 20 to 25 percent of their value. Additional protection was granted to iron and textiles in 1818 and 1819.

One of the greatest ambitions of the national-minded Republicans was frustrated by the lingering constitutional doubts of presidents Madison and Monroe. In the closing days of his administration, Madison vetoed as unconstitutional Calhoun's Bonus bill of 1817, a measure reserving $1.5 million, which the new national Bank paid the government for its charter, for beginning a great national system of roads and canals. Although he recognized that internal improvements were necessary to encourage national expansion and to cement the national union, Madison's strict-constructionist background asserted itself. While Calhoun found justification for the measure in the "general welfare" clause, Madison reluctantly concluded that, without a constitutional amendment, federal expenditures for internal improvements were unlawful. With this judgment, his successor, solemn, middle-of-the-road James Monroe, agreed fully.

JUDICIAL NATIONALISM

In the congenial atmosphere of Republican nationalism following the War of 1812, the Federalist nationalism of Chief Justice John Marshall and the Supreme Court he dominated came to full fruition. Having asserted the ' Court's authority on constitutional questions in Marbury *vs.* Madison back in 1803, Marshall now used this authority in a series of remarkable decisions to establish his Federalist and nationalist views on questions of property rights, constitutional interpretation, and federal and state powers.

In Dartmouth College *vs.* Woodward (1819), the Court overruled an attempt by the New Hampshire legislature to change the college's colonial charter. Marshall's Court had already made itself the defender of property rights against state legislatures in an earlier case, and now Marshall declared that charter rights, too, were sacred. This decision was to become increasingly significant with the growing importance of chartered corporations in American economic life.

The biggest corporation of Marshall's day, the Second Bank of the United States, was involved in his most far-reaching decision, McCulloch *vs.* Maryland (1819). This case arose from Maryland's attempt to tax out of existence the Bank's branch at Baltimore. The power to tax was the power to destroy, he argued, and no state could be allowed to destroy an instrumentality of the federal government. Perhaps the most important part of this decision was Marshall's argument, based on the doctrine of implied powers, that Congress had acted constitutionally in chartering the Bank. Here he echoed Hamilton's argument to President Washington at the time the first national Bank was chartered, maintaining that if the end Congress sought to attain was sanctioned by the Constitution, then "all means which are appropriate, which are plainly adapted to that end" are constitutional.

Of various other decisions affirming federal over state powers, one may be singled out as particularly important. In Gibbons *vs.* Ogden (1824), the Court invalidated a monopoly that New York had granted over steamboat service between New York and New Jersey. In giving Congress the power to regulate interstate commerce, Marshall declared, the Constitution meant that *only* Congress should have such power. Furthermore he defined "interstate commerce" so broadly as to include the carrying of passengers or any other variety of commerce between states. Marshall's sweeping extension of the commerce clause not only invalidated the New York monopoly as an invasion of Congress' exclusive power to regulate, but also laid the basis for the vast future extensions of federal regulatory powers.

Thus in the first flush of the market revolution, the spirit of enterprise and nationalism seemed pervasive everywhere in American life—in the entrepreneurial undertakings of countless citizens, in the efforts of the states to hasten progress through transportation projects and corporate charters, in the tariff and banking legislation of Congress, in the diplomacy of President Monroe's Doctrine, and in the decisions of the Supreme Court. The only marring note seemed to be the doubts of old-fashioned Virginia presidents about federal appropriations for roads and canals, and even this slight barrier to progress would be removed when one of the younger, national-minded Republicans entered the White House in 1825. Yet an unprogressive, agrarian society had not—could not have—changed so totally and quickly as this one momentarily appeared to have done. Two decades of crisis and conflict were to elapse before Americans would be at ease in the new world of enterprise.

FOR FURTHER READING:

A good introduction to American economic history is Stuart Bruchey, *The Roots of American Economic Growth, 1607–1861* (1965),* while the indispensable starting point for this period is Douglass C. North's somewhat technical but rewarding analysis of *The Economic Growth of the United States, 1790–1860* (1961).* These may be supplemented with the detailed accounts of the factors of economic growth in George R. Taylor, *The Transportation Revolution, 1815–1860* (1951).* and Paul W. Gates, *The Farmer's Age: Agriculture, 1815–1860* (1960).* Special aspects are well treated in Louis C. Hunter, *Steamboats on the Western Rivers* (1949); Carter Goodrich and others, *Canals and American Economic Development* (1961); Samuel Eliot Morison, *The Maritime History of Massachusetts, 1783–1860* (1921)*; Robert G. Albion, *The Rise of New York Port, 1815–1860* (1939); Robert W. Fogel, *Railroads and American Economic Growth* (1964); and Albert Fishlow, *American Railroads and the Transformation of the Ante-Bellum Economy* (1965). For western development, Frederick Jackson Turner's famous essay on "The Significance of the Frontier in American History" is reprinted, along with many of the arguments it has evoked from other historians, in George R. Taylor, ed., *The Turner Thesis Concerning the Role of the Frontier in American History* (rev. ed., 1956, Amherst Problems in American Civilization).* Francis Philbrick's *The Rise of the West* (1965) is a refutation of the Turner thesis; Ray A. Billington has written the best account of *Westward Expansion* (1949); Malcolm Rohrbough, *Land Office Business* (1968) and Francis Prucha, *Sword of the Republic* (1969) are important works on early white settlement of the west; Reginald Horsman's *The Frontier in the Formative Years* (1970) is a skillful synthesis; and Richard C. Wade describes early western cities in *The Urban Frontier* (1959).* *Flush Times of Alabama and Mississippi* (1853) by Joseph Baldwin is an absorbing contemporary account of the boom years in the Southwest. George Dangerfield has written two accounts of the political history of the era of Republican nationalism: *The Era of Good Feelings* (1952)* and *The Awakening of American Nationalism* (1965).

---

*Available in paperback edition.

PRESIDENTIAL ELECTIONS AND MAJOR EVENTS, 1816–1828

1816   **James Monroe** (Republican) elected over Rufus King (Federalist).

Tariff of 1816, the first deliberately protectionist tariff act.

1817   Second Bank of the United States chartered.

Madison vetoes Calhoun's Bonus bill for internal improvements.

1817–1826   Erie Canal constructed.

1818   National Road reaches the Ohio River.

1819   Dartmouth College *vs.* Woodward. John Marshall's Supreme Court defends charter rights against state legislation.

McCulloch *vs.* Maryland. John Marshall's Supreme Court upholds the constitutionality of the national Bank.

Panic of 1819 forces a general suspension of specie payments and inaugurates a long and severe economic depression.

1820   Land Act of 1820. Lower land prices and abolition of credit system.

Missouri Compromise.

James Monroe (Republican) reelected without opposition.

1824   Tariff of 1824. Higher protection.
Gibbons *vs.* Ogden. John Marshall's Supreme Court extends the federal power to regulate interstate commerce.

John Quincy Adams (Republican) elected over Andrew Jackson, William H. Crawford, and Henry Clay (all Republicans).

1826   Anti-Masonic movement begins.

1828   Tariff of Abominations. Extremely high protective duties.

Andrew Jackson (Democratic Republican) elected over John Quincy Adams (National Republican).

Depression Decade: Sectionalism and Democracy 1819–1828

10

The Panic of 1819 was the first severe economic crisis ever to seriously affect the American people as a whole. Part of an international economic dislocation following a long period of war, it was especially intense in the United States because of the reckless expansion of banks, credit, and entrepreneurial investment that preceded it. When the prices of cotton and other commodities suddenly plummeted on the world markets, countless Americans faced the loss of their homes, farms, workshops, and other property because they could not meet the debts they had incurred to finance their entrepreneurial ventures. The banks suspended specie payments, and bank notes, the only circulating medium, skidded toward worthlessness in the hands of their holders. Merchants went bankrupt, city workers lost their jobs, and the economy ground to a standstill. The paralysis maintained its grip through the early 1820s, and not until after mid-decade did prosperity return.

The economic effects of the Panic were no more momentous than its psychological and political effects. In rapid succession, the American people had been drawn from the settled ways of the old agrarian order into a national market economy of dizzying prosperity, unlimited optimism, and headlong change, and then suddenly plunged into privation and despair. The shock of this experience made the 1820s a decade of soul searching and tension. The postwar mood of generous nationalism evaporated as sections and interest groups became narrowly concerned with their own welfare and jealous of rival sections and interest groups. There was a striking revival of Jeffersonian orthodoxy as prodigal agrarians eschewed the fleshpots of the market and resolved to return to the old ways of frugality and honest toil. Class antagonisms sharpened as impoverished farmers and urban workers blamed political and business leaders—above all, the banking fraternity—for the disaster. And finally, there was a growing interest in politics, a dissatisfaction with the political leadership that had allowed hard times to come, and a demand for new leaders who would be more responsive to the popular will in using government to relieve the distress.

POLITICAL SECTIONALISM

The resurgence of sectional rivalries was dramatically demonstrated by the heated congressional controversy in 1820 over admitting Missouri as a slave state. Slavery had been a source of conflict in the constitutional convention and on several occasions since, but it had not yet become a major issue. The Quakers had been bearing testimony against human servitude for some time, and by 1804 every state north of Delaware had provided for the ultimate emancipation of slaves within its borders. But there was as yet no strong general movement against slavery as a moral and political evil, for most men of good will, both north and south, continued to indulge Jefferson's hope that it would eventually disappear everywhere through the gradual operation of economic and moral forces.

Thus when northern congressmen sought to amend the Missouri admission bill to require the gradual emancipation of Missouri slaves, they were acting less from moral repugnance to the institution than from a revival of the traditional northeastern resentment at southern political domination. Much of the South's political power was derived from the constitutional provision that three fifths of its slaves be counted in apportioning congressional representation and electoral votes. Northeasterners seized upon the Missouri question as a means of blocking the extension of this political injustice throughout the Louisiana Purchase. Southern congressmen, on the other hand, reacted violently to this attack on their vulnerable system of labor. Admission of Missouri as a free state would upset the even balance between slave and free states and destroy the protection that this gave the South in the Senate against any future antislavery measures.

A Missouri Compromise was finally reached because of the simultaneous movement to make the geographically separated eastern appendage of Massachusetts (now Maine) a separate state. Maine was admitted as a free state, Missouri was admitted as a slave state, and it was provided that no further slave states were to be created from that part of the Louisiana Purchase lying north of latitude 36°30' (the latitude of the southern boundary of Missouri).

What many northern congressmen had in mind when they opposed the admission of any more slave states was illustrated at this same session of 1820 by the fate of a bill to extend further tariff protection to the hard-pressed manufacturers. Representatives from slave-holding states voted almost five to one against this measure in the House and provided most of the votes that killed it in the Senate. By 1824, when the manufacturers tried again for higher duties, the South was opposed fifty-seven to one in the House. This time the Northeast was heavily in favor, the only opposition there coming from representatives of international merchants and shippers who resisted any diminution of international trade. But now western farmers had been convinced that the growth of manufacturing might create a flourishing home market for their unprofitable products, and western representatives provided the margin by which the tariff bill squeaked through Congress. The Tariff of 1824 raised duties on textiles to 33⅓ percent, sharply increased the rate on iron, and won rural support by duties on raw wool and hemp.

RELIEF AND DEMOCRACY

Manufacturers were not the only ones who had learned from the doctrines of Republican nationalism to look to government for aid. Thousands of western settlers were now unable to complete their payments for public lands under the credit system inaugurated by the Land Act of 1800. In response to their outcries, Congress forgave interest charges, extended payment periods, and allowed delinquent purchasers to retain an amount of land proportionate to the payments they had made. At the same time, in the Land Act of 1820, it abolished the credit system while lowering the minimum price of public lands from $2 to $1.25 an acre. The minimum tract that could be purchased had recently been reduced to eighty acres, and all these changes enabled a settler to buy a farm for as little as $100 cash.

But it was to the state governments that the people looked for relief from the most desperate problem created by the Panic, the disappearance of money and the collapse of the pyramid of debt that had been built up during the boom. Men could neither collect the debts owed them nor pay the debts they owed, property could not be sold, and a sweeping liquidation through foreclosures and bankruptcies threatened the whole community.

Legislatures, especially in the hard-hit South and West, responded to the demands of their aroused constituents by various schemes to circumvent the constitutional prohibition against issuing paper money or making anything except gold and silver legal tender. Some states established "banks" or "loan offices" to print state-backed paper money for loan to desperate debtors. Usually these measures were coupled with "stay laws" requiring creditors who refused to accept the state-backed paper money to delay executions on their debtors' property. Relief was also provided through "property laws" whereby a "disinterested" jury composed of the debtor's neighbors set a minimum value below which his property could not be forcibly sold to satisfy his debts.

The violent political struggles over debtor relief laws and the closely related banking question accelerated the drift toward a more democratic political system in many of the states. A few socially complex states like New

York and Pennsylvania were already far along the road toward a well-developed two-party or bifactional system in which evenly matched candidates campaigned against each other with the aid of party newspapers and stable party organizations expert in the techniques of garnering votes. Under such circumstances voter interest and participation were high, and public policy was responsive to majority wishes.

In most of the country, however, widespread interest in politics had appeared only sporadically before the 1820s. Having little sense that government—at least the remote state and national governments—affected them much anyhow, most people were willing to leave politics to those well-to-do and socially superior men in their communities who had something to gain from political power, whether land grants or bank charters or simply office. This resulted in a *personal-factional* political system in which a group of leaders allied through personal or family ties normally maintained unchallenged predominance in a county or other district. In the legislatures, representatives from the various local oligarchies formed shifting alliances, again based on personal or family ties.

This system was sanctioned by Jeffersonian political theory. Jefferson had never maintained that the people as a whole should decide public policy, but only that the people were wise enough and virtuous enough to select the wisest and most virtuous among them as political leaders. Candidates pretended that they did not seek office, certainly did not electioneer, but only reluctantly consented to serve when called upon by their fellow citizens. The voters did not tell their chosen representatives what to do once elected, and certainly the representatives did not seek votes by promising to do thus and so. Instead, according to Jeffersonian theory, these unusually wise and virtuous men should be left free to reach wise and virtuous decisions through rational debate and compromise with each other in legislatures and Congress.

The personal-factional system was best adapted to homogeneous communities where conflicts of interest were not very important. It mustered enough genuine wisdom and disinterestedness to function satisfactorily until the market revolution began multiplying the number of specialized economic roles and competing interest groups in the community, while at the same time making men more conscious of the connection between enterprise and public policy. This caused no difficulty during the boom years when there seemed to be enough for everybody. But the Panic made people suddenly aware of their separate and competing interests at the very moment they began looking to government for mutually contradictory kinds of aid. With debtors clamoring for stay laws and loan offices while creditors denounced them, the Jeffersonian notion of a harmony of interests served by wise and virtuous leaders could no longer be sustained. Voters wanted to know where candidates stood on questions of vital concern to them, and the more alert politicians began telling the voters what they thought a majority wanted to hear.

As elections began to be transformed into popular referenda on public policy, a current of discontent with the established political leadership manifested itself. The main target of popular resentment was the banking system, which was blamed for causing the collapse by its reckless overexpansion of credit. While the banks were refusing to pay their own debts by not redeeming their notes in specie and while the depreciation of bank notes was the most conspicuous source of loss to the whole community, the banks were foreclosing on the property of their debtors, continuing to pay dividends, and extending special accommodations to their favored borrowers. The state banks managed to shift some of the resulting resentment to the national bank against which they had similar complaints. But in the eyes of many newly aroused voters, the banking system as a whole was to blame and along with it the politicians and businessmen who had fostered it and profited from it. Moreover these same politicians and businessmen were often leading the opposition to debtor relief.

As voters came to the polls in increasing numbers to repudiate the established leaders, a new-style democratic politics began to supplant the personal-factional system. The new-style democratic politician not only promised the voters what they wanted, but also portrayed himself as fighting the battle of the plain people against a group of unscrupulous "aristocrats." The old loose and shifting factional groupings in state politics began to stabilize as "democratic" and "aristocratic" alignments. In Kentucky, and to a lesser extent in some other southern and western states, something very like a two-party system developed out of the violent conflict over debtor relief.

In the East, where debtor relief was not such a pressing problem, other issues led to similar results. In New York, DeWitt Clinton capitalized on some high-handed maneuvers by the long entrenched "Albany Regency" candidates to make a smashing political comeback as gubernatorial candidate for the "People's Party." In the same state in 1826, the disappearnace and presumed murder of a man who had revealed the secrets of the Masonic order caused an astonishing anti-Masonic outburst, which became a political movement and eventually a short-lived political party. Since Masonic lodges were usually composed of the most prominent men in their communities and since many of the dominant politicians were Masons, the anti-Masons attacked the order as a secret, aristocratic conspiracy against the rest of the community.

The urban counterpart of anti-Masonry was the labor movement that began to flourish late in the 1820s. By fostering larger and more specialized units of production, the market revolution was making it more difficult for artisans and mechanics to follow the traditional progression from apprenticeship through the wage-earning journeyman status to independent proprietorship. The depression and unemployment highlighted the insecurity of the permanent wage-earning status in which more and more workingmen were finding themselves. Journeymen organized labor unions and called strikes against the ten-hour day. On the political front, they joined with small entrepreneurs whose middle-class status was likewise threatened, to form workingmen's parties in Philadelphia and New York City. Under the banner of "Equal Rights," these parties advocated free public education, opposed imprisonment for debt, and agitated against banks and other "monopolies" through which a favored few could exploit the many.

Amid the frustrations and conflicts of the 1820s, the long drift toward popular sovereignty in the United States was reaching its culmination. From the beginning of settlement, the cheapness of land and the demand for labor had created an atmosphere of universal opportunity and rough social equality that was quickly reflected in the quasi-democratic political institutions of the colonies. The Revolution, consigning the destiny of Americans to their own hands, had cut off elitist tendencies and firmly established the ideal of equal political rights. In the following decades, state after state had alleviated restrictive suffrage requirements and other denials—often more symbolic than real—of the Revolutionary ideal. Meanwhile the egalitarian tendency of American life had been reinforced by the process of western settlement, and the new western states had been free to adopt constitutions reflecting the increasingly democratic tone of the country.

Yet it remained for the market revolution to democratize enterprise, to give a final push to the egalitarian tendency, and to arouse a hitherto apathetic electorate to the importance of public policy and politics. The boom-bust cycle made this popular political awakening more abrupt than it might otherwise have been. Appearing first at the local and state levels, the new-style democratic politics began to manifest itself at the national level in the presidential election of 1824.

THE ELECTION OF 1824

An institutional symbol of the established personal-factional system was the presidential caucus. Every four years, the Republican Senators and Representatives met in caucus at Washington to designate their party's presidential candidate, and since 1800 the caucus designation had been tantamount to election. As the election of 1824 approached, the foreordained choice of the caucus was William H. Crawford of Georgia, Monroe's Secretary of the Treasury and the favorite of the large congressional delegations representing Virginia and New York. Crawford's strongest support came from areas that had been relatively immune to the postwar boom and the Republican nationalism that accompanied it (landlocked North Carolina, the worn-out plantation country of eastern Virginia, and the conservative Dutch farming counties along the Hudson River), and he ran as the candidate of a resurgent Jeffersonianism.

This time, however, the caucus system itself was challenged by the sectional and personal rivalries that had rendered Monroe's second term anything but an "era of Good Feelings." Secretary of State John Quincy Adams came forward as the presidential choice of New England and Speaker Henry Clay as the choice of the West. In addition, Secretary of War John C. Calhoun proposed to take his state of South Carolina away from Crawford in the South and counted on his record of support for tariffs, internal improvements, and the national Bank to give him Pennsylvania's electoral vote and additional nationwide backing. All of these anti-Crawford candidates, in fact, were unrepentent champions of Republican nationalism. Calhoun led them in attacking the caucus as undemocratic, and the refusal of their supporters to attend it resulted in Crawford's being nominated by only a minority of the Republican Congressmen.

The ultimate beneficiary of all these currents was none of these candidates, but Andrew Jackson, hero of the Battle of New Orleans. In order to gain an advantage in a local factional struggle, some Tennessee politicians had pushed through their legislature a resolution nominating Jackson for president, never expecting him to be a serious candidate. But there was a surprising response to the nomination from quarters that politicians had not heretofore taken seriously. No one knew where the Tennessee general stood on public issues. To people disenchanted with the old leaders, it was enough that he was a popular hero, the people's man against the established leadership. The strength of this sentiment became apparent when a grass-roots movement swept the Pennsylvania Republican convention out of the control of the leaders who had intended to endorse Calhoun and forced them to pledge Pennsylvania for Jackson. Calhoun promptly withdrew from the presidential race, running unopposed for vice president and carrying South Carolina into the Jackson camp.

When the election took place, Jackson led the four-man field in both popular and electoral votes, but no one had a majority. The Constitution directed that the House of Representatives, voting by states, should choose among the three highest candidates. This eliminated Clay, low man in electoral votes, and Crawford was also removed from serious contention by a physical collapse. This left Clay to wield his great influence in the House on behalf of either Jackson or Adams. Clay chose Adams, and Adams was elected by the narrowest of margins.

THE TRIBULATIONS OF THE SECOND ADAMS

John Quincy Adams was among the ablest and most patriotic presidents, but also one of the least successful. Partly through circumstances and partly through insensitivity to public sentiment, he defied and was overwhelmed by the most powerful political currents of the 1820s.

The Jackson men regarded Adams' election, in any case, as a flouting of the people's will. But when he appointed Henry Clay as Secretary of State, traditional stepping stone to the presidency, their fury knew no bounds. The cry of "Bargain and Corruption" rang throughout the land, touching off a four-year campaign to vindicate popular sovereignty by placing Jackson in the White House.

Adams compounded his difficulties by underestimating the depression-bred reaction against Republican nationalism. Adams and Clay sought to build a National Republican party, based on a coalition of the Northeast and the Ohio Valley and dedicated to Clay's "American System" of protective tariff, national bank, and internal improvements. In addition, the President's first annual message called for a national university and federally sponsored scientific research and exploration, while cautioning Congressmen against being "palsied by the will of our constituents."

The Adams-Clay program outraged the neo-Jeffersonian Crawford men, now led by New York's Martin Van Buren, and drove them into alliance with the Jackson and Calhoun factions. Calling itself the Democratic Republican party, this Jacksonian doalition for four years blocked the President's program in Congress and harassed him in every way possible. The only significant legislative product of these four years was a tariff act passed in 1828. With both parties trying to win presidential votes by juggling complicated tariff schedules, this "Tariff of Abominations" pushed duties on both manufactured and agricultural products to absurdly high levels and satisfied almost no one.

The presidential election of 1828 was marked by the return of the two-pary system to national politics and by a scurrility on both sides that was unmatched since the last closely contested two-party election in 1800. Questions of public policy were hardly discussed, the real issue being whether the people's man Jackson should prevail over the seasoned statesman and old-style political leader Adams. This was enough to produce a substantial increase in the number of voters and a substantial majority for Jackson.

FOR FURTHER READING

Murray N. Rothbard focuses on the *The Panic of 1819* (1962). The best general account of the 1820s is Frederick Jackson Turner, *The Rise of the New West, 1819 1829* (1906).* Even more suggestive, though it deals only with the southern states, is Charles S. Sydnor, *The Development of Southern Sectionalism, 1819–1848* (1948). Glover Moore has carefully examined

---

*Available in paperback edition.

The Missouri Controversy, 1819–1821 (1953). James Sterling Young, *The Washington Community, 1800–1828* (1966), explains how the very organization of governmental activity and institutions in Washington reflected the pervasive fears of a vigorous national government. Some idea of the political transformations going on in the states in the 1820s may be gained from Dixon Ryan Fox, *The Decline of Aristocracy in the Politics of New York* (1919),* and from Charles Sellers, *James K. Polk, Jacksonian: 1795–1843* (1957). The presidency and subsequent political career of John Quincy Adams are splendidly narrated in Samuel Flagg Bemis, *John Quincy Adams and the Union* (1956). Robert V. Remini has written a lively scholarly account of *The Election of Andrew Jackson* (1963).*

PRESIDENTIAL ELECTIONS AND MAJOR EVENTS, 1828–1840

1828   **Andrew Jackson** (Democratic Republican) elected over John
        Quincy Adams (National Republican).

1830   Jackson vetoes the Maysville Road bill.

1832   Tariff of 1832. Remedies the worst abuses of the Tariff of Abomi-
        nations, but fails to satisfy the South Carolina Nullifiers.

        Jackson vetoes the bill to recharter the Second Bank of the
        United States.

        Andrew Jackson (Democratic Republican) reelected over Henry
        Clay (National Republican).

        South Carolina nullifies the tariff laws.

1833   Compromise Tariff. Gradual reduction of all tariff duties to 20
        percent.

        Force Act. Authorizes president to use military to enforce the
        laws.

        Jackson transfers the federal deposits from the national bank to
        selected state-chartered deposit banks.

1836   Jackson issues Specie Circular requiring specie for purchase of
        federal lands.

        Distribution Act distributing the federal surplus among the states.

        Martin Van Buren (Democrat) elected over William Henry Harri-
        son, Daniel Webster, and Hugh Lawson White (all Whigs).

1837   Panic of 1837 forces a general suspension of specie payments
        and initiates a severe and prolonged economic depression.

        Van Buren proposes the independent treasury system.

1838   New York Free Banking Act, a forerunner of general incorpora-
        tion laws. One of the many efforts by the states to reform
        and regulate banking.

1840   Independent treasury system finally approved by Congress after
        three years of debate.

        William Henry Harrison (Whig) elected over Martin Van Buren
        (Democrat).

The Jacksonian Era
1828–1840

11

With Andrew Jackson's inauguration, the forces of egalitarianism swept over the federal government. Though Jackson had risen to become master of a large plantation and one of the leading men of his state, he had never abandoned the egalitarian habits of his earlier surroundings in small-farmer North Carolina and frontier Tennessee. On Inauguration Day, he opened the White House reception to an unruly mob of the high and the low, shocking the older official society but unmistakably announcing the new regime's conviction that one man was as good as another.

The same point was made with more substantial effect by Jackson's extension of the "spoils system" and his frank advocacy of "rotation in office." The new President was accompanied to Washington by a host of new-style democratic politicians demanding office as a reward for their support. Jackson took the position that any honest citizen could discharge the duties of a government office as well as any other. Furthermore public offices should not be the property of their holders for life. They should be passed around, with a preference shown for friends of the administration that the people had elected. The numerous removals and appointments that Jackson made on these principles somewhat impaired the efficiency of government service, but also made it more representative of and responsive to the country as a whole. Moreover the spoils system helped make possible the new-style political parties through which the popular will could be translated into public policy.

Jackson was the first president to operate on the principle that the people themselves should decide public policy. Arguing that the president was the only federal official elected by the people as a whole, he was supremely certain that his policies represented the popular will. And so great was the popular confidence he inspired that the people, or a majority of them, usually agreed.

By assuming this role of democratic tribune, Jackson greatly increased the power of the presidency relative to Congress. All of his predecessors combined had vetoed only nine congressional measures, usually on the ground that they were unconstitutional. Old Hickory used the veto twelve times, against legislation he thought inexpedient as well as legislation he thought unconstitutional. And by taking his differences with Congress to the voters, he was highly successful in making recalcitrant legislators compliant or in getting them replaced.

JACKSONIAN POLICIES

Though the people's candidate had been elected, it was by no means clear what policies a people's administration would follow. Jackson himself had little political experience, and it was supposed that much would depend on whether Calhoun or Van Buren controlled his administration and became his heir for the presidential succession. Calhoun wanted to base the Jacksonian Democratic-Republican party (which gradually came to be called simply the Democratic party) on an alliance between the South and the West, which would reduce tariffs for the South and liberalize federal land policy for the West. A most embarrassing issue for Calhoun's plans was that of internal improvements, which the West favored and the South increasingly opposed.

Van Buren, on the other hand, wanted to resurrect the old Jeffersonian coalition between southern planters and the "plain Republicans" of the Northeast. Such a coalition could unite on neo-Jeffersonian grounds to oppose internal improvements (New York wanted no federally financed competition for its Erie Canal) and the national bank (New Yorkers resented the bank as a Philadelphia institution that gave New York City's rival an undeserved financial dominance). The one issue that was dangerous to Van Buren's plans was tariffs, over which Northerners and Southerners were disagreeing with mounting vehemence.

Although the Calhoun men had seemed to have the upper hand in the party, Jackson's inauguration produced a sudden reversal. Calhoun's friends were almost frozen out of the Cabinet, while Van Buren himself was given the Secretaryship of State. Relations between Jackson and Calhoun steadily deteriorated until the South Carolinian was finally driven from the party. This result was produced in good part by Van Buren's astute use of the information that Calhoun, while a member of Monroe's Cabinet, had advocated punishing Jackson for his rash invasion of Spanish Florida. The New Yorker was aided, too, by the "Eaton imbroglio," when the socially prominent women of Washington tried to ostracize the somewhat disreputable wife of Jackson's old friend and Secretary of War John Eaton. Mrs. Calhoun was among the ladies who angered the President by snubbing Peggy Eaton, while the widower Van Buren was free to treat her with conspicuous gallantry.

But more fundamental than any of these considerations was the fact that the old general found Van Buren more congenial than Calhoun, both personally and in political outlook. Jackson came to Washington without a very well-thought-out position on the major issues. But he did have some deeply rooted political instincts which he trusted implicitly, and it was these that determined the policies of his administration. His instinctive egalitarianism has already been noted. Joined to this was an instinctive neo-Jeffersonian agrarian-mindedness.

Jackson himself had once engaged in extravagant land and commercial speculations based on credit. The bankruptcy that ended these operations and the long struggle to pay off his debts and regain solvency through farming were the experiences that were most decisive for his political outlook. A thoroughly chastened advocate of the virtues of agriculture, hard work, and economy, abhorring debt and fearing the get-rich-quick atmosphere fostered by easy credit, he interpreted the boom-bust cycle of 1815–1819 as reproducing his own personal experiences on a national scale. Consequently when he assumed the presidency, his one clearly defined objective was to administer a simple, economical government so as to pay off the national debt as rapidly as possible.

Jackson's mood was more congenial with Van Buren's neo-Jeffersonianism than with the Republican nationalism that had heretofore been Calhoun's trademark. The influence that this gave Van Buren became most apparent when the advocates of a nationwide federal road system managed in 1830 to push through Congress the Maysville Road bill. Though this bill only provided that the federal government should buy stock in a company building a turnpike from Maysville to Lexington in Kentucky, it was regarded as the test measure for the whole internal improvements program. Expenditures for internal improvements would delay Jackson's cherished project for paying off the national debt, and Van Buren had little difficulty persuading him that the measure should be vetoed. The veto message not only condemned the Maysville project, but suggested that all federal expenditures for internal improvements were perhaps either unwise or unlawful. Yet, though it retarded for several decades the dream of a nationally financed transportation network, the Maysville veto had greater symbolic than practical effect. While it was a declaration that the Jacksonians favored not only frugal government but limits on federal powers, Jackson himself authorized some $10 million in improvement bills, including some for local projects.

THE TARIFF AND NULLIFICATION

Clearly, Jackson and Van Buren were not ready to assault all the works of Republican nationalism. To undertake a thoroughgoing downward revision of the Tariff of Abominations would be to delay payment of the public debt and to disrupt the North-South alliance that Van Buren sought to perfect. Consequently the President urged his first Congress to handle the question with "utmost caution," and the resulting tariff revisions of 1830 hardly touched the more abominable features (its outrageously high duties generally) of the system.

At this point South Carolina exploded. No state had enjoyed a more uninterrupted prosperity from colonial days to 1819 than South Carolina. First rice, indigo, and sea island cotton had created a wealthy ruling class in the lowcountry, and then the upland cotton boom had spread comparable riches through the rest of the state. No state, except perhaps Kentucky, was harder hit or more permanently damaged by the depression of the 1820s. The disruption of business coincided with the rise of more efficient cotton-producing areas in the Gulf States, and to make matters infinitely worse, a growing anxiety over the slavery issue made South Carolina particularly sensitive about state rights. South Carolina's reaction to its economic prostration was the more violent because of the long period of heady prosperity that had preceded it and because no state had developed a prouder or touchier group of political leaders.

Until the depression, the Republican nationalism of Calhoun and his friends had been ascendant in South Carolina. The hard times enabled a rival "state-rights" faction to blame Calhoun's favorite policies for all the state's woes. By the mid-twenties, the state-rights men had stirred up a storm of resentment against the protective tariff and were close to winning political control of the state. Calhoun and his friends were forced to retreat from Republican nationalism as rapidly and unobtrusively as possible. When Congress passed the Tariff of Abominations in 1828, the Calhoun men confounded their state-rights rivals by outdoing them in violent agitation against protection and by adopting an even more radical version of the state-rights doctrine.

The famous doctrine of nullification was announced in the South Carolina Exposition and Protest of 1828, secretly written by Calhoun and issued as a report of a legislative committee. The Nullifiers maintained that the Constitution was a compact among states that retained their essential sovereignty and that had delegated only limited and clearly specified powers to the federal government. The states themselves were the only proper judges of whether their common agent, the federal government, had exceeded the powers delegated to it by the constitutional compact. If a state judged that some federal law was a violation of the compact, it could declare it null and void whereupon the federal government must desist unless and until three fourths of the states, through the amending process, explicitly granted it the nullified power.

The South Carolinians counted on the Jackson administration to push tariff reform, and only after its failure to do so in 1829–1830 did Calhoun's friends begin a campaign in the state for actual nullification. The Jacksonian Congress responded by eliminating some of the worst excesses of the Tariff of Abominations in 1832, but the rates were still decidedly protectionist. Meanwhile Calhoun had openly broken with Jackson and put himself at the head of the Nullifiers; the Nullifiers won the two-thirds majority in the state legislature necessary to call a state convention; and in November, 1832, the state convention declared the tariff laws null and void, and forbade their enforcement in South Carolina.

When Congress met in December, Jackson called for thoroughgoing tariff reform but at the same time announced his determination to enforce all federal laws throughout the land, by military means if necessary. It was this situation that produced the Compromise Tariff of 1833. Snatching from the Jackson party the credit for tariff reform, Clay and Calhoun united to push through a measure by which all tariff rates were to be reduced by gradual steps over a ten-year period to a uniform rate of 20 percent. Congress also complied with Jackson's demand that it simultaneously pass a Force Act, authorizing him to use the armed forces to uphold the laws. The South Carolina convention then reassembled and rescinded its nullification of the tariff laws, but got in the last word by nullifying the Force Act.

The seemingly inconclusive outcome should not obscure the important long-range effects of this dangerous crisis. The fact that the Nullifiers could claim victory—the tariff had been reformed—heightened their uncompromising attitude toward the federal government and gave them complete dominance over South Carolina. From this time on, the state and its magnetic leader Calhoun sought to unite the South in radical resistance to federal tyranny, and the incessant agitation from this source was a major factor in producing the eventual secession of the southern states.

In the shorter run, nullification and disunion were discredited. Every other southern legislature denounced the South Carolina doctrine, the aged Madison denied that it derived from the Kentucky and Virginia resolutions of 1798, and the country as a whole responded enthusiastically to the nationalistic sentiments that Jackson expressed in opposing the Nullifiers. In fact, Jackson's zeal for preserving the Union led him to embrace a nationalistic interpretation of the Constitution that greatly embarrassed Van Buren and other state-rights Jacksonians. Heretofore the state-rights idea had been associated with democratic-mindedness in American politics, but now that the people's candidate was in the White House proclaiming federal preeminence over the states, federal power seemed less threatening. Perhaps the most significant result of the nullification crisis was the decline of state-rights sentiment in the face of a rising democratic nationalism.

INDIAN REMOVAL

Yet Jackson was not always a single-minded champion of federal prerogatives, as indicated by his handling of claims of the Cherokee nation, one of the Five Civilized Nations. A practical westerner who was not inclined to romanticize the "noble savage," the Tennessee president winked when the state of Georgia expropriated Cherokee lands in defiance of a federal court ruling. In *Cherokee Nation v. Georgia* (1831) and *Worcester v. Georgia* (1832), the Marshall Court sided with the Indians, invalidating the state's claim to Cherokee territory. But Jackson refused to enforce the ruling, reportedly saying: "John Marshall has made his decision, now let him enforce it."

That which followed, the forced removal of these native Americans to territory beyond the Mississippi, is one of the darker chapters in the nation's history. Amid scenes of indescribable suffering, some 4,000 of the 16,000 refugees died in 1838 and 1839 of cold, hunger, and disease along the 800-mile-long route known in Cherokee memory as the "Trail of Tears." By 1839, three more of the remaining Five Civilized Nations—Choctaw, Chickasaw, and Creek—had been forcibly removed to the West under the Congressional acts of 1830 and 1834. In 1843, the fifth nation, the resisting Seminoles of Florida, were all but exterminated by federal troops. Meanwhile, the Black Hawk War (1832) had ended effective Indian resistance to white settlement in the Old Northwest.

All told, more than 60,000 Indians were forced onto western reservations, thereby opening up millions of acres of fertile eastern land to land-hungry whites. Emerging as it did at the peak of the nullification crisis, the federal restraint implicit in Jackson's Indian policy may have confused some Jackson watchers. But southerners, westerners, and land speculators were delighted to find a president who shared their views of the Indian's place in an expanding nation. In fairness to Jackson, the policy of dispossession and relocation that he so vigorously enforced was begun well before his election. Moreover, given the social values of the age and a context of growing conflict between Indian nations and eastern states, it did not appear an unreasonable solution to the "Indian problem." Convinced that assimilation was impossible and that autonomous Indian enclaves were impractical, if not unconstitutional, Jackson seems genuinely to have believed that his was a "just and humane policy" that placed the Indian "beyond the reach of injury or oppression." That it proved to be none of these things is indisputable; that other, more enlightened alternatives were open to him is less certain.

THE BANK WAR

Simultaneously with the nullification controversy, another great conflict had begun to take shape, this one between Andrew Jackson and the Second Bank of the United States. Jackson's experience with debt and depression had made him distrustful of all banks. On the bank question, his democratic-mindedness merged with his agrarian-mindedness to produce the conviction that banks fostered an unhealthy atmosphere of speculation, created boom-

and-bust cycles, and transferred wealth from the many to the few. The national Bank was open to special objection because it concentrated so much power in private hands and because it violated the Jeffersonian principles of strict construction and limited government. Jackson's views in all these respects reflected the resurgent agrarian-mindedness and neo-Jeffersonianism produced by the depression, as well as the antibank animus of the emerging workingmen's movement.

Actually, since Nicholas Biddle had become president of the Bank in 1823, it had acted to restrain the numerous state-chartered banks from the tendencies Jackson feared, and most businessmen and politicians had become convinced that the Bank was indispensable to a soundly growing economy. Yet the opponents of banking in general saw the national Bank as the head of the whole odious system, and the only part of the system that the federal government could readily reach. As a new boom gathered strength in the early 1830s, they were aided by an incongruous ally, entrepreneurial democracy.

Once again, as in the boom years following the War of 1812, the glittering promise of profits held out by a rapidly expanding market economy was creating a host of new entrepreneurs. For these men of enterprise, easy credit was the key to success, and the more reckless of the state-chartered banks became the citadels of the entrepreneurial spirit. By restraining the state banks from overexpansion, the national Bank curtailed the profits and dimmed the prospects of the state banks and their borrowers. Consequently the new entrepreneurs, the more speculative elements of the economy, regarded the Bank as an aristocratic and repressive institution, representing established wealth and using its privileged position to hobble newcomers who attempted to join the race for success.

Both the new entrepreneurs and the agrarian-minded had been heavily attracted to Jackson's Democratic party. Both groups opposed the Bank on somewhat egalitarian grounds, but their common hostility to Mr. Biddle's institution could not indefinitely conceal the fact that their ultimate objectives were diametrically opposed.

When Jackson became president, Biddle was already thinking about getting a bill passed to renew the Bank's charter, which was due to expire in 1836. Jackson dismayed the Bank's supporters when he questioned its constitutionality and expediency in his first message to Congress. Their dismay turned to alarm when it became clear that Jackson would be a candidate for reelection in 1832. The old Adams-Clay alignment, calling itself the National Republican party, was planning to run Clay against Jackson, and Clay was urging Biddle to press for recharter before the election. Clay argued that this would force Jackson to approve a recharter bill, for a veto would be a damaging issue against him in the election. Biddle finally agreed, and in July, 1832, a recharter bill passed Congress by substantial majorities.

Jackson promptly returned the measure to Congress with a veto message declaring the Bank unconstitutional and demagogically denouncing the foreign ownership of much of the Bank's stock. At the heart of his message was an eloquent paragraph expounding the Jacksonian social philosophy. The President granted that natural inequalities existed in every society. "But," he said, "when the laws undertake to add to these natural and just advantages artificial distinctions, to grant titles, gratuities, and exclusive privileges, to make the rich richer and the potent more powerful, the humble members of society—the farmers, mechanics, and laborers—who have neither the time nor the means of securing like favors to themselves, have a right to complain of the injustice of their government."

Jackson's hostility to the bank was genuine, but his veto message was at least in part designed to make the Bank an election issue. The Bank men did not have the votes in Congress to override the veto, but they confidently expected that both the veto and its author would be repudiated in the ensuing presidential election. When the returns were in, Jackson's estimate proved to be the shrewdest as he won 219 electoral votes to Clay's 40.

Yet the Bank was far from dead. Jackson rightly feared that Biddle was determined to use the Bank's great economic and political power to push a recharter bill through Congress over his veto. Equally determined to cripple the Bank, the President resolved to remove the government's mounting deposits from its vaults. Federal receipts were booming along with the economy, the national debt had been paid off, and a federal surplus of millions of dollars was beginning to accumulate. These surplus federal deposits greatly extended the Bank's lending ability, profits, and power. It took the administration a year to find a way of removing surplus deposits from the Bank. After discharging two consecutive uncooperative Secretaries of the Treasury and after protracted negotiations with nervous state bankers, Jackson announced in September, 1833, that henceforth the Treasury would deposit the federal funds in selected state banks, so-called deposit banks or pet banks.

Enraged by the removal of deposits, Biddle recklessly threw the full economic power of the Bank against the government. Deposit removal and Jackson's hostility made some contraction of the Bank's loans necessary, but Biddle resolved to force such a severe loan contraction and to create such widespread distress that Congress would be compelled to restore the deposits and eventually recharter the Bank. As a result, the "Panic Session" of Congress was under intense pressure during the winter of 1833–1834 to restore the deposits to relieve the country from mounting bankruptcies, unemployment, and distress. But Jackson's anti-Bank majority held firm, Biddle was finally forced to relax the pressure, and the Bank's doom was sealed—partly because Biddle's panic helped to prove Jackson's case against the Bank's immense power.

BOOM AND BUST AGAIN

The destruction of the Bank was only a Pyrrhic victory in the Jacksonians' larger campaign to reform banking in general. Jackson and many of his principal followers were "hard-money" men who wanted all bank notes driven from circulation, leaving only gold and silver coin as a circulating medium. Their attack on the national bank was only the first step in their deflationary, agrarian-minded program, and they hoped to use the state-bank deposit system to reform the state banks. The deposit banks would be required, as a condition for receiving the deposits, to cease issuing notes in denominations under $5 or accepting such notes in their transactions with other banks. Gradually the prohibition would be extended to notes under $10 and then $20. Driving small notes from circulation would create a steady demand for specie for small transactions, and all banks would have to reduce their loans and note issues in order to have enough specie on hand to meet the demand.

But this scheme did not have time to get under way before it was overwhelmed by a massive inflation. The Jacksonians had destroyed the national Bank's stabilizing influence on the economy just at the moment when powerful inflationary forces were pushing the country into a boom even more wildly speculative than the one that followed the War of 1812. With the national Bank's restraining influence removed, the state banks expanded their loans, note issues, and profits; new state banks were chartered by the hundreds; the deposit banks themselves got out of control; and the wave of inflation and speculation rolled ominously higher toward its inevitable cresting and crash.

The hard-money men could only shout futile warnings. Their Jeffersonian constitutional scruples prevented them from attempting direct federal regulation of the state banks. Regulation at the state level was equally impossible because the uneasy alliance between hard-money (or agrarian-minded) Democrats and enterprise-minded Democrats began breaking down as soon as their common enemy, the national Bank, was finally defeated.

Nevertheless, in 1836, Jackson attempted a drastic remedy with his Specie Circular. The flood of bank notes had stimulated an especially frantic speculation in public lands, and the Circular directed that thenceforth lands must be paid for in specie or specie-redeemable bank notes. Coming too late, the Specie Circular succeeded only in putting a strain on the vastly overextended structure of credit. The strain was increased by the Distribution Act that Jackson had reluctantly signed a few weeks before. Congress had decided to distribute the bulging federal surplus, approaching $40 million, among the states; and the federal deposit banks were suddenly called upon to transfer vast sums to the state treasuries. Finally, in the spring of 1837, only weeks after Jackson left office, a financial crisis in England set off a wave of bankruptcies in the United States, the banks suspended specie payments, and the Panic of 1837 brought the whole towering pyramid of credit crashing down.

Jackson's hand-picked successor Van Buren was left to cope with a severe and prolonged depression. Aligning himself with the hard-money wing of the Democratic party, Van Buren proposed that the government sever its connections with all banks and keep its funds in its own "independent treasury" offices. He further proposed that the government accept and pay out only gold and silver coin, which would have some deflationary effect by creating a constant demand for specie. But in the main the proposal meant that the federal government would wash its hands of responsibility for the economy. Because of the split between hard-money and soft-money Democrats, Congress wrangled over the independent treasury throughout Van Buren's term. The bill was finally passed in 1840.

Meanwhile the depression had forced most state legislatures to attempt some kind of banking reform. A few states prohibited banks entirely, others gave a monopoly of the banking business to a state-owned or mixed public-private bank, and most states adopted stricter regulations to prevent an overextension of credit by private banks. New York's widely imitated Free Banking Act of 1838 sought to provide state regulation and at the same time to divest banks of the monopolistic special privileges they enjoyed through their legislative charters. Foreshadowing general incorporation laws for all kinds of enterprises, it provided that anyone could engage in the banking business if he complied with certain regulations. Thus by the early 1840s, the country had reached a practical compromise on the banking question: banks would continue to stimulate economic growth, but they would be restrained through free competition and state regulation rather than through a national bank.

The long and hotly contested struggle over banking was important in two respects. On the most obvious level, it reflected the efforts of an economy newly swept forward by the market revolution to develop a credit and currency system that would sustain growth and broaden opportunity without causing disastrous boom-and-bust cycles. But at a deeper level, it reflected the psychological ambivalence of a conservative, agrarian society toward the whole new world of rapid change and growth into which it had been suddenly thrust. During the first great boom, 1815–1819, the country as a whole succumbed with uncritical enthusiasm to the new spirit of enterprise. The depression of the 1820s produced an equally decided reaction in the other direction—against banks, easy credit, paper money, and entrepreneurial ambition. Thus the return of prosperity and the second great boom, 1834–1837, evoked more ambivalent reactions. Some again saw unlimited opportunity and clamored for unlimited credit; others, the neo-agrarians who remembered the 1820s, championed hard money; still others, perhaps the majority, oscillated between the two extremes. By the time of the second great depression following 1837, the ever-advancing market had sufficiently undermined agrarian-mindedness, and the boom-bust cycle had sufficiently chastened the enterprise-minded to make a rough consensus possible. The American people had finally made their adjustment to the new world of enterprise created by the market revolution.

THE NEW POLITICS

Just as the Jacksonian era saw the evolution of financial institutions and practices to serve the emerging spirit of enterprise, so did it see the evolution of political institutions and practices to serve the emerging spirit of egalitarian democracy. The basic feature of the new politics was the two-party system, which had flourished briefly and imperfectly around 1800 and which ree-merged to reach its full development only in the 1830s.

Carrying to the national level the new-style democratic politics that had emerged in the states during the 1820s, the Jacksonians created a strong political party and forced their opponents to imitate their organization and techniques for wooing a mass electorate. The anti-Jacksonians were at first an ill-organized coalition of Clay-Adams National Republicans, Nullifiers, and—out of hostility to the Van Buren organization in New York—the demo-cratic-minded anti-Masons. These elements were unable to unite to stem the Jacksonian tide in the presidential election of 1832, but they were already beginning to learn the lessons of Jacksonian politics. In fact the anti-Masons had anticipated the Democrats in calling a national party convention repre-senting the grass-roots elements of the party to replace the discredited caucus method of nominating candidates.

A powerful, unified opposition party developed only in 1833–1834 when Jackson's removal of deposits caused the defection of many business-minded Democrats and enabled his opponents to unite on the platform of resistance to executive tyranny. Taking the name "Whigs," to identify them-selves with earlier defenders of liberty, they stood for sound business enter-prise and a program of Republican nationalism. Though the Whigs drew increasing support from all sections and classes, they appealed especially to the wealthier and more established members of the business community, to the manufacturing interests, and to the larger southern planters whose staple crops involved them extensively in the commercial network. Calhoun's Nullifiers cooperated with the Whigs for a few years, but after 1837 returned to the Democratic party.

In 1836, the new Whig party sought to capitalize on political sectional-ism by running three presidential candidates, hoping to throw the election into the House of Representatives. But the magic of Jackson's popularity was sufficient to win his candidate, Van Buren, a slim majority over all three

Whigs. The Whigs' day finally came in 1840 when the Democrats were discredited by the depression and when the Whigs outdid the Democrats at the game of democratic politics. Running the popular old Indian fighter William Henry Harrison as the people's candidate against the "aristocratic" Van Buren, the Whigs whipped up enthusiasm with monster rallies, torch-light parades, songs, and log-cabin symbolism to win a sweeping majority.

The presidential election of 1840 also produced by far the largest out-pouring of voters yet seen. Only 27 percent of the estimated eligible voters had voted for president in 1824; the Jackson-Adams contest of 1828 had raised the figure to 56 percent; but the contest of 1840 brought out 78 percent of the eligible electorate, a proportion that may never have been equaled since. This dramatic rise in political interest was a result of the full development of the two-party system. By 1840 the two parties were almost equally strong not only at the national level but also in every section, in most of the states, and in a majority of counties. This meant closely contested elections for all offices from sheriff to president with no efforts being spared to woo hesitant voters. Each party maintained an elaborate network of stridently partisan newspapers in Washington, the state capitals, and count-less villages and towns. Rival orators stumped every neighborhood for months before every election. Competing systems of party committees at county, state, and national levels issued a constant stream of broadsides and pamphlets, organized parades and rallies, and made sure that no voter stayed away from the polls on election day. This incessant political activity not only brought voters to the polls in droves, but also made politics a leading form of American recreation, while providing the population with a massive political education.

But the parties were as much affected by the voters as they affected the voters. The new-style democratic politicians of both parties developed an acute sensitivity to shifts in public opinion and became expert in building coalitions that would yield a majority or near-majority. The Whigs continued to appeal more strongly to businessmen, the well-to-do, manufacturing inter-ests, and large planters, while the Democrats attracted smaller farmers, workingmen, and frontier areas. But both parties needed additional support to achieve a majority, and both quickly learned the techniques for constantly adjusting their positions to changing public moods. As a result the parties tended not to differ sharply in normal times and to maintain a nearly even balance of strength. From Jackson's day to our own, with only brief interrup-tions, this two-party system has remained a reasonably sensitive instrument for translating majority opinion into public policy while moderating the sharpness of conflict among the diverse groups that compose American society.

CONFLICTING HISTORICAL VIEWPOINTS

4. What Was Jacksonian Democracy?

In his Life of Andrew Jackson *(3 vols., 1860), the nineteenth-century historian James Parton concluded that the seventh president was "a patriot and a traitor. . . . A democratic autocrat. An urbane savage. An atrocious saint." On this note of paradox, scholarly investigation of Jacksonian politics began and to the present day Old Hickory's administration remains among the most controversial in American history.*

Parton, the earliest and most distinguished nineteenth-century Jackson scholar, represented the patrician school of historians. Sons of affluent and often aristocratic eastern families, deeply suspicious of popular democracy and the common man, these early historians viewed Jacksonianism as the degradation of American government. Jackson, they affirmed, was an illiterate backwoods barbarian, the agent of the unwashed and ignorant masses.

Soon after 1900, a generation of reform-minded scholars challenged this decidedly conservative "Whig" interpretation. Countering the antidemocratic views of the patricians with prodemocratic views of their own, these progressive historians generally celebrated Jackson as the champion of the popular will. Thus, in his distinguished Life of Andrew Jackson *(2 vols., 1911), John Spencer Bassett praised the rustic Tennessee president for his "brave, frank, masterly leadership" of a broad democratic movement. Generally agreed on the nature of Jacksonian democracy, the progressives nevertheless often argued about its origins. In* The Frontier in American History *(1920) and* The United States, 1830–1850 *(1935) Frederick Jackson Turner, one of the earliest of the great progressive scholars, emphasized the influence of frontier democracy in the development of Jacksonianism. In Turner's view, Jacksonian Democracy was a sectional rather than a class movement. It was inspired and sustained, he believed, by the pioneer societies of the new states of the West and Southwest. To Arthur M. Schlesinger, Jr., on the other hand, Jacksonianism was "a problem not of sections but of classes." In his Pulitzer Prize-winning* Age of Jackson *(1945), the younger Schlesinger included eastern wage earners as well as western farmers among the supporters of the Old Hero. The movement, he argued, pitted "noncapitalist groups, and laboring men, East, West, and South" against "capitalist groups, mainly Eastern."*

In recent years, the critics of the progressive interpretation, and particularly of Schlesinger's labor thesis, have been numerous. Bray Hammond (Banks and Politics in America *[1957]) and Edward Pessen* (Jacksonian America *[1969]), for example, denied that Jackson's was a working-class* movement. *Arguing that his supporters were not common men at all but incipient entrepreneurs, Hammond characterized the Jacksonians as "newer, more aggressive . . . businessmen" who clashed with "an old and conservative merchant class." According to Pessen, Old Hickory was antilabor, and workingmen opposed him at the polls. Marvin Meyers (The Jacksonian Persuasion [1957]) and John W. Ward (Andrew Jackson, Symbol for an Age [1955]), on the other hand, have fastened on symbolism and psychology to explian the Jacksonian phenomenon. In differing though complimentary studies, these scholars concluded that in Jackson, Americans found neither a champion of class nor section, but the embodiment of old-fashioned republican virtues. But the ultimate refutation of the Schlesinger interpretation—and all others for that matter—came from Lee Benson, who argued in* The Concept of Jacksonian Democracy *[1961] that Jacksonianism existed only as a figment of the historical imagination. Indeed, if historians followed the advice of this historical quantifier, they would forget altogether about the concept of Jacksonian Democracy.*

Benson's thesis has some support, but the imminent demise of Jackson studies is most unlikely. Today, more than two centuries after the Old Hero's birth, the man and the movement continue to provoke lively controversy.

FOR FURTHER READING

Robert V. Remini's *Andrew Jackson* (1966)* is both brief and excellent, and Glyndon G. Van Deusen's *The Jacksonian Era, 1828–1848* (1959)* provides a generally whiggish overview of the entire period. Richard McCormick's *Second American Party System* (1966) describes party formation in the Jacksonian era; Robert V. Remini has analyzed *Andrew Jackson and the Bank War* (1967); Peter Temin focuses on *The Jacksonian Economy* (1969); and Edward Pessen's *Riches, Class, and Power Before the Civil War* (1973) provides a valuable social portrait of the era. William W. Freehling has written the *Prelude to Civil War: The Nullification Controversy in South Carolina* (1966)* and Charles M. Wiltse focuses on *John C. Calhoun: Nullifier, 1829–1839* (1949). Other important biographies of Jackson's contemporaries include William N. Chambers, *Old Bullion Benton: Senator from the New West* (1956); Thomas P. Govan, *Nicholas Biddle: Nationalist and Public Banker* (1959); Glyndon G. Van Deusen, *The Life of Henry Clay* (1937)*; and Glyndon G. Van Deusen, *Thurlow Weed, Wizard of the Lobby* (1947). The consequences of Jackson's Indian policies may be traced in Thurman Wilkins, *Cherokee Tragedy* (1970), and Arthur DeRosier, *Re-*

*Available in paperback edition.

moval of the Choctaw Indians (1970). Francis Paul Prucha's *American Indian Policy in the Formative Years* (1962) is an important revisionist work. A firsthand impression of Martin Van Buren can be gained from his *Autobiography* (published in the *Annual Report of the American Historical Association,* 1918); and James Curtis's *The Fox at Bay* (1970) examines Van Buren's presidency. The analyses of Jacksonian America by European observers are extremely illuminating. Here the classic is Alexis de Tocqueville, *Democracy in America* (2 vols., 1835–1840)*; but also fascinating are Michael Chevalier, *Society, Manners, and Politics in the United States* (1839)*; Francis J. Grund, *Aristocracy in America* (1839)*; Harriet Martineau, *Society in America* (1837)*; and Frances Trollope, *Domestic Manners of the Americans* (1832)*. The Bank War can be analyzed in Frank Otto Gatell, *The Jacksonians and the Money Power, 1829–1840* (Berkeley Readings in American History, 1967).*

Romanticism, Reform, Slavery

12

The country had no sooner developed a two-party system for reflecting the majority will while moderating conflict, than it ran head-on into the one conflict that could be neither resolved by majority will nor moderated: the conflict over Negro slavery. The age of enterprise and egalitarianism that produced the two-party system had also brought Americans to their highest pitch of confidence about the possibilities of individual men and of optimism about the future of their society. It was a reforming age, abounding in schemes for wiping out the remaining blemishes that marred the full perfection of man. It was a utopian age, spattered with perfectionist communities and looking forward to the early perfection of the whole society. Such an age was bound to find intolerable the most glaring affront to the liberal principles of the Declaration of Independence. Yet Negro slavery was so deeply rooted as a social and economic institution that the slaveholders, though themselves heirs of the American liberal tradition, could not surrender it.

ROMANTICISM

Underlying the reformist spirit of the age was a new configuration of ideas and attitudes called *Romanticism.* A vast and complicated movement in the intellectual and literary history of the Western world, Romanticism took different forms and led toward different conclusions in different countries, periods, and individuals. As used here, the term denotes the central tendencies of thought in the United States in the first half of the nineteenth century.

Romanticism grew out of the eighteenth-century Enlightenment and was akin to it. Both assumed that the world was designed for man's happiness and both emphasized man's ability. In America, at least, both led in the direction of optimism, individualism, and liberal political principles. But Romanticism was a reaction against the Enlightenment's mechanical view of the natural world and its emphasis on intellect. Where the Enlightenment ascribed man's competence to his ability through reason to understand the natural laws by which a watchmaker Creator regulated both the physical and moral universes, Romanticism distrusted intellect and valued man's emotional and intuitive qualities. Regarding the natural world as the embodiment of a divine spirit, Romanticism held that the natural and the spontaneous were the good and that the highest truth was derived through the instantaneous spiritual intuition of the individual.

American Romanticism reached its most sophisticated and self-conscious form in the Transcendentalism of Ralph Waldo Emerson and the group of New England intellectuals he inspired. While most of Emerson's contemporaries were probably unaware of Transcendentalism or Romanticism as an explicit body of doctrine, the pervasive Romantic assumptions were apparent in every aspect of American life. The overwhelming theme of popular literature and the popular stage was the primacy of feeling over intellect. In more serious writing, James Fenimore Cooper celebrated the moral perfection and superior wisdom of the "natural" but untutored woodsman Leatherstocking and the "noble savage" Chingachgook, while Nathaniel Hawthorne and Herman Melville explored, from a Romantic standpoint, some of the darker implications of Romantic doctrine. The landscape painters of the Hudson River School sought to capture on their canvases the emotion of the "sublime" evoked by natural scenes. Architects turned from the intellectually satisfying simplicity, harmony, and proportion of the eighteenth century's "colonial" or "Georgian" style to exotic and more titillating models—Gothic, Moorish, and Egyptian. Even in laying out gardens and parks, Americans abandoned formal patterns and tried to reproduce artificially the wildness and irregularity of nature, as in Frederick Law Olmsted's design for Central Park in New York City.

The influence of Romanticism extended far beyond intellectuals, writers, and artists. Jacksonian egalitarianism was reinforced by some widely accepted Romantic assumptions. The Enlightenment's emphasis on reason and education, its insistence that reason was more highly developed in some men than in others, had prevented even the more liberal men of the eighteenth century from endorsing full egalitarianism and popular sovereignty. Thus Jefferson had relied on a "natural aristocracy" to rule, trusting the people to elect the "natural aristocrats" to office, yet not trusting them to dictate public policy. But when intuition rather than reason was seen as the source of truth, the situation changed. The Romantic doctrine of democracy was expounded most baldly by the Jacksonian politician and distinguished historian George Bancroft: "if the sentiment of truth, justice, love, and beauty exists in every one then it follows, as a necessary consequence, that the common judgment in taste, politics, and religion is the highest authority on earth." Indeed, by Jackson's time, the semiliterate farmer who lived simply and close to nature was often regarded as being superior in virtue and real wisdom to a city dweller whose "natural" impulses had been stifled by the artificialities of education and culture.

Jackson's enormous popularity may be attributed in considerable measure to the prevalence of such attitudes. The contest between Jackson and John Quincy Adams in 1828 was widely interpreted as pitting a "natural" man of virtue, a product of the American frontier, against the well-educated, highly cultured, and therefore suspect Adams, who had the additional disadvantage of having spent much of his early life in the artificial surroundings of an overcivilized and decadent Europe. To Harvard-trained John Quincy Adams, Jackson was "a barbarian who could not write a sentence of grammer and hardly could spell his own name." But the people found in him the embodiment of all the natural wisdom of the common man. In the presidential election of 1840, the Whigs turned the tables by using, in naked parody, the Jacksonian political formula. Deftly exploiting a hard-cider and log-cabin symbolism, they presented William Henry Harrison, "the Ohio Plowman," as the representative of the "hardy yeomanry" whose "primitive" qualities contrasted sharply with the city-slicker airs of the Jacksonian candidate, Martin Van Buren. The voters who responded enthusiastically to these appeals had never heard of Romanticism as a body of doctrine, but the smashing victory they gave Harrison at the polls demonstrated their unconscious conversion to some key Romantic assumptions.

ROMANTIC CHRISTIANITY

Apart from political behavior, extensive popular acceptance of Romantic assumptions was most evident in religious behavior. Well into the nineteenth century, the story of religion in the United States was a story of the gradual erosion of the originally dominant Puritan-Calvinist strain of Protestant Christianity. In an increasingly self-reliant, optimistic, and individualistic society, it continually became more difficult to sustain a view of life that emphasized the awful sovereignty of God, the sinfulness and helplessness of man, and the necessity for salvation by God's miraculous and arbitrary grace.

Under the impact of the eighteenth-century Enlightenment, some members of the more sophisticated classes had abandoned the inscrutable, omnipresent God of the Calvinists for Deism's remote and kindly Creator. Others had moved in the same direction more gradually, retaining the outward forms and language of orthodox Christianity, but coming to believe that a reasonable God was favorably disposed toward all men, that men were sufficiently endowed with reason to be capable of goodness, and that the objective of a religious life ought to be goodness in this world rather than God's arbitrary salvation in a world to come. Such opinions spread rapidly even among the direct descendants of seventeenth-century Puritanism, the

New England Congregationalists. However, violent controversy broke out between the liberal and orthodox factions. By the end of the century, the liberal Congregationalists, who tended to be the wealthier and better educated, were breaking off to form separate churches and taking the name Unitarians.

While Unitarianism was a minority movement in the churches, Christian orthodoxy unquestionably was at a low ebb in the last quarter of the eighteenth century. The mighty orthodox counteroffensive, the Great Awakening of the 1730s and 1740s, had spent its force; the Revolution had brought with it the spiritual and moral laxity usual in wartime, Deism was growing popular and militant, and the orthodox themselves had become listless and begun to acquiesce in compromises with the spirit of the age.

It was under these circumstances that the orthodox clergy resorted to the emotional techniques of the Great Awakening to launch another vigorous counteroffensive known as the Great Revival. Really a series of revival movements beginning around the turn of the century, the Great Revival kept the country in religious ferment for twenty-five years, obliterating the last traces of Deism and bringing a majority of Americans into the Protestant churches. America did not return to Calvinism, for in the process of capturing America, Protestant Christianity was itself captured and transformed by the Romantic optimism and individualism of American culture.

One phase of the Great Revival began with a series of spectacular "camp meetings" in Kentucky. These week-long extravaganzas of religious enthusiasm spread rapidly over the West, spawning a host of poorly educated but highly effective revival preachers. Traveling up and down the West, these emotional revivalists left in their wake a host of new churches, mainly of the less sophisticated popular denominations, Baptists and Methodists.

Meanwhile President Timothy Dwight of Yale and his protégé Lyman Beecher were showing the conservative clergy in the East how to use a more restrained revivalism as a technique for combating Unitarianism and maintaining the hegemony of orthodox Congregationalism. At the same time, the Congregationalists were cooperating with the Presbyterians in a joint campaign to evangelize the frontier areas of western New York and the Old Northwest. The revival movement and the western missionary effort both culminated in the 1820s in the spectacularly successful evangelism of Charles Grandison Finney. This former lawyer combined emotional intensity with some shrewdly devised new techniques—cottage prayer meetings preceding his revival meetings, the full participation of women, the "holy band" of zealous young helpers to pray individually with the religiously smitten—to produce an explosion of emotional piety that entrenched a revivalistic "Presbygationalism" in the western regions. Although he was ordained a Presbyterian minister, Finney's "New School" Calvinism led him far from the hell-fire and damnation of an orthodox past. Preaching neither God's inscrutable sovereignty nor man's ineradicable depravity, he embraced the doctrine of free will and laced his sermons with a perfectionism that directed his followers not only to personal salvation but social reform.

Most of the revivalists started from positions they would have regarded as theologically orthodox, but like Finney they were more interested in the effectiveness, the preachability, of what they were saying than in its theological correctness. They quickly found that it was easiest to evoke the desired emotional response by preaching that God was anxious to save sinners, that sinners need only accept God's love. Many Presbyterians and the more conservative Protestants of all denominations in the South resisted this tendency, but the main body of American Protestantism moved gradually and unconsciously toward a Romantic theology. Love was viewed as the essence of the Christian life. God was love, freely offering his love to all who would accept it. Conversion was the emotional experience of acceptance and loving response. In some versions, as with many Methodists and in the theology that Finney himself taught, conversion was viewed as carrying with it a kind of spiritual perfection. The tone of this Romantic Protestantism was clearest perhaps in hymns like "O Love That Will Not Let Me Go" and its juvenile counterpart "Jesus Loves Me."

UTOPIANISM AND HUMANITARIANISM

Wherever the Great Revival burned—and especially in the frequently ravaged "burned-over district" of western New York—it left behind a bed of glowing embers ready to be fanned into all kinds of extravagant perfectionist and utopian movements. Most of these movements were millennialist, expecting Christ's early return to establish the Kingdom of God on earth. There was an excited outburst of expectation when the Reverend William Miller calculated from Biblical prophecies the time of Christ's return, but believers were disillusioned when the event did not occur, either in the originally predicted spring of 1844 or, after Miller had corrected his calculations, on October 21 of that year.

Various groups that looked forward to an early millennium sought in the meantime to gather together those who had been "perfected" through conversion into communities that would be without sin or blemish. Because they emphasized the primacy of love in all relationships and the freedom from sin that comes with salvation, these perfectionist utopians had particular difficulty with conventional notions about the proper relations between the sexes. One group, led by John Humphrey Noyes, established a flourishing community at Oneida, New York, that rejected private property for common ownership and exclusive marriage for a carefully regulated system of "complex marriage." A more successful group, the Shakers, solved the problem of exclusive love by practicing celibacy in their many communities.

The most durable of all these movements was Mormonism, which derived from Joseph Smith's claim that he had discovered in upstate New York some golden plates containing new revelations from God, and which for a time sanctioned the practice of polygamy.

In addition to the religiously oriented utopian movements, the Romantic age produced many secular utopian communities. Perhaps the best known was Brook Farm at Roxbury, Massachusetts, which was supported by many people on the fringes of the Transcendentalist movement. A more ambitious community at New Harmony, Indiana, was founded by Robert Dale Owen, son of the English textile manufacturer and social reformer Robert Owen. The most extensive movement in secular communitarianism was inspired by Charles Fourier, a French social philosopher who had calculated rationally the optimum size and organization for the ideal socialistic community, which he called a "phalanx." Attracting the support of the prominent New York editor Horace Greeley, the Fourierists established some forty or fifty phalanxes in the United States. In general, the secular utopias did not fare as well as those that had a religious motivation to keep their members loyal to the communitarian ideal. Many of the latter survived late into the nineteenth century, dwindling away only as the ebbing of religious revivalism dried up their source of recruits.

The perfectionist impulse that produced the utopian communities also inspired a broader series of movements aimed at wiping out every individual and social evil that the age could identify. Much of this reformist activity was devoted to previously neglected classes of unfortunates. Dorothea Dix led the crusade that persuaded state legislatures to establish institutions for the care of the mentally ill. A related movement induced a number of states to undertake extensive programs of penal reform, emphasizing rehabilitation rather than merely punishment of criminals. For the first time, facilities were developed for educating the deaf, dumb, and blind. Indeed, the great movement for publicly supported common schools for all children got its real start in this perfectionist age with Horace Mann's ambitious program in Massachusetts leading the way.

The reform movements that had the greatest impact were those most closely associated with the Great Revival. In the early stages of his revivalist campaign in Connecticut, Lyman Beecher devised the technique of organizing through local churches voluntary societies of laymen to promote various moral and evangelical objectives. By the late 1820s, these local societies had developed into a group of regional and national federations with paid agents to organize new local societies, raise funds, and carry out the various objectives of the federations. The American Home Missionary Society, which hired evangelists to carry the Great Revival into the West, was one of the first of the national federations. It was soon joined by other national societies that devoted themselves to such religious objectives as foreign missions, distributing Bibles and religious tracts, promoting Sunday schools, and saving sailors. Leadership and financing for all these societies came from the same group of revivalistic "Presbygational" ministers and philanthropists led by Beecher and Finney.

The developing Romantic theology of the Great Revival soon inspired a reform impulse that went beyond the evangelical objectives of the earliest societies. Finney in particular was preaching that conversion caused a disposition of "disinterested benevolence" in the converted, and his revivals left behind numbers of converts anxious to find some object on which to lavish their disinterested benevolence. The first object to be discovered was the drunkard.

The fantastic consumption of alcoholic beverages in the early republic unquestionably constituted a serious social problem. Lyman Beecher had early been shocked by the extent of drunkenness at ministerial ordinations, and as the revival spirit spread, he helped inspire the organization of local temperance societies, which aimed at moderation rather than complete abstinence in the consumption of alcohol. When this proved ineffective, Beecher began campaigning for total abstinence, and in 1826 the American Society for the Promotion of Temperance was organized with total abstinence as its goal. Sending evangelists through the country to persuade people to sign a pledge of total abstinence, the Society claimed five thousand local branches with a million members by 1834.

Turning to politics, the temperance forces secured a local option law in Massachusetts in 1838 and the first statewide prohibition law in Maine in 1846. Soon most of the northern states had legislated against alcohol. In contrast to twentieth-century prohibitionism, the nineteenth-century movement was much weaker in the South, where only the border states of Delaware and Tennessee resorted to legislative prohibition.

The temperance movement was merely the first of the reform movements inspired by the Great Revival. By the 1830s, the headquarters for the benevolent societies had shifted from Boston to New York City, where Finney had been established as pastor of a great "free" church (charging no pew rents) for the poer and where resided the two leading financial angels of the general benevolence movement, the merchant brothers Arthur and Lewis Tappan. Into New York every May poured an army of the benevolent-minded from every part of the country to attend a series of annual conventions of all the societies. New societies were continually being organized for every conceivable purpose: to promote peace, to stop the carrying of mails on Sunday, to stop the wearing of corsets.

WOMEN'S RIGHTS

Animated by the same humanitarian and moral impulses as men, women played significant roles in the reform movements of the age. Very often, however, their effectiveness was severely limited by the fears and prejudices of the men with whom they sought common cause. Angelina and Sarah Grimké, for example, left their South Carolina home and went north to aid in the antislavery cause. But their efforts to speak in its behalf were often opposed by male abolitionists and frequently howled down by audiences unaccustomed to such "unladylike" endeavors. In 1840, Lucretia Mott, Elizabeth Cady Stanton, and half a dozen other American women traveled to London to attend the World Anti-Salvery Convention only to be excluded because of their sex. In the 1850s, Susan B. Anthony had much the same experience in the temperance movement, where "ladies" were expected to be seen but not heard. The irony of such discrimination by men and by organizations dedicated to humanitarian causes was not lost on this generation of women. With Angelina Grimké, not a few of them would ask: "What can a *woman* do for the slave when she herself is under the feet of man and shamed into silence."

The sexual prejudices of the male reformers were mirrored and magnified by the larger society they sought to uplift. In the eyes of the law, women were perpetual minors, the wards of male guardians without whom they had no separate legal identity. Denied the right to vote, hold office, or sit on juries, they enjoyed few property guarantees, suffered gross educational and job discriminations, found divorce a virtual impossibility, and were legally subject even to corporal punishment by their husbands. Until 1850, nearly every state permitted wife beating "with a reasonable instrument" (defined by one Massachusetts judge as a "stick no bigger than my thumb").

Confronted by such disabilities, women (usually of the upper-middle class) organized for their own relief, often combining women's rights with temperance, abolition, public education, and prison reforms. Except for some highly significant breakthroughs in the fields of literature and education, their successes were few; throughout the period, feminism remained little more than an attitude shared by a few intrepid social pioneers. Sarah Grimké's *The Equality of the Sexes* (1838) and Margaret Fuller's *Women in the Ninteenth Century* (1844) were important early woman's manifestoes; Amelia Bloomer's sensible but much-ridiculed crusade for dress reform, Lucy Stone's repudiation of marriage laws that gave a husband "injurious and unnatural superiority" over his wife, and Stanton and Mott's Seneca Falls declaration of woman's independence ("We hold these truths to be self-evident: that all men *and women* are created equal") symbolized a heightening feminist consciousness. But the work of these early feminists scarcely touched the lives of the vast majority of the nation's women. Sisterhood was not powerful in antebellum America. For all the vigor of their protest, the Susan B. Anthonys and the Angelina Grimkés of that era organized more effectively for causes other than their own.

ABOLITION

While the woman's movement probably owed little to evangelical Christianity, religion was clearly a principal engine of abolition. Before 1830, the organized antislavery movement had been small and ineffectual, drawing its support mainly from those persons, notably Quakers, with strong religious scruples against human bondage. A scattering of manumission societies, principally in the upper South, sought to encourage owners to free their slaves, and Benjamin Lundy had maintained for some years an antislavery journal. In addition, the American Colonization Society had been seeking without much success to promote the migration of free Negroes to Africa, a conservative approach to the problem that aroused the suspicion of both the defenders and critics of slavery.

Only when the British Parliament's widely-publicized debates over emancipation caught the attention of the leaders of the American benevolence movement did antislavery begin to become a major force on this side of the Atlantic. In 1830, the Tappan brothers helped organize an antislavery society in New York. The following year young William Lloyd Garrison left Benjamin Lundy's employment to set up his own militant antislavery newspaper *The Liberator* in Boston. Over the years to come, Garrison and the small group of zealous antislavery men he inspired in New England were to furnish an uncompromising ideology for the growing antislavery movement, while the Finney-Tappan benevolence movement was to commit its mass of support, stretching west from New York, almost wholly to the cause.

At first antislavery was only one among the many causes espoused by the Tappans and their associates. A turning point came when one of Finney's ablest young converts and apprentice evangelists, Theodore Dwight Weld, became wholly committed to the antislavery cause. In 1833, Weld enrolled at Lane Seminary in Cincinnati, a school that had just been established under Lyman Beecher's presidency to train Finney's converts for the ministry. Proselytizing among his fellow students, Weld provoked the famous Lane Debate, a revivalistic discussion of slavery that lasted for eighteen days and nights and ended with the conversion of virtually the entire student body to the abolitionist cause. Meanwhile the Tappan and the Garrison groups had come together in uneasy alliance to form the American Anti-Slavery Society, which now employed Weld and his fellow Lane converts as agents. During the mid-1830s these men and others conducted a whirlwind evangelistic campaign through New England, New York, Pennsylvania, and the Old Northwest, which resulted in the conversion of some whole communities to antislavery and the organization of over a thousand local antislavery societies with more than one hundred thousand members.

The abolitionism preached by Weld and his associates emphasized the moral evil of slavery and the religious duty of good men to align themselves against it. In fact, most abolitionists were intensely pious people, driven by religious sentiments that portrayed good works as the result of salvation. At first they naively hoped to persuade slaveholders to abandon the institution by sending into the South tons of pamphlets portraying the sin of holding human beings in bondage.

Despite the rapid growth of the movement, abolitionism remained highly unpopular in much of the North. Many Northerners who had no great fondness for slavery feared that antislavery agitation endangered the Union. Still others were deeply infected with the same race prejudice that bolstered slavery in the South. Prominent abolitionists had to face hostile mobs, and one editor, Elijah Lovejoy, was actually killed for his antislavery views.

Yet the abolitionists gained support far beyond their own ranks when they moved into politics in the mid-1830s with a petition campaign asking Congress to abolish slavery and the odious slave trade in the District of Columbia. Many Northerners who shied away from the constitutionally difficult question of abolition in the slave states were glad to support the abolitionist petitions with reference to the national capital over which Congress had unquestioned jurisdiction. Northern opinion was generally indignant when Congress responded to southern pressure in 1836 by adopting a "gag rule" refusing to consider petitions relating in any way to slavery. At this point, ex-President John Quincy Adams, serving out the remainder of his life in the House of Representatives, took up the cause. Originally not an abolitionist, "Old Man Eloquent" was infuriated by this denial of the constitutionally guaranteed right of petition. Supported by a growing body of northern opinion, he carried on a dogged fight against the gag rule until it was eventually repealed in 1844. Though the North was still far from abolitionized, the steady agitation of the question was gradually conditioning increasing thousands of voters to view the slaveholding section of American society with hostility.

THE SOUTH AND SLAVERY

Meanwhile white Southerners were being forced to reexamine their attitudes toward their "peculiar institution." Christianity and the liberal principles of the Declaration of Independence affected Southerners just as much as Northerners. During the latter part of the eighteenth century, many of the South's outstanding leaders had emancipated their slaves, denouncing slavery as incompatible with the ideals of the Revolution. Thomas Jefferson and other liberal Southerners had counted on the gradual operation of economic forces to eliminate slavery in the South as was already being done in the North. As late as the Missouri debate in 1820, southern Congressmen refused to defend slavery in the abstract, arguing instead that the unfortunate institution had been inherited and was difficult to eradicate.

Yet southern opinion had already begun to shift in a direction that would ultimately lead to civil war. The fundamental cause for change was the market revolution. Until the end of the eighteenth century, the stronghold of slavery had been in the Chesapeake tobacco region of Virginia and Maryland. The economic depression in this region following the Revolution had encouraged the spread of antislavery sentiment and afforded some grounds for Jefferson's hope that the institution might wither away. But farther down the coast the great plantations of South Carolina had continued to flourish; and with the perfection of the cotton gin in 1793, high profits stimulated the rapid spread of plantation slavery into the up-country. South Carolina was the only state that permitted a resumption of the barbarous foreign slave trade before its prohibition by Congress in 1808.

The most spectacular expansion of plantation slavery came during the boom years following the War of 1812 when it flooded over the newly opened lands of Alabama, Mississippi, and Louisiana. Taking deep root as a flourishing economic system, the chief source of wealth, and a spur to enterprise, slavery became increasingly impossible for white Southerners to surrender. The cottom boom in the lower South dampened antislavery tendencies in the upper South by creating a heavy demand at high prices for the surplus slaves of the declining tobacco kingdom. Nonslaveholders, too, came to feel that they had a stake in the institution. Only about a fourth of the white families in the South ever owned slaves, and even among the slaveholding minority only 12 percent owned as many as twenty slaves. But the South was as deeply infected as any other part of the country with the spirit of enterprise that the market revolution generated, and in the South the acquisition of slaves was becoming the primary and almost the exclusive means of raising one's economic and social status.

At the same time, another factor was reinforcing the white South's growing economic attachment to slavery. Thomas Jefferson had assumed that deep antipathies between white men and black men would make emancipation unthinkable without some plan for removing the emancipated slaves from the United States. This conviction that the two races could not live side by side in freedom received a powerful impetus in the 1790s when the slaves on the nearby French West Indian island of Santo Domingo rose in rebellion, murdering or forcing into exile thousands of their former masters. From this time on, the more the white South became attached to slavery as an economic institution, the more it feared its slaves, and consequently, the more it insisted on slavery as an institution for controlling this dangerous population. Alarms over threatened slave insurrections became more frequent, some with a basis in fact and others arising more from imaginations made excitable by fear and guilt.

A real insurrection finally came in August, 1831, when a slave named Nat Turner led an uprising in Southampton County, Virginia. Over sixty whites were killed before the rebels were crushed. A wave of hysteria washed over the whole domain of slavery, and the Virginia legislature was frightened into the Old South's only full and free debate over the peculiar institution. Not a voice was raised to justify slavery in the abstract, and proposals for gradual emancipation were barely defeated.

The entire South sensed that a fateful choice had been made. The fears of slave insurrection had culminated just at the time when slavery was becoming too entrenched as an economic institution to be surrendered and at the very moment when the American antislavery movement was launching a massive propaganda barrage against slavery, appealing to Christian and liberal values that white Southerners shared. Slowly and reluctantly, Southerners faced the fact that, if slavery were to be retained, they could no longer ease their consciences with hopes for its eventual disappearance or tolerate the expression of such hopes in their midst. Southern minds must be nerved for a severe struggle in defense of the institution to which they now saw themselves committed. So southern leaders of the Calhoun school began trying to convince themselves and others that slavery was a "positive good," while southern legislatures abridged freedom of speech and the press, made manumission difficult or impossible, and imposed tighter restrictions on both slaves and free Negroes.

Proslavery arguments never succeeded in relieving the majority of white Southerners from varying degrees of moral uneasiness or feelings of guilt. Like all men unsure of their ground but unable to change it, Southerners responded to attacks on slavery with mounting vehemence. Even in the 1830s, when both Southerners and Northerners were still preoccupied with the Jacksonian political issues, the abolitionists' petitions provoked such violent congressional debates that the gag rule had to be imposed. Within another decade, the explosively emotional quarrel over slavery would move to the center of the political stage, there to remain until blood was shed.

CONFLICTING HISTORICAL VIEWPOINTS

5. How Brutal Was Slavery?

In his monumental studies, American Negro Slavery *(1918) and* Life and Labor in the Old South *(1929), Ulrich B. Phillips set forth the classic defense of slavery as a labor system beneficial to both master and man. A tireless researcher and a prolific writer, Phillips uncovered a wealth of new material and contributed enormously to our factual knowledge of the "peculiar institution." But the work of this Georgia-born scholar was seriously flawed by racial prejudice. The Negro slave, he believed, was innately inferior and naturally submissive. In his view the plantation was a school in which primitive and uncouth blacks were purged of their African savagery and offered the blessings of western civilization and Christianity.*

This sympathetic interpretation of a benign and paternalistic institution dominated American historical writing for nearly three decades. But in the increasingly enlightened climate of racial opinion following World War II, historians began reassessing traditional assumptions about the antebellum South's labor system. In American Negro Slave Revolts *(1943), Herbert Aptheker, a Marxist historian and a passionate civil rights advocate, portrayed a rebellious and discontented slave work force that contrasted sharply with the carefree darky bondsmen of Phillips' idyll. The most sweeping revision, however, was Kenneth Stampp's broad synthesis,* The Peculiar Institution *(1956). A distinguished liberal scholar who argued that "Negroes are, after all, only white men with black skins," Stampp viewed slavery as a harshly cruel system degrading to both exploiter and exploited. The typical slave, he concluded, hated both the institution and his master.*

Not all of Phillips' critics agreed with Stampp. In Slavery *(1959), Stanley Elkins, for example, offered a controversial study that blended Stampp's harsh criticism of slavery with Phillips's view of the slave as contented Sambo. Using social science and comparative history techniques, Elkins concluded that the labor system of the Old South was so brutal and dehumanizing that it infantilized its victims. According to this interpretation, the typical slave was, thus, childlike, docile, and convinced of his own inferiority.*

In the 1970s, historians have rejected Elkins's conclusions and moved beyond Stampp's. Increasingly the direction has been away from the study of slavery as an institutional problem toward an analysis of day-to-day life in the quarters. Masters now attract less scholarly attention than slaves. John Blassingame's Slave Community *(1972), for example, offers a fascinating view of plantation life and labor from the vantage point of the bondsman himself; and Eugene Genovese's* Roll, Jordan, Roll *(1974) brilliantly portrays (as its subtitle promises) "the world the slaves made." Although not understating its unjust and often unspeakably cruel dimensions, both Blassingame and Genovese conclude that slavery permitted its victims a heretofore unsuspected degree of cultural autonomy and sense of community.*

The most provocative recent study is Robert Fogel and Stanley Engerman's Time on the Cross *(1974), a book that has attracted perhaps more public interest and more scholarly criticism than any other work of history in memory. A computer study by two gifted "cliometricians,"* Time on the Cross *contends that slave labor was more efficient and productive than free labor and that slaves lived comparatively well-provisioned, secure, and comfortable lives. "Over the course of his lifetime," the authors argue, "the typical slave field hand received about 90 percent of the income he produced." These conclusions, although less novel than the authors claim, provoked a storm of controversy. Many blacks found them offensive, and many scholars—including most historical quantifiers—faulted the data and research procedures upon which they were based.*

FOR FURTHER READING:

In the absence of an adequate general account of Romanticism in American thought, much can be learned from the splendid segment of a study left uncompleted by Perry Miller, *The Life of the Mind in America from the Revolution to the Civil War* (1965). An older work by Octavius B. Frothingham is still the fullest account of *Transcendentalism in New England* (1876)*; and Henry Steele Commager's *Theodore Parker: Yankee Crusader* (1936)* describes a major figure on the fringes of the Transcendentalist movement. A general account of religion, utopianism, and reform in this period is Alice Felt Tyler, *Freedom's Ferment: Phases of American Social History to 1860* (1944)*; and Daniel Boorstin, *The Americans, The National Experience* (1965) sets these and other social movements in a broad historical context. For the Great Revival in the East and revivalism's connection with perfectionism and reformism, see Whitney R. Cross, *The Burned-over District* (1956)* and Timothy L. Smith, *Revivalism and Social Reform in Mid-Nineteenth Century America* (1957).* The flavor of revivalism in the West is reflected in the *Autobiography* (1856)* of Peter Cartwright; while the beginnings of Mormonism are traced in Fawn M. Brodie, *No Man Knows My History: The Life of Joseph Smith* (1945).

Outstanding studies of the Old South include: the early chapters of W. J. Cash, *The Mind of the South* (1941)*; Clement Eaton, *The Growth of Southern Civilization, 1790–1860* (1961)*; Clement Eaton, *The Freedom-of-Thought Struggle in the Old South* (1964)*; Clement Eaton, *The Mind of the Old South* (rev. ed., 1967)*; Frank L. Owsley, *Plain Folk of the Old South* (1949)*; and William R. Taylor, *Cavalier and Yankee: The Old South and American National Character* (1961).* Some aspects of slavery not included in the essay above are analyzed in: David Brion Davis, *The Problem of Slavery in Western Culture* (1966); Winthrop. D. Jordan, *White Over Black: American Attitudes toward the Negro, 1550–1812* (1968); William K. Scarborough, *The Overseer* (1966); and Robert S. Starobin, *Industrial Slavery in the Old South* (1970). Differing views on the origins of abolitionism are offered in Gilbert H. Barnes, *The Anti-slavery Impulse* (1933)* and Louis Filler, *The Crusade Against Slavery* (1960). Benjamin Quarles has written about the *Black Abolitionists* (1969); Bertram Wyatt-Brown is the author of *Lewis Tappan* (1969); and Aileen Kraditor, *Means*

---

*Available in paperback edition.

and Ends in American Abolitionism (1969) emphasizes variety and conflict within the abolitionist movement. The interpretations of a number of scholars on various aspects of abolitionism are presented in a volume of essays collected by Martin Duberman, ed., *The Anti-Slavery Vanguard* (1965).* A leading proslavery theorist is described in Harvey Wish, *George Fitzhugh: Propagandist of the Old South* (1943).

PRESIDENTIAL ELECTIONS AND MAJOR EVENTS, 1840–1852

1840   **William Henry Harrison** (Whig) elected over Martin Van Buren (Democrat).

1841   Vice President **John Tyler** becomes president on death of Harrison.
Whig Congress repeals the independent treasury system.
Land Act of 1841. Preemption principle allows settlers to buy public lands they occupy at minimum price.
Tyler vetoes successive bills chartering a national bank and is disowned by the Whig party.

1842   Tariff of 1842. Whig measure extending substantial protection to American manufactures.
Webster-Ashburton Treaty with Great Britain, settling the Maine boundary and other disputed matters.

1844   Tyler's treaty for the annexation of Texas defeated in the Senate.
James K. Polk (Democrat) elected over Henry Clay (Whig).

1845   Texas annexed by joint resolution of Congress.

1846   Democratic Congress reinstitutes the independent treasury system.
Tariff of 1846. Substantial reduction of rates.
Polk's veto of Rivers and Harbors bill checks policy of internal improvements.
Oregon controversy with Great Britain compromised.
Polk precipitates Mexican War by insisting on extreme Texas boundary claim.
Wilmot Proviso proposed to bar slavery from any territories acquired from Mexico.

1848   Treaty of Guadelupe Hidalgo. Ends Mexican War, with the United States paying Mexico for a vast cession in the Southwest.
Zachary Taylor (Whig) elected over Lewis Cass (Democrat) and Martin Van Buren (Free Soiler).

1849   Gold Rush to California.

1850   Vice President **Millard Fillmore** becomes president on death of Taylor.
Compromise of 1850: (1) California admitted as free state; (2) Utah and New Mexico territories organized on principle of squatter sovereignty; (3) Texas surrenders claims to area in New Mexico, and United States assumes Texas debt; (4) slave trade abolished in the District of Columbia; (5) a more stringent Fugitive Slave Law enacted.

1852   **Franklin Pierce** (Democrat) elected over Winfield Scott (Whig).

Manifest Destiny
and Sectional Conflict
1840–1852

13

Though the Whig and Democratic leaders continued to battle each other in the early 1840s over tariff, national bank, and internal improvements, these old issues no longer excited Americans as they had in Jackson's day. The market revolution had completed its psychological conquest of the country, and with hard times receding, an enterprising generation was engrossed in the pursuit of wealth and status.

For countless thousands, the pursuit led west toward the perennial American goal of cheap land and a fresh start. But now, for the first time in the American experience, there seemed a limit to the supply of cheap, fertile land. In the South the tide of settlement rolled up to the boundary of the Mexican province of Texas. Farther north it was nearing the treeless Great Plains which were thought unfit for cultivation.

Yet neither political nor geographical boundaries were to halt the two-hundred-year advance of the American frontier. Since the 1820s, American settlers had been pouring into Texas, where in 1836 they rebelled against Mexican authority, defeated a Mexican army, and set themselves up as an independent republic looking toward union with the United States. During the same period, wagon trains from the Missouri frontier had been crossing the Plains along the northern borders of Texas and pushing on to trade with the ancient Spanish-Mexican settlement of Santa Fe on the upper Rio Grande. Still farther north, fur traders had followed in the tracks of Lewis and Clark, exploring the Rocky Mountains and bringing back tales of new promised lands beyond in the Oregon country and Mexican California. Meanwhile, the enterprising merchants of Boston and Salem and New York were sending their ships around the Horn to pick up hides on the California coast and were becoming excited about the possibility of dominating trade with the Orient from the magnificent Pacific harbors at San Diego, San Francisco, and Puget Sound.

While Americans were discovering the farther West, romantic assumptions were intensifying their faith in the superiority and glorious destiny of their free institutions. Rapidly the idea grew that it was the "manifest destiny" of these free institutions to spread over all the vast, thinly inhabited, and lightly held territories between the Mississippi Valley and the Pacific Ocean.

The growing enthusiasm for territorial expansion further confused an already tangled political situation while raising an ominous question. The decade of the 1840s opened with the Whigs and Democrats still battling inconclusively over old issues that no longer stirred the voters, and both parties were for different reasons somewhat demoralized. Under these circumstances the issue of expansion was a godsend to ambitious politicians with various axes to grind. But it was a dangerous issue. The controversy over slavery was making the country edgy. The mounting hostility between North and South was becoming too apparent to be wished out of consciousness. A great crusade to fulfill the manifest territorial destiny of the United States might reunite Americans in enthusiastic patriotism. But it could also incite a disastrous sectional conflict over the territorial spoils.

TIPPECANOE—AND TYLER TOO

Such possibilities were still far from most men's minds as the Whigs took over the national government following their great victory in the presidential election of 1840. President Harrison called a special session of Congress to pass the traditional Whig program—repeal of the independent treasury system, a new national bank, a higher protective tariff, and a scheme for distributing the federal land revenues among the states. Yet the Whigs were the unluckiest of the major political parties. Within a month after his inauguration, "Old Tippecanoe" died, leaving the Whig program at the mercy of the vain, stubborn Vice President, John Tyler of Virginia.

Tyler had left the Democratic party when Jackson threatened to coerce the South Carolina Nullifiers in 1832, and he retained much of the old-fashioned Virginian attachment to state rights. He went along with Clay in repealing the independent treasury system, but after indicating a willingness to approve a national fiscal agency, he vetoed two successive bills chartering a new national bank. By other vetoes, Tyler made it clear that Clay could have either a higher protective tariff or distribution, but not both. Clay chose increased protection for manufacturers, and the Tariff of 1842 raised duties generally to the levels that had existed before the Compromise Tariff of 1833. Meanwhile, in a futile effort to secure distribution, the Whig Congress included in the Land Act of 1841 the principle of *preemption*. Preemption enabled any head of a family to settle on 160 acres of the public domain before they were offered for sale at the customary auction and then to bid them in at the minimum price of $1.25 an acre.

Thus the stubborn Virginia President frustrated every part of the Whig program except the higher tariff and caused Clay to accept a preemption system for which he had no great enthusiasm. The overwhelming majority of the Whig Congressmen, both northern and southern, turned on Tyler in fury and read him out of the Whig party. Every member of his Cabinet resigned, Secretary of State Daniel Webster tarrying only a little longer than the others. Webster's delay was partly to enable him to complete the negotiations with England that led up to the Webster-Ashburton Treaty of 1842, compromising a dispute over the boundary between Maine and Canada. Bereft of party support, Tyler took up the issue of expansion, hoping that it might enable him to run for president in 1844. Secretly, his administration began negotiating with the Texas authorities for a treaty of annexation.

The Texas question had long been regarded as a threat to the delicate sectional balances that held the two parties together as national organizations. From the moment of the Texas Revolution in 1836, antislavery men had been denouncing it as a plot by southern filibusterers to extend the area of slavery, and even Jackson, despite his warm friendship for the Texas leader Sam Houston, had delayed recognition of the new republic until after Van Buren was safely elected. Van Buren had similarly avoided the question of annexation during his administration as being too dangerous to the harmony of the Democratic party.

Thus, by pushing the Texas question to the fore, Tyler hoped to embarrass greatly the old party leaders and either run for president as the candidate of a pro-Texas third party or displace Van Buren as the Democratic nominee. The potential for sectional conflict over the Texas issue was increased when Tyler brought in Calhoun as his Secretary of State to complete the secret negotiations for an annexation treaty. The treaty was signed and sent to the Senate in April, 1844. Along with it, Calhoun sent a copy of a dispatch he had written to the British minister, Richard Pakenham, denouncing British interference in Texas, defending slavery as a positive good, and justifying annexation mainly as a measure in defense of slavery. Calhoun's Pakenham letter, irritating even moderate antislavery men, doomed the treaty to defeat in the Senate and produced violent political turmoil on the eve of the presidential nominating conventions.

THE PRESIDENTIAL ELECTION OF 1844

Clay and Van Buren had both seemed assured of nomination by their respective parties, and both wished to keep the Texas issue out of the campaign.

At the end of April, hard on the heels of Calhoun's Pakenham letter, they published simultaneous letters opposing immediate annexation. Shortly thereafter, Clay was nominated by the Whig convention, but Van Buren's Texas letter aroused a storm of opposition against him at the Democratic convention.

Although a majority of the delegates to the Democratic convention had originally been instructed for Van Buren, the late-developing Texas excitement had produced, especially in the southern and western states, a decided popular reaction in favor of a pro-Texas candidate. Van Buren's Texas letter was the signal for Texas men and anti-Van Buren men to join forces in a last-ditch fight to block his nomination. Their strategy was to insist on a two-thirds majority for nomination. Many delegates who felt bound by their instructions to vote for Van Buren on the early ballots were nevertheless able to vote for the two-thirds rule that made his nomination impossible.

But if Van Buren could not muster a two-thirds majority, neither could his leading rival Lewis Cass of Michigan. The deadlock might have destroyed the Democratic party if the convention had not finally hit upon a compromise candidate. James K. Polk had recently suffered two successive defeats in campaigns for governor of Tennessee, but he was almost the only Democrat of any prominence who could command the confidence of all the feuding factions. The hard money Van Buren wing of the party respected him as a protégé of Jackson and able leader of the Democratic forces in the House of Representatives during the Bank War, while as a slaveholding Southerner and outspoken advocate of immediate annexation, he was acceptable to the expansionist, anti-Van Buren wing.

Having nominated Polk by acclamation, the convention adopted a platform calling for "the reoccupation of Oregon and the reannexation of Texas, at the earliest practicable moment." The Oregon question had recently generated considerable enthusiasm in the Northwest, but even there it had been overshadowed by the Texas question. The Oregon plank seems to have been included primarily to remove the sectional sting from the inescapable Texas issue.

The ensuing election reflected the nearly equal division of popular strength that the matured two-party system had by this time produced. In the closest presidential result to this time, Polk received 49.6 percent of the popular votes to 48.1 percent for Clay. Polk's majority margin in the electoral college was provided by New York, where the diversion of a small number of normally Whig votes to an antislavery third-party candidate swung the balance in favor of the Democrats.

The Texas men interpreted this narrow victory as a mandate for annexation. Just before Polk's inauguration in early 1845, Congress approved, by joint resolution rather than treaty, the admission of Texas as one of the United States.

THE POLK ADMINISTRATION

Polk was one of the hardest working and most effective men ever to occupy the White House. Unimaginative, undramatic, and without much prestige when he entered office, he was nevertheless spectacularly successful in getting what he wanted from a deeply divided Democratic party and Congress and from other countries. And he wanted a great deal.

Polk was first of all an old-fashioned, doctrinaire, Jacksonian Democrat. He wanted an independent treasury system reinstituted, and from his first Congress in 1846, he got it. He wanted a drastic downward revision of the tariff, and the same Congress gave him a tariff act incorporating the antiprotectionist principle of moderate rates designed chiefly for revenue and expressed in uniform percentages with only moderate discrimination in favor of the most important American manufactures. He wanted an even further reduction in the already circumscribed federal expenditures for internal improvements, and his vetoes of long-sanctioned appropriations for river and harbor improvements were sustained. Thus under Polk, the traditional Democratic policies were finally established, to remain substantially unchanged until the Civil War.

While cleaning up this unfinished Democratic business, Polk was simultaneously moving aggressively along the new line of expansionism. With the Texas issue settled, he wasted not a moment in turning his attention to the Oregon country. This vast expanse of territory, stretching from the Rockies to the Pacific and from the border of Mexican California at 42° on the south to Russian Alaska at 54°40' on the north, had been jointly occupied by the United States and Great Britain with the proviso that either nation could terminate the joint occupation by giving one year's notice. In the early 1840s, American settlers began finding their way to Oregon in substantial numbers and disputing possession of the land with the well-established British posts of the Hudson's Bay Company. This migration had created considerable interest in Oregon in the states of the upper Mississippi Valley, northwestern Democrats had begun agitating for a more vigorous assertion of American claims to the country, and the Democratic platform had declared that "Our title to the whole of the Territory of Oregon is clear and unquestionable."

Polk's inaugural address echoed the Oregon plank in the Democratic platform, but he felt bound to renew once more his predecessors' offer of a compromise boundary along the forty-ninth parallel, an offer the British had rejected several times. When the British minister rudely rebuffed this proposal without even referring it to his government, Polk took a more bellicose line. Calling on Congress to give notice of the termination of joint occupancy, he asserted the American claim to the whole of the territory.

For a time war threatened, but both sides were ready for any face-saving solution along the forty-ninth parallel. Polk allowed intimations to reach the British that if they made a proper proposal he would submit it to the Senate for advice. Such a proposal came in June, 1846, and the Senate advised its acceptance. The 49° boundary already established east of the Rockies was extended west to the Pacific with a short detour down the Strait of Fuca to leave Britain the whole of Vancouver Island.

THE MEXICAN WAR

Polk's bold Oregon game with the British was rendered more dangerous by his bellicose diplomacy in another quarter. For a time, he seemed to be courting simultaneous wars with Great Britain and with Mexico. The principal prize in the latter case would be Mexican California with its splendid Pacific harbors. There can be little doubt that Polk was determined to secure the vast domain between the southwestern borders of the United States and the Pacific and that he deliberately provoked war when the Mexicans refused to sell it.

Having won its independence from Spain in 1821, Mexico was a proud young republic with a political system so unstable that any government compromising the national honor was sure to be driven from office. The Texas Revolution had been a severe blow to Mexican pride. Stubbornly refusing to recognize Texan independence, the Mexicans regarded the annexation of Texas by the United States as an act of aggression and had broken off diplomatic relations.

It was at this point that Polk entered the White House. One of his first acts was to order an American army to the western frontier of Texas to ward off any attack by Mexico while the formalities of annexation were being completed. He was less justified in authorizing the army to advance beyond the traditional Texan boundary at the Nueces River and in announcing his determination to enforce the unfounded Texas claim that its territory extended to the Rio Grande River. Then he sent a minister to Mexico with an offer that the United States would assume the unpaid claims of American citizens against Mexico for property losses during the Mexican Revolution in return for Mexican acceptance of the Rio Grande boundary. In addition, the envoy was to try to purchase New Mexico and California.

Since the Mexicans had not indicated any willingness to reopen regular diplomatic negotiations, it should not have been surprising that they refused to receive Polk's minister. Nevertheless Polk chose to regard this rebuff as a cause for war. He had already ordered the American army to advance to the Rio Grande, and he prepared to ask Congress for a declaration of war. The Mexicans saved him the trouble by precipitating hostilities. A Mexican force encountered an American patrol just east of the Rio Grande, and in

THE TRANS-MISSISSIPPI WEST
after the Kansas-Nebraska Act (1854)

the ensuing skirmish sixteen Americans were killed or wounded. Polk got the news just in time to modify his war message. Mexico, he told Congress, "has invaded our territory, and shed American blood upon the American soil." War was declared on May 13, 1846.

The Mexican War, whatever its morality, was militarily the most success-ful of American wars. General Zachary Taylor led the army on the Rio Grande into north central Mexico and at Buena Vista in February, 1847, won a brilliant victory over a superior Mexican force commanded by General Santa Anna. Shortly thereafter, another American army under General Win-field Scott landed at Vera Cruz on the Gulf Coast and by September had occupied the enemy capital, Mexico City. Meanwhile Colonel Stephen Kear-ney had led another American army across the plains from Missouri, seizing Santa Fe on the upper Rio Grande, and then moving on west across the mountains and deserts to establish American authority in California.

When General Scott captured Vera Cruz, President Polk sent Nicholas P. Trist, chief clerk of the State Department, to accompany Scott's army and seize upon any opportunity for negotiating a peace that would give the United States the territory it wanted. The fall of Mexico City reduced that country to political chaos, and by the time Trist found a government stable enough to negotiate, he had infuriated President Polk by insubordinate be-havior. Defying an order to return home, Trist went ahead and negotiated the Treaty of Guadelupe Hidalgo, signed in February, 1848. By this treaty, Mexico recognized the Rio Grande boundary and ceded New Mexico and California, while in return the United States was to assume the claims of its citizens against Mexico and pay Mexico $15 million. Since these were the terms Polk had instructed the repudiated diplomat to secure, he signed Trist's treaty, and the Senate ratified it.

TOWARD THE FIRST SECESSION CRISIS

Despite the brilliance of its military victories and the vastness of its territorial acquisitions, the United States emerged from the Mexican War more deeply divided and distracted than ever. The enthusiastic expansionism of men like President Polk had been partly an effort to find a cause that would unite all Americans in a new burst of patriotic nationalism and furnish a vaccine against the insidiously spreading infection of sectional enmity. But the infec-tion had already taken too firm a hold, and the remedy served to intensify rather than alleviate the disease.

The enthusiasm for expansion was most widespread in the Northwest and the Southwest and among Democrats; in the East and among Whigs, the transparently aggressive character of the Mexican War had made it unpopu-lar with many from the beginning. The Whigs carried on a constant criticism of the administration's war policy, and Northern Whigs began to denounce the war as a southern project for expanding the area of slavery. Northern voters were told, too, that a slavery-dominated Democratic party had demonstrated its indifference to the interests of the free states by reducing the tariff, cutting off appropriations for rivers and harbors, and surrendering the American claim to the whole of Oregon. The war helped to crystallize in thousands of northern minds the conviction that the area of slavery and the political power of slavery must not be allowed to expand.

In the summer of 1846, while Congress was debating a bill appropriating money for negotiations with Mexico, a Pennsylvania Democrat named David Wilmot offered an amendment declaring that slavery should be forever barred from any Mexican territories to be acquired. The Wilmot Proviso, though defeated when first introduced, infuriated southern Congressmen and provoked a struggle of such mounting violence that within three years it would bring the country to the brink of secession and civil war.

The end of the Mexican War made it indispensable to enact some legislation for government in the new territories, but no legislation could be passed without settling the status of slavery there. Northerners dominated the House of Representatives and insisted on the Wilmot Proviso while Southerners, relying on a Senate still evenly balanced between slave and free states, asserted their right to migrate with their property, including slaves, into the territory they had helped to win. President Polk urged that the Missouri Compromise line of 36°30' be extended to the Pacific as the boundary between slave and free territory, telling Northerners that slavery could never get a foothold in the arid Southwest no matter what Congress provided. But Polk made the serious blunder of announcing that he would under no circumstances accept a second term. Having expended his patronage in getting his ambitious program through his first Congress, he was less and less able to control Democratic Congressmen as his term neared its end, and the extremists, both North and South, defeated his and all other efforts to reach a compromise solution.

It was in this atmosphere that the presidential election of 1848 occurred. The free-soil issue had split both parties deeply along sectional lines. The rift was potentially deeper among the Whigs because antislavery sentiment was stronger in the northern wing of their party, but they successfully obscured their differences by again adopting the strategy of nominating a military hero. This time he was General Zachary Taylor, the hero of Buena Vista, a plain, honest old soldier who owned a plantation and slaves in Louisiana. Democratic differences were more conspicuous because Polk's no-second-term position had prompted a prolonged intraparty struggle over the nomination. At the cost of great bitterness, the Democratic convention finally nominated Senator Lewis Cass of Michigan, hated by the Van Burenites for his role in blocking their chieftain's nomination four years previously.

The major-party nominations provoked the formation of a formidable antislavery third party. Deeply suspicious of the slaveholding Taylor, the more fervently antislavery Whigs organized a Free Soil party with the Wilmot Proviso as their platform. They were quickly joined by the "Barnburners," or Van Buren Democrats, who were just as anxious for revenge against Cass and the rival "Hunker" faction of the New York Democratic party as they were to stop the spread of slavery. The new party nominated Van Buren for president and Charles Francis Adams, Whig son of John Quincy Adams, for vice president.

Taylor's personal popularity, his nonpartisan posture, the special appeal that his slaveholding status gave him in the South, and the Barnburner secession from Cass in the North made the outcome a foregone conclusion. "Old Rough and Ready" did not have to say where he stood on the territorial question, while Cass advanced a compromise solution of great future significance but little immediate appeal to the more zealous defenders of the southern and northern positions. This was the doctrine of popular sovereignty by which the settlers in the territories would be left to settle the status of slavery for themselves. Taylor won handily, while the Free Soilers garnered a substantial popular vote and elected nine congressmen.

THE COMPROMISE OF 1850

By the time Taylor took office in March, 1849, the discovery of gold in California had attracted a horde of unruly immigrants and created a desperate need for legislation providing government in the new territories. Meanwhile Southerners had been further infuriated by proposals in Congress to abolish slavery and the slave trade in the District of Columbia. Calhoun was passionately exhorting Southerners to abandon the old parties and unite in a new sectional party to defend the South's rights and safety. The more radical Southerners were demanding that the South secede if the Wilmot Proviso were applied in any form to any territory, and a number of southern governors and legislatures took measures looking toward secession in such an eventuality. In this crisis, the new President, to the shock of those Southerners who had supported him because he was a slaveholder, encouraged the Californians to bypass the territorial stage, to draw up a state constitution without congressional authorization, and to apply directly for admission as a free state. Thus Taylor's first Congress met in December, 1849, to find a free California waiting on its doorstep and passions running so high that members carried Bowie knives and revolvers and the House of Representatives took three weeks and sixty-three ballots to elect a Speaker.

The aged Henry Clay now stepped forward to rally the forces of moderation and compromise, presenting a series of proposals as an "omnibus" settlement of all the disputed questions arising from the slavery issue. (1) California was to be admitted as a free state. (2) The remainder of the Mexican cession was to be organized into two territories, Utah on the north and New Mexico on the south, leaving the status of slavery for their inhabitants to settle. The Utah territory was to provide a government for the large body of Mormons who had migrated to the shores of the Great Salt Lake in 1846 after being driven out of their settlements in Missouri and Illinois. The New Mexico territory involved an additional complication because Texas claimed that its territory extended to the upper Rio Grande, embracing Santa Fe and half of the old Spanish-Mexican province of New Mexico. Clay therefore further proposed that (3) Texas should give up its claims to the New Mexican area in return for which the United States would assume the Texas public debt; (4) the slave trade but not slavery should be abolished in the District of Columbia; (5) the old federal fugitive slave law of 1790, the enforcement of which had been increasingly defied and impeded in the North, should be strengthened.

Southerners complained that Clay's compromise would cost the South its equal strength in the Senate while making only the single concession to the South of a stronger fugitive slave law. Formidable opposition also came from President Taylor and the bulk of the northern Whigs, who were determined that the advance of slavery should be decisively halted. Even after Taylor died in July, 1850, and was succeeded by the procompromise Vice President Millard Fillmore, Clay was unable to gain a majority for his omnibus proposal. Only when the Illinois Democrat, Stephen A. Douglas, took command and broke Clay's omnibus bill into separate proposals did the various compromise measures pass.

The success of the Compromise depended on the willingness of the aroused lower South to accept it. In Georgia, Mississippi, and other states, party lines broke down as Whigs and moderate Democrats joined forces to defeat the advocates of secession. The country breathed sighs of relief, and the majority of politicians everywhere committed themselves to the Compromise measures as a "final solution" of the slavery controversy.

In the presidential election of 1852, the Democratic nominee, Franklin Pierce of New Hampshire, won because of his allegiance to the Compromise. Again the Whigs had turned to a military hero, nominating General Winfield Scott. But Whigs in the South could no longer sustain themselves as copartisans of the increasingly antislavery northern Whigs. With southern Whigs being forced into the Democratic party, the Whig party was already dying as a national entity, and Scott was its last presidential candidate.

FOR FURTHER READING:

Frederick Merk has written an important work on *Manifest Destiny and Mission in American History* (1963); Ray A. Billington is the author of the best general account of *The Far Western Frontier, 1830–1860* (1956)*; and Henry Nash Smith, *Virgin Land* (1950),* is a brilliant interpretation of the meaning of the West for the American imagination. The trade between Missouri and Santa Fe is described by a participant in Josiah Gregg, *Commerce of the Prairies* (1844)*; the fur trade is vividly and soundly reconstructed in Robert G. Cleland, *This Reckless Breed: Trappers of the Southwest* (1950), and in Bernard De Voto, *Across the Wide Missouri* (1947)*; and Francis Parkman's account of his experiences along *The Oregon Trail* (1849)* is a classic. Bernard De Voto has written a distinguished book about the momentous developments on the western and expansionist fronts during *The Year of Decision, 1846* (1943)*; Marquis James's *The Raven* (1929)* is a vivid biography of the Texas leader Sam Houston; Frederick Merk has collected essays on *The Oregon Question* (1967); and Norman Graebner is the author of *Empire on the Pacific* (1955). The political history of the 1840s is best followed through three biographies: Robert Seager, II, *And Tyler Too: A Biography of John & Julia Gardiner Tyler* (1963); the third volume of Charles M. Wiltse's *John C. Calhoun* (3 vols., 1944–1951); and Charles Sellers, *James K. Polk, Continentalist: 1843–1846* (1966). Alfred H. Bill, *Rehearsal for Conflict* (1947), describes the war with Mexico; and Holman Hamilton's *Zachary Taylor* (2 vols., 1941, 1951) covers both the war and the Taylor administration. Allan Nevins's biography of *Frémont, Pathmarker of the West* (1955) throws light on many aspects of western exploration and the Mexican War; Nevins's *Ordeal of the Union* (2 vols., 1947) is a full analysis of the developing sectional controversy of the late 1840s; Chaplain Morrison's *Democratic Politics and Sectionalism* (1967) closely examines the Wilmot Proviso; and Holman Hamilton's *Prologue to Conflict: The Crisis and Compromise of 1850* (1964)* explains the temporary resolution of the controversy.

---

*Available in paperback edition.

PRESIDENTIAL ELECTIONS AND MAJOR EVENTS, 1852–1860

1852   **Franklin Pierce** (Democrat) elected over Winfield Scott (Whig).

Harriet Beecher Stowe publishes *Uncle Tom's Cabin*.

1854   Kansas-Nebraska Act. Repeals Missouri Compromise and organizes Kansas and Nebraska territories on principle of squatter sovereignty.

1856   **James Buchanan** (Democrat) elected over John C. Fremont (Republican) and Millard Fillmore (American).

1857   Dred Scott *vs.* Sandford. Roger B. Taney's Supreme Court declares that Congress cannot bar slavery from the territories.

Buchanan fails to force the admission of Kansas to statehood under the proslavery Lecompton Constitution.

Hinton Rowan Helper publishes *The Impending Crisis of the South*.

1858   Lincoln-Douglas Debates. In his contest with Abraham Lincoln for Senator from Illinois, Stephen A. Douglas argues, in his "Freeport Doctrine," that slavery cannot survive in a territory without positive supporting legislation.

1859   John Brown's Raid.

1860   Radical Southerners break up the Democratic party by withdrawing when the Charleston convention refuses to endorse their demand for a congressional slave code.

Abraham Lincoln (Republican) elected over Stephen A. Douglas (Northern Democrat), John C. Breckinridge (Southern Democrat), and John Bell (Constitutional Unionist).

1860–1861   Seven states of the lower South secede and organize the Confederate States of America.

A House Dividing
1843–1860

14

Hoping that the Compromise of 1850 had finally settled the slavery controversy, the American people again turned their energies to the march of
enterprise. The fifties were a decade of unprecedented economic growth
and prosperity, the climax of the market revolution and the beginning of the
industrial revolution. Yet the very process of economic growth and physical
expansion provoked a renewal of sectional conflict that could be resolved
only by civil war.

CULMINATION OF THE MARKET REVOLUTION

The exuberance of the forces generating the market revolution had also
generated boom-and-bust cycles that had periodically inhibited the country's full potential for economic growth. Not until the years between 1843
and 1857 did the developed market economy have a chance to show what
it could do in an extended period without a major depression.

The results were spectacular. Between 1844 and 1854, the total value
of all commodities produced rose by 69 percent, the highest gain for any
decade until the 1880s. Accompanying this rise in gross production was an
equivalent gain in the efficiency of production with output per worker increasing by 10 percent in the 1840s and 23 percent in the 1850s, the latter
increase again to be unequaled until the 1880s. This rapid economic growth
was in part simply a further acceleration of the market revolution in its
various aspects after a slackening of pace during the depression of 1837–
1843.

Commercial agriculture resumed its growth at a faster rate than ever. By
1846, the formerly protectionist Northwest was exporting so much wheat
to foreign markets that it turned toward free trade and provided the votes
by which the tariff reductions of that year were passed. By 1850, the North-

west exceeded the Northeast in wheat production, and this was only a prelude of things to come. The advance of the agricultural frontier north into Wisconsin and west across Iowa into eastern Kansas and Nebraska, coupled with the widespread use of Cyrus McCormick's mechanical reaper, pushed northwestern wheat production from some thirty million bushels in 1850 to almost one hundred million bushels in 1860. Meat packing and the production of corn and hogs expanded almost as spectacularly.

Similarly in the South, the cotton crop increased by 60 percent in the 1840s and 100 percent in the 1850s. Sugar production in Louisiana rose fourfold between the mid-1830s and 1859. The increasing productivity and profitability of southern agriculture were reflected in the rising price of slaves. In the 1790s, a prime field hand could have been bought for $300; by 1840, the price had risen to $1,000; and by 1860, it ran up to $1,500.

The impressive growth of a regionally specialized commercial agriculture was closely related to the perfection of a national system of transportation and communication providing facilities for swift, cheap, and efficient interregional and international exchanges of goods and services. Turnpikes, canals, and steamboats had been effective enough for the earlier stages of the market revolution, but not until the 1850s was the transportation system brought to full efficiency by the creation of a great railroad network.

Although railroad construction had received a start in the 1830s, only local lines had been completed before the depression of 1837–1843 stalled further progress. As late as 1848, the country had only six thousand miles of track. Mileage doubled in the next four years and reached thirty thousand by 1860. By 1857, the country had invested a billion dollars in railroads, two thirds during the preceding seven years.

Particularly important was the completion in the early 1850s of five great trunk lines connecting the Atlantic ports of Boston, New York, Philadelphia, Baltimore, and Charleston with the Ohio and Mississippi valleys by way of Albany and Buffalo, Pittsburgh, Wheeling, and Atlanta and Chattanooga. From these terminals the eastern trunk lines rapidly developed new western railroads to the emerging transportation and commercial centers of Chicago, St. Louis, and Memphis. By 1855, a passenger could travel in two days from one of the Atlantic cities to Chicago or St. Louis for a fare of $20. Radiating out from the trunk lines were a series of feeder lines bringing cheap transportation and commercial production to virtually every part of the country.

The flood of products harvested by an expanded agriculture and brought to the coast by a perfected transportation system helped push American exports from $144 million worth of commodities in 1850 to $334 million in 1860. Imports climbed to an even higher level, the trade deficit being bridged by exports of California gold, which rose from $5 million in 1850 to $58 million by the end of the decade. This swelling of foreign commerce brought with it a vigorous revival of the American carrying trade.

Another element in the economic expansion was the upsurge of immigration from abroad, especially from Ireland and Germany after the potato famine created widespread destitution in 1846. Immigrants to the United States had not numbered more than ten thousand a year before 1825, but exceeded one hundred thousand in the mid-1840s and reached an annual level of around four hundred thousand in the early 1850s. Between 1844 and 1854 nearly three million new Americans arrived from abroad. Many of these people supplied the labor for the factories that were springing up in the East, others did the hard, dirty work in railroad and canal construction. The Germans established strong colonies in such northwestern cities as Cincinnati, St. Louis, and Milwaukee, while still other immigrants swelled the tide of agricultural migration into Wisconsin, Iowa, and beyond.

THE RISE OF INDUSTRY

The impressive economic gains of the late 1840s and the 1850s were more than a matter of growth along established lines. The rounding out of the vast and lucrative national market set the stage for the industrial revolution in the United States. A new sector of the economy was moving into the dynamic role. Earlier, the profits of the American carrying trade during the Napoleonic Wars had provided the initial impetus that jarred the economy out of its static staple-exporting phase. Then the swelling flood of commercial crops, cotton above all others, had fueled the transportation revolution and the creation of a national market economy. Now, from the 1850s on, industry was to be the primary stimulant for a sustained and massive expansion of production that would create the most abundant economy that history had yet known.

Large-scale factory production had been developing gradually since the War of 1812, but not until the 1840s did the expansion of the industrial sector spurt ahead. The value of manufactured products in 1850 for the first time exceeded the value of agricultural products, and between 1850 and 1860 it nearly doubled from just over $1 billion to just under $2 billion. Probably the best measure of industrial growth is the increase in the difference in value between raw materials used and final manufactured products. Between 1839 and 1849, this difference, or the value added by American manufacturing, is estimated to have risen by 157 percent, and between 1844 and 1854 by 134 percent. These ten-year increases were not to be equaled in any subsequent decade of the nineteenth century.

Cotton textile manufacturing had been the pioneer industry in the United States. In 1791, the successful Rhode Island merchant Moses Brown had employed Samuel Slater, who understood the recently developed English textile machinery, to set up a small spinning plant. Soon there were a number of such small enterprises putting out the yarn they spun to be woven into cloth on hand looms in homes. When imports of English cloth were cut off during the War of 1812, the infant American textile industry spurted ahead to meet the demand.

Besides giving American manufacturers a temporary monopoly of the domestic market,the war also caused large amounts of capital to be diverted from the disrupted shipping business to manufacturing. Beginning in 1813, a group of wealthy Boston merchants led by Francis Cabot Lowell poured the unprecedented capital of $600,000 into the Boston Manufacturing Company at Waltham, Massachusetts. This was the first really large-scale and completely integrated manufacturing enterprise in the United States. The Waltham operation included every step in the manufacturing process from raw cotton to the final printed cloth, with the most advanced machinery used at every stage. The healthy profits at Waltham encouraged the promoters to erect similar plants at Lowell and other places in New England where water power was available.

The example of the Waltham system hastened the development of large plants using power-driven machinery in other industries: woolens, flour, shoes, carpets, stockings, and paper. The assembly-line or continuous-process system was even adopted for nonmachine operations, as in the great pork butchering and packing establishments that grew up at Cincinnati and, later, Chicago. The small, scattered iron works of the colonial period expanded, with the adoption of the rolling mill and the substitution of coal for charcoal fuel, into larger-scale enterprises. The demand for iron created by the railroad boom helped quadruple the output of pig iron between 1842 and 1860.

By the 1840s stationary steam engines had been developed to the point where they could substitute for water power in industrial production. This strengthened the tendency for industry to locate in cities, and industrial growth contributed greatly to urbanization. In 1820, only 6 percent of the American people had lived in places of 2,500 or more population. By 1860, the figure had risen to nearly 20 percent, and New York had become the first city to pass the 1,000,000 mark. The greater part of this urban growth had occurred during the 1840s and 1850s. Much of it was produced by the increased volume of international and interregional trade that funneled through the cities, but industrial development was becoming almost as important. Five of the fifteen largest cities in 1860 had more than 10 percent of their population engaged in manufacturing, while some of the newer and smaller cities like Newark, Lowell, and Lynn were almost wholly industrial.

The steady trend toward concentrating production in larger and larger industrial units had undermined the independence of the old artisan class and created a growing new working class of permanent wage earners. This shift in the status and prospects of workingmen had given rise in the 1820s and 1830s to a number of labor unions of skilled artisans in such crafts as printing, shoemaking, and the building trades. The craft unions had organized city federations in New York and Philadelphia, workingmen's parties had entered local politics, there had been strikes for the ten-hour day, and in 1834 a National Trades Union had been formed.

This early labor movement was swept under by the Panic of 1837, but as prosperity returned in the 1840s, so did the craft unions. Strikes became numerous and successful enough so that the ten-hour day was general by the middle 1850s. Again a National Trades Union was organized, and again, in 1857, a depression wiped out labor's organizational gains. This time, though, several nationally organized craft unions survived the debacle.

The union movement largely bypassed the growing body of unskilled or semiskilled workers who manned the new mechanized factories. For several decades after the establishment of the Waltham plant, the New England cotton mills recruited their labor force mainly from young New England girls, who lived in paternalistically managed company boarding houses and worked in the mills until they married. This system broke down after the Panic of 1837, and from this time on, the labor force for all kinds of factories was recruited increasingly from unskilled immigrants. Factory hours were long, and factory wages provided only a mean living. Not for many decades would the industrial worker begin to share in the vastly expanded wealth created by the industrial revolution.

CONFLICT AGAIN

With North and South riding the greatest tide of prosperity either section had ever known, it may seem strange that the decade of the 1850s ended in civil war. Indeed direct conflicts of economic interest between the sections over national legislation seemed at the lowest ebb since the Panic of 1819. Southerners were no longer frustrating the Northwest's demands for federal aid to internal improvements; between 1850 and 1860, the federal government granted eighteen million acres of the public lands to aid construction of forty-five railroads in ten states. The tariff issue no longer engaged men's passions as northern industry continued to flourish under the low rates of 1846.

Yet the very lushness of prosperity and growth was fostering imperial visions in the two sections: in the South visions of an expanding cotton-slavery empire and in the North visions of an expanding free-soil empire. As these competing expansionist impulses headed toward a collision, they were inevitably intensified by the moral dimensions of the slavery question.

The South's growing insecurity over the institution of slavery was particularly dangerous. By the 1850s, the North was rapidly outstripping the South in population and potential political power, while Northerners were demonstrating their deepening disapproval of slavery by blocking enforcement of the stringent new Fugitive Slave Law, one of the few concessions to the

South in the Compromise of 1850. These circumstances help explain the mounting stridency with which southern spokesmen proclaimed the merits of slavery—and more specifically the South's hysterical reaction to two famous books published during the 1850s. The first, Harriet Beecher Stowe's novel *Uncle Tom's Cabin* (1852) was a sentimental portrayal of slavery's brutal impact on some appealingly drawn slave characters. The second, Hinton Rowan Helper's *Impending Crisis of the South* (1857) was an all too effective argument by a nonslaveholding North Carolinian that slavery was disastrous to the nonslaveholding white majority in the South. Both books were not only denounced but violently suppressed in the South, while in the North they won wide audiences and helped harden antislavery sentiment.

Paradoxically, the South had more power in the federal government in the 1850s than it had had since Jeffersonian days. The campaign of 1852 demonstrated that the northern and southern wings of the Whig party were too far apart on the slavery question to hold together any longer, leaving the Democrats as the one great national party. Northern Democratic politicians competed against each other for promotion in the party and the federal government by going as far as they could toward satisfying southern demands and thereby winning southern support. Therefore the South came to have the dominant voice in the Democratic presidential administrations of Franklin Pierce and James Buchanan. As long as the Democrats remained a national party and the South's northern Democratic allies could win elections in a good part of the North, the South could in effect control the country and counteract the northern advantage in population and representation. But eventually the South, out of its insecurity, demanded more from its northern Democratic allies than they could grant without losing elections in the North.

What the South was demanding in the 1850s was the right for slavery to expand. This insistence grew out of complicated motives. It was in part simply the cotton-slavery imperialism of a prosperous and expansive social and economic system. It was also an effort to bolster the South's slipping proportion of representation in the federal government through the creation of additional slave states so as to defend slavery better from political attack. It was finally a demand that Northerners recognize the moral legitimacy of slavery by acknowledging its right to grow and thus relieve the white South from the intolerable burden of justifying and defending an unjustifiable and indefensible social system.

THE TERRITORIAL QUESTION

It seemed clear by the 1850s that there was no further room for new slave states within the territorial limits of the United States under the political arrangements that prevailed. The Missouri Compromise barred slaves from the remaining unorganized parts of the Louisiana Purchase, the Oregon territory had been organized on free-soil principles, and geography seemed to prohibit slavery's spread over the arid wastes of the New Mexico and Utah territories.

Under these circumstances, expansionist Southerners turned their attention to the Caribbean area, and the Pierce administration attempted to purchase Cuba from Spain. This effort had the advantage of appealing on nonsectional grounds to a nationalistic "Young America" group who wanted to continue the expansionism of the 1840s. But when a trio of southern-oriented diplomats issued the Ostend Manifesto proposing that Cuba be seized if it could not be purchased, there was such a reaction in the North and in Spain that the Cuba project had to be dropped. Despite this setback, many Southerners continued to agitate throughout the 1850s for expansion into the Caribbean area and to support illegal filibustering expeditions that sought to overturn weak Central American governments and pave the way for American annexations.

With the outlook for foreign expansionism dim, a small group of southern politicians began a fateful effort to push slavery into that part of the Louisiana Purchase hitherto reserved as free soil. Democratic Senator Stephen A. Douglas of Illinois was anxious to pass a bill providing territorial government for the Kansas and Nebraska country, partly to facilitate the start of a transcontinental railroad that might terminate in his home town of Chicago. Senator David R. Atchison of Missouri, representing a slaveholding constituency across the Missouri River from the area in question, had staked his political life on a promise that his constituents would be able to take their slaves into the new territory. Atchison joined with a group of powerful southern Senators to insist that no territorial bill would pass unless it contained a clause repealing the Missouri Compromise prohibition of slavery. Douglas gave in to their demand, a weak President Pierce was persuaded to use all the power of the national administration to secure enough northern Democratic votes to pass the bill, and the Kansas-Nebraska Act of 1854 was the result.

Douglas argued that the Act was simply an extension of the democratic "popular sovereignty" principle already applied to the New Mexico and Utah territories by the Compromise of 1850. But indignation blazed up in the North at this cynical abrogation of a sacred compromise and at the servile northern Democrats who obeyed an "aggressive slavocracy." While only a small minority of Northerners were disposed to interfere with slavery where it already existed, far more were ready to stop its further spread. With the Kansas-Nebraska Act, cotton-slavery imperialism provocatively challenged free-soil imperialism. The immediate response was the organization of a new sectional party in the North calling itself "Republican" and vowing its opposition to the least extension of the area of slavery.

Meanwhile Kansas, the more southerly of the two new territories, was filled with violence and bloodshed as proslavery and antislavery factions contended for control of the territorial government. New England abolitionists contributed guns and funds for free-soil immigrants, while "border ruffians" from Missouri crossed the river to furnish illegal ballots and armed support to the proslavery faction. When President Pierce again yielded to southern pressure and recognized a proslavery legislature elected largely by illegal voters from Missouri, the enraged free-soilers elected their own legislature and governor. A proslavery force raided the free-soil capital, and in retaliation, a fanatical free-soiler named John Brown invaded an isolated proslavery settlement and butchered five inoffensive residents. In the sporadic violence that followed, more than two hundred people were killed.

In retrospect, the demand for repeal of the Missouri Compromise appears to have been a suicidal strategy for southern interests. Southern opinion generally was not strongly in favor of such a demand, and even many of the more radical Southerners admitted that slavery would probably never be established in any of the disputed territories. What the South was really demanding was an acknowledgment of its technical right to take slaves into all territories, an acknowledgment of the legitimacy of slavery. For the sake of this technical right, southern leaders put their northern Democratic allies in an untenable position in their home constituencies and called into existence a formidable antislavery party that would soon destroy their control of the federal government.

BUCHANAN RIDES THE STORM

The new Republican party, drawing heavily from former Whigs and outraged Democrats, grew by leaps and bounds in the North. As the presidential election of 1856 approached, the Democrats were also threatened by another new party, the Americans or Know-Nothings, who appealed to anti-immigrant, anti-Catholic sentiment. To meet this double challenge, the Democratic national convention dropped the discredited Pierce and nominated the cautious, conservative, and prosouthern James Buchanan of Pennsylvania. The new American party nominated ex-President Fillmore and drew a substantial vote, especially from former Whigs in the South, but carried only one state. The major feature of the election was the strong showing of the new Republican party, which carried all but five of the free states for its candidate John C. Frémont. Only by the lavish use of money in Pennsylvania and Indiana and by the support of an almost solid South did the Democrats squeak through with a bare electoral majority.

Meanwhile the attempt to apply the popular sovereignty principle was deepening the chaos in Kansas and Washington. Southerners were insisting that popular sovereignty did not allow the people of a territory to bar slavery until they came to draft a constitution preparatory to admission as a state. Shortly after Buchanan's inauguration in March, 1857, a southern majority on the Supreme Court upheld this southern contention in the celebrated case of Dred Scott. Chief Justice Roger B. Taney's opinion denied the slave Scott's contention that he had been made free by residence in the free territory of Iowa, saying that Congress could not bar slavery from the territories—and it was a logical inference that territorial legislatures could not either.

While northern opinion was reacting to this further evidence of slave power aggression, President Buchanan was trying to remove the issue from politics by pushing Kansas into statehood. Failing in his efforts to get a fair referendum on slavery in Kansas, the President unwisely succumbed to southern pressure and endorsed a proslavery state constitution drafted by a notoriously unrepresentative convention at Lecompton. At this point, Senator Douglas and a number of other northern Democrats, fighting for political survival at home, revolted against the President and blocked the admission of Kansas under the Lecompton Constitution.

At the height of the Kansas crisis in 1857, the country's nerves were further strained by a severe financial crisis. The Republicans capitalized on the hard times to broaden their appeal. The southern-dominated Democratic Congress had just passed the Tariff of 1857, reducing protection to the lowest level since 1812. It was easy to blame the depression on the new tariff and to win support from hard-hit manufacturers and industrial workers by promises of higher rates. At the same time, the Republicans made themselves more appealing to northwestern farmers by agitating for a homestead act giving free homesteads of 160 acres to actual settlers on the public lands. A wave of religious revivals following the financial crash further excited the public mind and intensified the North's moral sensitivity on the slavery question.

THE ELECTION OF 1860

Under these unsettling circumstances, the slavery debate began to be dominated by the approaching presidential election of 1860. Stephen A. Douglas of Illinois was the leading aspirant for the Democratic nomination and perhaps the only one who could win enough support in the North to be elected. But Douglas was in an exceedingly difficult dilemma, reflecting the dilemma of the Democratic party. In order to be nominated, he had to allay southern suspicions arising from his opposition to the Lecompton Constitution, but it was questionable whether he could allay these suspicions and win the nomination without taking a position so prosouthern that he would lose the subsequent election. And in the meantime, he had to win reelection to the Senate against the leading Illinois Republican, a shrewd Springfield lawyer named Abraham Lincoln.

In his famous series of debates with Lincoln across Illinois in 1858, Douglas sought to escape his predicament by taking an ambiguous position. On the one hand, he maintained his doctrine of popular sovereignty, which would technically permit Southerners to take their slaves into the territories and deny territorial legislatures the right to bar slavery before statehood. But at the same time he assured the Illinois voters, in what came to be called the Freeport Doctrine, that slaves could never be successfully held in a territory unless the territorial legislature had passed a slave code or positive legislation for protecting and policing slave property. Douglas won the senatorial election by a narrow margin, but his Freeport Doctrine made him even less acceptable to Southerners as a presidential nominee.

By now southern demands were reaching an extreme of presumption and folly. The more radical Southerners had already begun to suspect that slavery, as Douglas claimed in the Freeport Doctrine, could not be sustained in the territories without a slave code. Now they moved beyond the claim that neither Congress nor territorial legislatures could bar slavery from the territories and began demanding that the federal government positively protect and guarantee slavery in the territories through enactment of a congressional slave code. Most Southerners were not insistent on this radical demand, and certainly very few Southerners had any real thought of taking slaves into any of the territories in any case. But as tension increased and excitement mounted, southern politicians feared to be outdone in defending their constituents' supposed interests, and the most extreme positions came to the fore. Southern insecurity had generated demands for more and more guarantees and assurances, these apparently aggressive movements of the slaveholding section had frightened the North into more determined resistance and spawned the Republican party, and this hardening resistance in the North had intensified southern insecurity and generated even greater demands.

Southern insecurity reached a peak of near hysteria in October, 1859, when the violent abolitionist John Brown, of Kansas fame, led a raid on the federal arsenal at Harper's Ferry, Virginia, seizing guns and ammunition with which he planned to arm a wholesale slave rebellion. Though Brown and his followers were quickly subdued, a paroxysm of terror ran through the South, and terror quickly turned to rage when it was learned that respectable antislavery men in the North had backed the plot.

Against this background, the Democratic national convention assembled at Charleston, South Carolina, in April, 1860. Radical Southerners insisted that the convention endorse their demand for a congressional slave code. When the pro-Douglas majority refused, after violent debate, the delegates from eight states of the lower South withdrew, and the convention had to adjourn. Two separate Democratic conventions then met in Baltimore, the northern-dominated one nominating Douglas and the southern-dominated one nominating John C. Breckinridge of Kentucky. Meanwhile the Republicans had met in Chicago to nominate Abraham Lincoln, and union-minded old-line Whigs from the border states, calling themselves the Constitutional Union party, had put John Bell of Tennessee into the running as a fourth candidate.

Lincoln had no support outside the free states, but there he made an almost clean sweep that was by itself enough for a majority in the electoral college. For the rest, Breckinridge carried most of the South handily; Bell won three border slave states; and Douglas, though running second to Lincoln in popular votes, won the electoral votes of only Missouri and half of New Jersey.

SECESSION

For years the small but steadily growing body of radical southern fire-eaters had been looking forward to this day, and they lost no time in making the most of their opportunity. South Carolina had been in a secessionist mood since the days of nullification, impatiently waiting for her stolid sister-states to awaken to their danger. At last enough of the southern population was sufficiently aroused by the election of a "Black Republican," and South Carolina could lead the way. Hastily calling a state convention, the Palmetto State formally repealed its ratification of the federal constitution on December 20, 1860. Within six weeks, she had been followed by the six Gulf States: Mississippi, Florida, Georgia, Alabama, Louisiana, and Texas.

As the border states hesitated, the waning Buchanan administration fretted in helpless impotence. The politicians at Washington scurried about seeking a formula for compromise, but the victorious Republicans would not listen to a proposal that countenanced the slightest extension of slavery, while the Southerners demanded at least a token concession on the territorial question. Meanwhile the seceded states had sent delegates to Montgomery, Alabama, organized themselves as the Confederate States of America, and chosen Jefferson Davis of Mississippi as their president.

CONFLICTING HISTORICAL VIEWPOINTS

6. What Caused the Civil War?

The Civil War is perhaps the best illustration of the ancient truism that the historian's view of the past is colored by his perception of the present. Southerners and Northerners debated the causes across regional lines.

State rightists, nationalists, and economic determinists offered their own predictable explanations for the catastrophe's origins.

The first scholarly assessment came from the pen of James F. Rhodes, a turn-of-the-century historian with a strong nationalist persuasion. In his History of the United States *(7 vols., 1893–1906), Rhodes argued that the war was fought over the issue of slavery: "of the American Civil War it may safely be asserted [that] there was a single cause, slavery." Almost universally accepted for two decades, Rhodes's thesis was disputed and ultimately displaced during the 1920s and 1930s. But during the period of civil rights activism following World War II, his interpretation won renewed support. In the most authoritative modern reaffirmation of the slavery hypothesis, Allan Nevins concluded that "The main root of the conflict . . . was the problem of slavery with its complementary problem of race-adjustment." Nevins's magisterial* Ordeal of the Union *and* The Emergence of Lincoln *(4 vols., 1947–1950) also identified "minor roots," including constitutional, political, and economic factors. But the issue of slavery and the future of blacks in American society, he insisted, were fundamentally the causes of the Civil War.*

On the eve of the Great Depression, Charles and Mary Beard argued that economic conflict, not slavery, caused the war. In The Rise of American Civilization *(2 vols., 1927), the Beards viewed the conflict as one between rival forms of capitalism. According to this reform-minded husband-and-wife team, the Civil War was a "Second American Revolution" in which northern industrialists sought successfully to dominate southern agriculturists. Although Charles Beard would later abandon this interpretation, it has remained popular among radical scholars. Both William A. Williams's,* The Contours of American History *(1961) and Barrington Moore's,* Social Origins of Dictatorship and Democracy *(1966) offer variations on the Beardian theme.*

Other historians interpreted the war as an inevitable clash of regional rivals. Arthur C. Cole, for example, argued in his The Irrepressible Conflict *(1934) that the North and the South were two distinct civilizations, two separate societies drawn ineluctably into conflict by the very nature of their differences. But other scholars denied that there were irreconcilable ideological, institutional, or economic differences between the sections. Indeed, James G. Randall* (The Civil War and Reconstruction *[1937]) and Avery Craven* (The Repressible Conflict *[1939]) viewed the Civil War as an avoidable conflict. Writing on the eve of Pearl Harbor, these antiwar historians blamed blundering politicians and moral fanatics for a holocaust that should never have happened.*

In one form or another, each of these major interpretations has supporters among the present generation of historians. Perhaps inevitably the conflict that divided the Union more than a century ago continues to divide the scholarly community. As Thomas J. Pressly remarked in his analysis of how Americans Interpret Their Civil War *(1954), "the further the Civil War receded into the past, the greater the strength of the emotions with which these divergent viewpoints were upheld."*

FOR FURTHER READING:

For economic development in the 1840s and 1850s, the references listed at the end of Chapter 9 will continue to be useful. Marcus Lee Hansen, *The Atlantic Migration, 1607–1860* (1940),* has a good account of the upsurge of immigration during these years. John R. Commons and others have written the standard *History of Labour in the United States* (4 vols., 1918–1935); and Hannah Josephson's *The Gold Threads* (1949) is a good account of the girl workers in the New England textile mills. William O. Scroggs describes the Caribbean adventures of various Americans in *Filibusters and Financiers* (1916). The drift toward Civil War is traced in Avery O. Craven, *The Growth of Southern Nationalism, 1848–1861* (1953), and in Roy F. Nichols, *The Disruption of American Democracy* (1948).* In *Crisis of Fear* (1970), Steven A. Channing offers a superb account of the secession movement in South Carolina. Thomas B. Alexander has analyzed Congressional voting in the 1850s as an index to *Sectional Stress and Party Strength* (1967); and Eric Foner's *Free Soil, Free Labor, Free Men* (1970) is a major study of early Republican ideology. The more illuminating biographies include: David Donald, *Charles Sumner and the Coming of the Civil War* (1950); George Fort Milton, *The Eve of Conflict: Stephen A. Douglas and the Needless War* (1934); Glyndon G. Van Deusen, *William Henry Seward* (1967); and Laura A. White, *Robert Barnwell Rhett* (1931). Indispensable to an understanding of secession is Ollinger Crenshaw, *The Slave States in the Presidential Election of 1860* (1945). Modern readers will gain much insight from those two famous books of the 1850s, Harriet Beecher Stowe, *Uncle Tom's Cabin* (1852),* and Hinton Rowan Helper, *The Impending Crisis of the South: How to Meet It* (1857).*

---

*Available in paperback edition.

PRESIDENTIAL ELECTIONS AND MAJOR EVENTS, 1860–1865

1860   **Abraham Lincoln** (Republican) elected over Stephen A. Douglas (Northern Democrat), John C. Breckinridge (Southern Democrat), and John Bell (Constitutional Unionist).

1860–1861   Seven states of the lower South secede and organize the Confederate States of America.

1861   Confederates bombard Fort Sumter, beginning the Civil War.
Virginia, North Carolina, Tennessee, and Arkansas secede and join the Confederacy.
Morrill Tariff. Substantial upward revision of duties, beginning a long period of high protection.
Trent affair. Union naval officer seized two Confederate diplomats from a British vessel.

1862   Homestead Act. Free farms of 160 acres to actual settlers.
Morrill Land Grant Act. Land grants to the states for agricultural and mechanical colleges.
Pacific Railroad Act. Federal subsidies for a railroad from Omaha to California.
Slavery abolished in the territories and the District of Columbia.
Second Confiscation Act. Freeing escaped or captured slaves of Confederates.

1863   Lincoln's Emancipation Proclamation. Declaring free all slaves in Confederate areas.
National Bank Act. With a supplementary act of 1864 establishes a system of banks issuing a uniform paper currency based on holdings of federal bonds.
Turning point of the war in July, when Union forces capture Vicksburg on the Mississippi and stop Lee's invasion at Gettysburg.
Lincoln announces his "ten percent plan" for the easy restoration of the seceded states to the Union.

1864   Lincoln vetoes the Wade-Davis bill, containing a harsher congressional plan for restoration of the seceded states to the Union.
Abraham Lincoln (Republican) reelected over George B. McClellan (Democrat).

1865   Lee surrenders to Grant at Appomattox Courthouse.
Lincoln assassinated.
The Thirteenth Amendment abolishes slavery throughout the United States.

The Civil War
1861–1865

15

When Abraham Lincoln arose to deliver his inaugural address on March 4, 1861, few people had any very clear idea of how the secession problem should be handled. Some voices in the North counseled letting the "erring sisters depart in peace." The abolitionist minority called for a holy war to free the slaves. Majority opinion in the North was increasingly convinced that the Union must somehow be preserved, but there was no clear mandate for military coercion of the seceded states. The war that finally came, like most wars, came not because anyone deliberately willed it, but out of a fortuitous chain of circumstances whose result reflected only imperfectly the conscious collective will of North or South. Insofar as a guiding will affected the outcome, it was the will of Abraham Lincoln.

LINCOLN AND THE SECESSION CRISIS

The new President was known to the country only as a lanky and apparently uncultivated lawyer-politician from the prairies of Illinois. He had won brief notice years earlier when his opposition to the Mexican War caused Illinois voters to repudiate him after a single term in Congress. Not until his debates with Douglas in the senatorial campaign of 1858 had he attracted national attention. Elected president by a minority of the voters, he had given little public indication of his policy in the months between the election and the inauguration. Actually he had blocked all efforts at compromise by privately opposing any arrangement that left the slightest room for the expansion of slavery. But this position could be put down to political expediency—compromise on the territorial question would have left the infant Republican party little reason for existence—and gave no clue as to what he would do when he assumed office.

Certainly Lincoln was not prepared to lead a crusade to free the slaves. He had insisted that slavery was wrong and that its expansion should be stopped so that the country might look forward to its eventual peaceful extinction. But he had repeatedly denied any disposition to interfere with slavery where it already existed. He had also denied in his debates with Douglas that he was "in favor of bringing about in any way the social and political equality of the white and black races." A "physical difference" would prevent the two races from ever living together on equal terms, he had said, and, therefore, "I, as much as any other man, am in favor of having the superior position assigned to the white race." He wanted slavery excluded from the territories so that "white men may find a home—may find some spot where they can . . . settle upon new soil and better their condition in life . . . as an outlet for *free white people everywhere.*"

The inaugural address revealed both a leader of unsuspected stature and a position around which northern opinion could rally. With an eloquence that no president since Jefferson had attained, Lincoln pleaded for preservation of the Union. "The mystic chords of memory," he said, "stretching from every battlefield and every patriot grave to every living heart and hearthstone all over this broad land, will yet swell the chorus of the Union, when again touched, as surely they will be, by the better angels of our nature." In trying to touch these chords, he reassured the South in the most positive terms that he would countenance no act against slavery in the states where it already existed.

But the address also had a vein of iron. The Union, said Lincoln, was perpetual, any violent acts against the authority of the United States were "insurrectionary or revolutionary," and these statements were to be taken "as the declared purpose of the Union that it *will* constitutionally defend and maintain itself." Though the federal government would not initiate hostilities, the President told the South, it would "hold, occupy, and possess" the federal forts and other property in the seceded states and collect the import duties there.

It is clear in retrospect that Lincoln thus committed himself to a course that led directly to one of the bloodiest wars in history. But war was not his purpose. Eight of the fifteen slave states were still in the Union. By refusing to recognize secession while at the same time declining to proceed forcibly against the secessionists, Lincoln was seeking to reinforce the manifest Unionist sentiment in the upper South. Apparently he wanted to keep the upper South from seceding, hoping that latent Unionism would eventually overcome secessionism in the seven seceded states of the lower South.

There were several difficulties with this Union-saving strategy. One was that Lincoln exaggerated the strength of Unionist sentiment in the lower South. Another was the likelihood that the effort to hold the federal forts in the seceded states would lead to armed conflict. Armed conflict was the more likely because many of the secessionists were quite ready to provoke a crisis that would force the upper South to choose sides.

The issue of peace or war came to a focus in the harbor of Charleston, South Carolina. Practically all the federal forts and other property in the lower South had been taken over by the seceding states before Lincoln's inauguration. Of the few posts remaining in federal hands, the unfinished and lightly garrisoned Fort Sumter, located in the entrance to Charleston's harbor, had become the symbolic focus of the whole controversy over federal property. Sumter had sufficient supplies to hold out only six weeks, and a decision about its future could not be postponed. Lincoln finally informed the Confederate authorities that he was sending a naval expedition to re-provision Sumter. They in turn ordered their general at Charleston to demand the fort's immediate evacuation and in case of refusal to bombard it. The demand was made and refused, and on April 12, 1861, the Confederate shore batteries opened fire.

Lincoln responded by calling on the states for seventy-five thousand troops. Rather than make war on their fellow Southerners, four states of the upper South—Virginia, North Carolina, Tennessee, and Arkansas—now reluctantly followed the lower South out of the Union. The four slave states of Delaware, Maryland, Kentucky, and Missouri remained with the Union, though the last two had strong secessionist movements and furnished many soldiers to the Confederacy. The tables were turned on the secessionists when the strongly Unionist western section of Virginia seceded from Virginia and laid the basis for the new state of West Virginia under the aegis of the Union. Meanwhile the Confederacy acted to consolidate the adhesion of the upper southern states by moving its capital from Montgomery to Richmond.

THE WAR BEGINS

A spirit of martial ardor swept over both sections in the spring of 1861. Northerners expected a short and easy war, while Southerners seemed oblivious of the overwhelming superiority in human and material resources against which they would have to contend. The five and one-half million free people of the eleven Confederate states faced a population of twenty-two million in the twenty-three Union states. The North had a four-to-one advantage in free males of fighting age and would muster twice as many soldiers. Even if one southern soldier was worth two Yankees (as Southerners loudly proclaimed), how were southern armies to be supplied and transported? The North had 80 percent of the country's factories and most of the coal and iron. Twenty-two thousand miles of railroad traversed the North as compared with nine thousand in the South, and the North's rail network included a series of vital trunk lines between East and West while the sprawling southern regions were but circuitously and inefficiently bound together.

Under the circumstances, the South made a remarkable military showing. This was due in part to the advantage of fighting a defensive war. The
North was compelled not only to invade but occupy the South, and southern
commanders had the additional advantage of shorter interior lines of communication for shifting troops from one front to another. Moreover Jefferson
Davis could utilize from the beginning a galaxy of outstanding generals,
Albert Sidney Johnston, Joseph E. Johnston, Thomas J. ("Stonewall") Jackson, and, preeminently, Robert E. Lee; while Lincoln spent several years
trying a succession of variously unsatisfactory commanders before he found
a really able one.

The Appalachian highlands, thrusting deep into the South, divided the
theater of war into two zones. Throughout the conflict, the greatest public
attention was focused on the East, where the rival armies menaced each
other's capitals, only a hundred miles apart. Here the Confederate armies,
magnificently led by Joseph E. Johnston and then by Robert E. Lee, repeatedly repelled Union invasions aimed at Richmond. General Irvin McDowell's army was turned back at Bull Run in northern Virginia in July, 1861.
Lincoln's next general, George B. McClellan, tried another tack, ferrying an
enormous invasion force down Chesapeake Bay and up the York River to
the eastern outskirts of Richmond only to be beaten off in the series of
hard-fought battles that constituted the Peninsula Campaign of May-June,
1862. later that summer, Lee trounced another Union army led by John Pope
in the second battle at Bull Run and followed up this victory with an audacious advance across the Potomac River into Maryland. McClellan caught
up with him at Antietam Creek, some fifty miles northwest of Washington,
in September, 1862, and in a closely contested battle inflicted so much
damage that the Confederates had to withdraw to Virginia.

Back on his home ground, Lee was again invincible, defeating Ambrose
E. Burnside at Fredericksburg in December and Joseph E. Hooker at nearby
Chancellorsville the following May. Once again the great Confederate general sought to capitalize on his success by invading the North, gambling on
the hope of a decisive victory that would cut the east-west trunk railroads
in Maryland and Pennsylvania, imperil Washington, and persuade the North
to make peace before its superiority in manpower and material became
irresistible. On July 1, 1863, Lee's seventy thousand men and the ninety
thousand Union soldiers of George G. Meade faced each other from opposing ridges outside the little town of Gettysburg in southern Pennsylvania. For
three days, wave after wave of Confederates swept up against the strong
Unionist position, only barely failing to flood over it. Lee was again forced
to retreat to Virginia, and the South's last hope of victory was gone.

While Lee's brilliant gamble was failing in the East, the Confederacy's
military doom was being more plainly spelled out in the West. Here the
Mississippi, Tennessee, and Cumberland rivers afforded natural invasion
routes for the combined operations of Union gunboats and armies, and here

an obscure Union commander, Ulysses S. Grant, steadily and inexorably crunched deeper and deeper into the South. Forts Henry and Donelson, guarding the Tennessee and Cumberland rivers, fell in February, 1862. Pressing on south up the Tennessee River, Grant inflicted a severe blow on the main Confederate army in the west at Shiloh in April and moved on into northern Mississippi. Meanwhile Union gunboats had steamed up the Mississippi from the Gulf to take New Orleans and down the Mississippi from the north to take Memphis. The last Confederate stronghold on the Mississippi, Vicksburg, fell to Grant in July, 1863, while Meade was turning back Lee at Gettysburg; thus the Confederacy was cut in two.

THE CONFEDERACY AT WAR

The burden of directing the Confederate war effort fell amost wholly on the shoulders of Jefferson Davis. Lacking able subordinates in his cabinet and in the Confederate Congress, Davis perhaps took on too much of the burden of detailed administration and sometimes exercised poor judgment in decisions about military strategy and commanding officers. But only an able and conscientious executive could have kept the Confederacy operating and its armies in the field under the staggering difficulties that he faced for as long as he did.

At the beginning of the war, Davis had high hopes of aid from Europe. France's Napoleon III was openly sympathetic as were the ruling upper classes in Great Britain, and both of these countries went so far as to recognize the Confederacy's belligerent status. But Davis was counting on the economic power of the South's cotton to produce more substantial aid—full diplomatic recognition, financial assistance, and perhaps even military intervention. The South might have built up large credits for the purchase of supplies in Europe by shipping its cotton abroad. Instead, the Confederate authorities placed an embargo on cotton exports, expecting that this would force British cotton mills to close and thus bring pressure on the British government to intervene more openly on behalf of the Confederacy. Unfortunately, the British mills had a year's surplus of raw cotton on hand, some alternative sources of supply were available, and although some of the cotton mills eventually shut down, their unemployed workers remained sympathetic to the more democratic North and exerted their influence against any aid to the South.

The South's best chance to drive a wedge between Great Britain and the North came in November, 1861, when a United States naval vessel stopped the British ship *Trent* on the high seas and took off the Confederate diplomats James M. Mason and John Slidell. But the United States promptly released Mason and Slidell, and Lincoln's skillful minister in London, Charles Francis Adams, was increasingly successful in preventing the British from aiding the Confederacy either directly or indirectly. And France refused to act without British support.

Meanwhile Lincoln had ordered the Union navy to blockade southern ports; by the time the Confederacy decided to ship cotton to Europe in exchange for supplies, this was no longer possible. Cut off from all outside goods (except a trickle brought in by swift blockade runners), the Confederacy was increasingly hard put to supply its armies with munitions or its people with the ordinary necessities of life.

As the war wore on and as the Confederacy's prospects dimmed, the early enthusiasm was replaced by growing discouragement, apathy, and disaffection. The Confederate conscription law, which exempted overseers and owners of twenty slaves, was especially resented by poorer Southerners who began to say that this was "a rich man's war and a poor man's fight." Desertions became an increasingly serious problem. The South's state-rights tradition was also a source of weakness as fractious governors like Joseph E. Brown of Georgia and Zebulon B. Vance of North Carolina defied the policies of the Richmond government. It seems fair to conclude that the South's commitment to the war had been less than wholehearted in the beginning and that a growing disenchantment with it was a major factor in the Confederacy's eventual collapse.

LINCOLN AND THE WAR

Lincoln was having his problems too. The North had a large contingent of "Peace Democrats" who, as the war dragged unsuccessfully on, demanded a negotiated settlement. The draft law of 1863, from which the wealthy could escape by paying $300 or hiring a substitute, provoked a bloody two-day riot in New York City. At the other end of the political spectrum, Lincoln was ceaselessly hounded by a group of "Radical" Republicans who wanted to make the war an antislavery crusade and who advocated a punitive policy toward the South. Under the leadership of men like Senator Charles Sumner of Massachusetts and Representative Thaddeus Stevens of Pennsylvania, the Radicals gained great power in Congress where they set up a Joint Committee on the Conduct of the War, which constantly criticized and interfered with the President's conduct of military operations.

The split between Radical Republicans and moderate or administration Republicans was not related, however, to the series of major laws passed by the wartime Congresses. The Morrill Tariff Act of 1861 marked a turn toward higher protective duties, and subsequent legislation of 1862 and 1864 pushed duties to unprecedented levels, inaugurating an era of extravagant protectionism that would last into the twentieth century. The long fight for free land culminated in the Homestead Act of 1862, granting 160 acres to any family that wished to settle on the public domain. The Morrill Land

Grant Act of 1862 donated public lands to the states for support of agricultural and mechanical colleges. In the same year Congress finally authorized the long-projected transcontinental railroad, granting thirty million acres and millions in federal bonds to the Union Pacific and Central Pacific railroad companies to build a line from Omaha to the Sacramento River. By an act of 1863 Congress established a national banking system with member banks issuing a stable currency of uniform national bank notes on the basis of their holdings of federal bonds.

In passing these important measures to serve the interests of northern farmers and business enterprise, the Congress was simply legislating the Republican platform now that the Southerners were no longer there to oppose. None of these measures aroused the controversy in the Republican party that the subject of slavery created. Anxious to mollify the loyal slave states of Delaware, Maryland, Kentucky, and Missouri, Lincoln stoutly resisted doing anything to suggest that abolition of slavery was a northern war aim. In the fall of 1861, he removed the Radicals' favorite general John C. Frémont from command in Missouri for declaring that the slaves of rebels were free. Meanwhile he sought unsuccessfully to interest Congress and the loyal slave states in a plan of gradual, compensated emancipation with the federal government footing the bill.

The Radicals were determined to force the issue, and in 1862 pushed through Congress legislation abolishing slavery in the territories and in the District of Columbia. More important was the Second Confiscation Act of 1862, declaring forfeit the property of all persons supporting the rebellion and proclaiming escaped or captured slaves to be "forever free." By this time, Lincoln was becoming aware that an emancipation policy would be of value in helping to win the war, especially by gaining friends for the Union in Europe. Finally, on January 1, 1863, he issued his Emancipation Proclamation. This famous proclamation freed only those slaves living in rebel areas and justified the action on the ground of "military necessity." Only as the Union armies advanced did the freedom proclaimed by the proclamation become an actuality for the slaves. Not until 1865 did the Thirteenth Amendment, forbidding slavery throughout the country, become a part of the Constitution.

The Emancipation Proclamation did not allay the Radicals' suspicion of Lincoln, but they failed to block his renomination for President in 1864. In this wartime election, the Lincoln Republicans ran as the Union party, appealing to War Democrats by nominating for vice president Andrew Johnson, the Tennessee Senator who had remained loyal to the Union. The regular Democratic nomination went to General McClellan, many of whose supporters were calling for peace negotiations. The long string of Union defeats in the East had so strengthened antiwar sentiment that Lincoln might have been defeated but for some timely military successes in the West on the eve of the election.

TOWARD APPOMATTOX

It is now clear that the fall of Vicksburg and Lee's failure at Gettysburg in July, 1863, had destroyed the last chances of a Confederate victory. And by this time, after trying a long succession of commanders, Lincoln had finally found a general who would justify his confidence. Ulysses Grant, who had capped his doggedly successful western campaigns with the victory at Vicksburg, was called to the East and in the spring of 1864 made general-in-chief of all the Union armies. Before leaving the West he had consolidated Union control of Tennessee with a victory at Chattanooga. Now his grand strategy was a two-pronged final offensive against the South with General William T. Sherman leading one great Union army south from Chattanooga into Georgia and himself leading another south from Washington toward Richmond.

The twin offensives were launched simultaneously in May, 1864, the two Union armies of around one hundred thousand men each pressing back Confederate armies of around sixty thousand. In the West, Sherman steadily pushed the Confederates south and by September won the important rail center of Atlanta. Here he made his audacious decision to abandon his line of supply and wage a war of destruction between Atlanta and the sea. Devastating the countryside as he went, he was in Savannah by December, and the Confederacy was further segmented. Turning north, Sherman reached Columbia, South Carolina, in February, 1865, and by March was in east central North Carolina.

By demoralizing the Confederate areas south of Virginia, Sherman greatly facilitated Grant's advance on Richmond. In the Spotsylvania Wilderness and at Spotsylvania Courthouse in May, 1864, Lee inflicted heavy casualties on the invading Yankees as he had so often done in the past. But this Yankee general did not withdraw to lick his wounds as had all his predecessors. By flanking movements, he kept pressing south toward Richmond. At Cold Harbor, Lee again inflicted frightful losses on the Union army, but still Grant pushed inexorably south, passing just east of Richmond and crossing the James River. Lee managed to shield Richmond as Grant moved around it to the south and southwest toward Petersburg. By June, the two armies were entrenched facing each other in a long line bending from Richmond southward around the southern side of Petersburg.

Grant simply would not let go, and as the siege went on through the summer and fall and winter his superiority in manpower began to tell. Remorselessly he kept extending his line to the west, and Lee's line became steadily thinner and more vulnerable as he had to keep stretching it farther. By April Lee could extend his line no more and had to pull out of his entrenchments, abandoning Richmond and Petersburg. But by this time Grant had cut all the roads leading south over which Lee might effect a junction with the only remaining Confederate army of any strength. On April

9, 1865, at Appomattox Courthouse Lee bowed to the inevitable and surrendered. One month later the fleeing Jefferson Davis was captured in disguise in Georgia and imprisoned at Fortress Monroe. The Confederacy was dead.

LINCOLN AND THE SOUTH

The treatment of the vanquished South had long since become a new bone of contention between Lincoln and the Radicals. Lincoln wished to bring the rebellious states back into full membership in the Union as rapidly and painlessly as possible. By the time Union forces occupied Arkansas in December, 1863, the President was ready with his "ten percent plan" of reconstruction. Under this plan he proposed to extend amnesty and restore confiscated property to all Confederates who would take a simple loyalty oath, excluding only high civil and military officers of the Confederacy or its states. As soon as 10 percent of a state's 1860 electorate had taken the oath, the state could write a new constitution and rejoin the Union.

The Radicals, however, feared with considerable reason that if the southern states were reconstructed on this basis, the old ruling class would return to power and the Negro freedmen would be little better off than they had been under slavery. Anxious for a thoroughgoing reconstruction of southern society, they insisted that black men be given the ballot and that the old rebel leadership be effectively excluded from political life. As a counter to Lincoln's plan they secured the passage in 1864 of the Wade-Davis bill. This measure required a majority, rather than 10 percent, of the 1860 voters to take a loyalty oath before reconstruction could begin and further insisted on disfranchisement of ex-Confederate leaders.

Lincoln allowed the Wade-Davis bill to die by pocket veto, but the Radicals had one tactical advantage. A state would not be fully restored to the Union until its representatives were seated in Congress, and the Radical-controlled Congress had full power over the admission of members. This power the Radicals used to deny admission to the first southern representatives who appeared under Lincoln's 10 percent plan. In March, 1865, as the war drew to a close, they gave a further indication of their objectives by creating the Freedmen's Bureau to assist the ex-slaves in adjusting to freedom and to protect their rights in their new state.

The sharpening struggle between Lincoln and the Radicals was suddenly cut short on Good Friday, April 14, 1865, five days after Lee's surrender at Appomattox, when a demented actor and southern sympathizer, John Wilkes Booth, shot a fatal bullet into the President's head as he sat in a box at Ford's Theater.

A grieving nation suddenly discovered a great tragic hero. To Lincoln's strength and humility and eloquence and magnanimity was now added the quality of martyrdom. He had presided over the bloodiest war in the American experience, preserving the Union as the land of liberty and last best hope of man. Hesitantly and grudgingly but in the end unmistakably, he had also made the war a struggle to include *all* male Americans within the sphere of American liberty. Yet the Emancipation Proclamation and the Thirteenth Amendment were only a beginning. It was Lincoln's Radical critics who saw most clearly that the task of completing emancipation still lay ahead, and even his great talents could hardly have been equal to this Herculean task. Perhaps it was a timely martyrdom that translated Abraham Lincoln—a man groping toward an ideal only dimly perceptible in his society and age—into the Great Emancipator. For a century and more to come, Lincoln, the symbol, would remind his countrymen that the egalitarian dream was still unfulfilled.

FOR FURTHER READING:

The standard work on the Civil War era is Allan Nevins *The War for the Union* (4 vols., 1959–1971), but James G. Randall and David Donald, *The Civil War and Reconstruction* (1961) is also indispensable. Divergent interpretations of the North's reaction to secession are presented in David M. Potter, *Lincoln and His Party in the Secession Crisis* (1950).* The northern conduct of the war is best followed through the biographies of Lincoln, the best single-volume one being Benjamin P. Thomas, *Abraham Lincoln* (1952). For greater detail, see Albert J. Beveridge, *Abraham Lincoln, 1809–1858* (2 vols., 1928); and the chronologically succeeding volumes by James G. Randall (completed by Richard N. Current) on *Lincoln the President* (4 vols., 1945–1955).* Current has also written a fine interpretive essay on *The Lincoln Nobody Knows* (1958).* Special aspects of the North during the war are treated in John Hope Franklin, *The Emancipation Proclamation* (1963); George M. Frederickson, *The Inner Civil War* (1965)*; James McPherson, *The Struggle for Equality* (1964); T. Harry Williams, *Lincoln and the Radicals* (1941)*; and T. Harry Williams, *Lincoln and His Generals* (1952).* The Negro's role in the struggle is analyzed in Dudley Cornish, *The Sable Arm* (1956) and Benjamin Quarles, *The Negro in the Civil War* (1953). Clement Eaton has written a *History of the Southern Confederacy* (1954),* and Frank E. Vandiver's *Their Tattered Flags* (1970) is a sprightly history of the secession government. Rembert W. Patrick describes *Jefferson Davis and His Cabinet* (1944); and the Confederacy's *King Cotton Diplomacy* (1931) has been analyzed by Frank L. Owsley. The military history of the war from the point of view of the northern armies may be followed in the vivid volumes by Bruce Catton: *Mr. Lincoln's Army* (1951),* *Glory Road*

---

*Available in paperback edition.

(1952),* and *A Stillness at Appomattox* (1954).* A more detailed and professional evaluation of the northern military effort through 1863, with greater attention to the western campaigns, is Kenneth P. Williams, *Lincoln Finds a General: A Military Study of the Civil War* (5 vols., 1949–1959). *The Gettysburg Campaign* (1968) is examined by Edwin B. Coddington. The fighting as viewed from the southern side is best followed in the distinguished studies by Douglas Southall Freeman: *R. E. Lee, a Biography* (4 vols., 1934–1935), and *Lee's Lieutenants* (3 vols., 1942–1944); and Tom Henderson Wells has written an excellent history of *The Confederate Navy* (1971). Also outstanding are two works by Frank E. Vandiver, *Rebel Brass* (1956) and *Mighty Stonewall* (1957). Bell I. Wiley has described the common soldiers in *The Life of Johnny Reb* (1943)* and *The Life of Billy Yank* (1952). Edmund Wilson's *Patriotic Gore* (1962) brilliantly portrays the human and literary dimensions of the era. Of the multitude of personal accounts of contemporaries, three very different ones may be singled out as having special interest: the *Personal Memoirs* (2 vols., 1885–1886) of General Grant; *A Diary from Dixie* (1905)* by Mary Boykin Chesnut; and *The Diary of Edmund Ruffin* (2 vols., 1972–1976).

EVENTS OF RECONSTRUCTION

National	General Tendency	Date	State
Lincoln Plan announced.	**Presidential Reconstruction**	1863	Governments set up in Louisiana, Arkansas.
Wade-Davis Plan pocket-vetoed by Lincoln.		1864	
Lee surrenders. Lincoln shot. Johnson Plan announced.		1865	Governments partly functioning in Virginia, Tennessee.
Freedmen's Bureau bill and Civil Rights bill vetoed. Fourteenth Amendment submitted to states. Congressional elections: Radical gains.		1866	All remaining states reorganized under Johnson Plan.
Reconstruction Acts. Tenure of Office Act.	**Height of Radical Reconstruction**	1867	Tennessee readmitted. Military Rule in effect.
Impeachment of Johnson. Fourteenth Amendment in effect. Grant elected.		1868	North Carolina, South Carolina, Florida, Alabama, Louisiana, Arkansas, readmitted under Radical governments.
Fifteenth Amendment in effect. First Enforcement Act.		1869	Conservative government restored in Tennessee.
Congressional elections: Republican majorities reduced.	**Conflict**	1870	Virginia readmitted under moderate government. Moderate government restored in North Carolina. Mississippi, Texas, Georgia, readmitted under radical government.
Second and third Enforcement Acts.		1871	Conservative government restored in Georgia.
Grant reelected.		1872	
		1873	
Congressional elections: Democrats gain control of House.	**Restoration of White Rule**	1874	Conservative government restored in Arkansas, Alabama, Texas.
Civil Rights Act (Declared invalid 1883).		1875	Conservative government restored in Mississippi.
Hayes-Tilden disputed election.		1876	Federal troops removed from Louisiana, South Carolina.
		1877	Conservative government restored in Florida, South Carolina, Louisiana.

Reconstructing the Union 1865-1890

16

In the generation after the Civil War, economic expansion absorbed most of the nation's energies. The people's attention, however, centered at first on a more traditional kind of problem, the Reconstruction of the Union and the new order in the defeated South.

THE PROBLEM

The problem of Reconstruction was manifold. Most obvious, and easiest, was the physical rebuilding of shelled cities and ruined railroads. Harder to reconstruct was the defeated section's economic life. The South's industry was at a standstill; much of her farming land was lying idle. Her labor system was destroyed, investment capital was lacking, the savings of many people were wiped out by the collapse of Confederate currency and bonds. Beneath every other problem lay that of a new relation between the South's two races. All that was clear about the country's 4,500,000 Negroes was that none of them remained a slave. Some 286,000 were Union soldiers; a few were settled on confiscated plantations in the Sea Islands of the Carolinas; and many were simply wandering, drifting from Union army camps to southern cities with great hopes and no means of support. Nearly everybody assumed that they were to continue to work on the land. A few radicals had suggested that they would become landowners and the Sea Islands experiment raised some hopes. White Southerners assumed that Negroes would work as laborers for white landowners.

In this politically minded country, most people approached such problems in political terms. By 1865, three southern states were already reconstructed under the easy terms offered by President Lincoln, which demanded only that 10 percent of the citizens take an oath of future loyalty and recognize that slavery was ended. Once this was done, elections were held for both state governments and federal Congressmen. But Congress refused to admit these delegates.

To settle this difficulty, Americans turned to the Constitution. In this unheard-of situation, however, it offered little help. What was the status of a sovereign state that had seceded and been forced to return to the Union? Was it still a state, since secession had been illegal, or was it merely a conquered province? Who could decide: Congress or the president? The president was commander-in-chief of the armed forces and had the power to pardon. But Congress had the right to admit new states, to make rules for territories, and to judge the qualifications of its own members. Long before Lincoln's death, the two branches of government had been at loggerheads over these issues.

More important in the long run than even the constitutional question was the state of mind of three main groups: the ex-slaves, the defeated southern whites, and the citizens of the victorious North. Though able Negro leaders shortly appeared, most of the ex-slaves were not only illiterate but completely inexperienced, both in politics and in dealing with such economic institutions as wages and rent. Many pathetic stories are told about the strange hopes and fears of these displaced people. Yet the basic desires of the freedmen were clear and by no means foolish. What they wanted was real freedom, and the signs of that freedom were the right to move around, access to education, and ownership of land.

Right after the war, according to northern travelers in the South, shock rather than bitterness was the most common state of mind among southern whites. With their institutions destroyed, what was to become of them? Most pressing of all, without slavery, how was the cotton going to be picked and planted? At first, many looked northward for their answers.

The third and largest group, the victorious northern whites, were by no means a united body. Nearly half were Democrats. Only a few Democrats had been willing to accept the breakup of the Union, but many had sharply criticized the conduct of the war and had opposed emancipation. The sole purpose of the fighting, the party's leaders had insisted, should have been the restoration of "the Union as it was." In the 1864 elections, the Democrats had lost some ground, yet they still mustered a formidable 45 percent of the votes.

Not even the Republicans were sure of what they wanted. The group called "Radicals" agreed that Lincoln had been too weak and lenient, but they agreed on little else. Republicans were also divided on such matters as the tariff and finance, and few had thought through the future status of the Negro.

Two paradoxes made constructive action inordinately difficult. First, slavery had been abolished and the ex-slaves armed by a nation that believed overwhelmingly in the inferiority of the Negro race. This belief, now discredited, was centuries old and almost universal. Even among the abolitionists, only a few had accepted the Negro as an intellectual and political equal. Only part of New England permitted Negroes to vote. Starting with Connecticut, Wisconsin, and Minnesota in 1865, one northern state after another continued to deny Negro suffrage in the years after the war.

Second, during Reconstruction the government had to undertake a program of drastic, even revolutionary measures. Yet nearly all nineteenth-century Americans had been taught that government action should be sharply limited. This had been said by Jefferson, Jackson, and Lincoln. Schools and colleges taught as gospel truth the maxims of *laissez faire* political economy.

The choice faced by the North, in its simplest terms, was the choice offered to every victor: occupation or conciliation. All the feelings of nineteenth-century Americans were against continued military occupation. Somehow, most agreed, the South must be forced to see its errors and govern itself—according to northern ideas.

Yet to whom in the South could government be confided? To the ex-rebels who were, many Northerners believed, still rebels at heart? To the ex-slaves whom most Northerners regarded as members of an inferior race? Even if they were given the vote, the freedmen, inexperienced in politics and a minority in all but two states, could hardly govern alone. They would have to have the support either of a substantial number of southern whites or of sufficient occupying forces. With or without Negro suffrage, the same choice existed: conciliation or occupation.

PRESIDENTIAL RECONSTRUCTION

The first alternative, conciliation, was attempted under the authority of presidents Lincoln and Johnson and is often referred to as Presidential Reconstruction. It is hard to tell how Lincoln's "ten percent plan" might have worked if it had been continued. As we have seen, this was already sharply challenged by Congress, and Lincoln himself had said it was only one of many possible devices. The Wade-Davis bill, Congress' more drastic substitute, had been left unsigned by Lincoln.

Like Lincoln, Andrew Johnson embodied the log-cabin presidential tradition. He had been a tailor by trade and had learned to read only as an adult. A resident of eastern Tennessee, where slaves were few, and a former Jacksonian Democrat, he had been an outspoken opponent of secession and a lifelong enemy of the southern planter class. Yet he had no real commitment either to Negro rights or to the Republican party. Like Lincoln, Johnson was honest and able, but he proved completely lacking in Lincoln's gifts of patience and political realism.

Like his predecessor, Johnson started by offering amnesty to those who would sign an oath of allegiance. Exceptions to the offer, more numerous than in Lincoln's plan, included important Confederate officials and Confederates who owned more than $20,000 worth of property. This seemed to exclude from participation the leaders of the Old South. Those who had taken the oath were to vote for a constitutional convention in each state. The conventions were to repeal the state's ordinance of secession, abolish slavery, and repudiate the Confederate and state debts. Then the state could elect a new government and send representatives to Washington. By the end of 1865, all the states had actually passed through either the Lincoln or the Johnson version of this process, and in conservative and southern eyes, Reconstruction was over.

Government was functioning in the South, and the people, Negro and white, were getting back to work. Yet much in the new order was deeply disturbing to northern opinion. Some of the reconstituted states elected prominent Confederates to state and federal office. Most enacted special "Black Codes" to regulate the conduct of freedmen. To former slaveholders, such rules seemed natural and necessary; to freedmen and many northerners, they looked like the next thing to slavery. In some states, blacks were not allowed to assemble; in others, the labor of petty offenders could be sold at auction; in some, Negro children could be apprenticed to white men without the consent of indigent parents. Most of the codes provided for strictly enforced compulsory labor contracts. In South Carolina, the code spelled out the intent of such contracts: Blacks were to engage only in agricultural labor or domestic service.

In 1865–1866, northern opinion was further affronted by outbreaks of racial violence in the South. Responsibility for race riots was of course disputed, but the victims nearly always turned out to be Negroes or pro-Negro whites. To Radical Republicans, it seemed that life was not safe in the South for those who really supported a change in southern society, and this change they were determined to bring about. To some this was a moral duty; to others a political necessity.

In the spring of 1866, Congress extended the life of the Freedmen's Bureau, a wartime organization designed to supervise and aid the ex-slaves, and passed a Civil Rights Act prohibiting many kinds of discriminatory legislation. It also refused to admit the representatives of the new southern state governments. Clearly, the President could not hope to carry forward his policy without regard for such formidable opposition. Yet Johnson, like other presidents in other battles with Congress, seemed to grow steadily more stubborn. He blamed the race riots on Radicals, minimized southern denial of Negro rights, and pardoned thousands of southern leaders. In the spring of 1866, he vetoed both the Freedmen's Bureau bill and the Civil Rights Act.

By this time, Johnson had gained the support of Democrats and solidified the Republican party against him. In the fall, he toured the country, violently denouncing his opponents as traitors. In the November Congressional election, the voters gave their answer. The Republicans won two thirds of both

Houses and the Radical leadership moved into key positions of power. A new phase of Reconstruction was clearly at hand.

CONGRESSIONAL RECONSTRUCTION

During Congressional, or Radical, Reconstruction, the second alternative, military occupation, was finally given a trial. The purpose behind it was still reform; the South was to be occupied only until her society could be altered and a new electorate formed. This meant attempting something like social revolution, and it was clear that in this revolution the Negroes must play a major part.

The Freedmen's Bureau and Civil Rights bills, both repassed over the President's veto, established that the former slaves were to be protected by the federal government during a transitional state. (They were not, however, to be given land; in this property-loving age only a few suggested such an extreme measure and local experiments in this direction were abandoned.)

Federal protection for the Negroes already implied a change in the relation of the federal government and the states, and this change was spelled out in the Fourteenth Amendment submitted to Congress in June, 1866. The first section of this amendment provided that no state should infringe any citizen's "privileges or immunities," nor "deprive any person of life, liberty or property, without due process of law," nor deny to any person "the equal protection of the laws." Thus individuals were guaranteed by the *Union* against oppression by the *states.* (The Bill of Rights already protected individual liberties from the federal government.)

The second section of the amendment edged toward Negro suffrage. It provided that if a state denied the vote to any of its male inhabitants, its representation should be reduced accordingly. The third and fourth sections barred leading Confederates from Congress or federal office and forbade states to repudiate the federal or recognize the rebel debt.

Obviously this all-important amendment could not be ratified by three-fourths of the states without some southern support. As President Johnson urged southern states not to ratify, Congress moved on to still more drastic action.

The First Reconstruction Act, passed in March, 1867, divided the South into five military districts, wiping out the existing state governments. Under military supervision, each state was to elect a constitutional convention. Delegates to these conventions would be chosen by vote of the whole male population, including the freedmen and excluding leading Confederates. Each constitution was to be ratified by a majority of the state's new electorate and approved by Congress. When the new state had ratified the Fourteenth Amendment, its representatives might be admitted to Congress. This Act was clarified and tightened by further legislation, and in 1870 Radical

Reconstruction was completed by the ratification of the Fifteenth Amendment, once and for all forbidding suffrage discrimination on the basis of "race, color, or previous condition of servitude."

All these actions were taken against the firm opposition of the President and in the face of the nearly certain disapproval of the Supreme Court. To safeguard Radical Reconstruction, Congress made the most drastic attempt in American history to establish the dominance of a single branch of government.

To disarm the Court, Congress simply withdrew certain kinds of cases from Supreme Court jurisdiction, and the Court prudently refrained from challenging this action. Johnson, however, could be rendered powerless only by impeachment and conviction for "treason, bribery, or other high crimes or misdemeanors." Failing after much effort to find serious evidence of "crimes," Congress saw its best chance for impeachment in the Tenure of Office Act passed in 1867. This Act, of dubious constitutionality, forbade the removal of cabinet officers without congressional sanction. Johnson challenged it by trying to remove Secretary of War Edwin Stanton, an appointee of Lincoln. In the spring of 1868, the House of Representatives impeached the President in a long, confused, and shaky set of charges. Anger ran so high that his accusers failed by only one vote to secure the two-thirds of the Senate necessary for conviction.

RADICAL RECONSTRUCTION IN ACTION

How did the Radical program actually work in the South? To this crucial question, historians have developed two opposite answers. A generation ago, most accounts said that Radical Reconstruction had been a dreadful mistake. Southern state governments, dominated by ignorant Negroes, self-seeking carpetbaggers, and despicable southern "scalawags" ("collaborationists" would be the modern term), had imposed a reign of terror, extravagance, and corruption. Finally, the South, supported by a revival of decent moderate opinion in the North, had risen in revolt and thrown off the yoke.

More recently this version has been challenged by an opposite one. According to this second, neo-Radical view, Radical Reconstruction was a long-overdue attempt to bring justice and progress to the South. It was sustained in the South not only by federal forces but by determined Negro support. Its defeat was brought about by brutal terrorism and northern betrayal.

The truth about this abortive social revolution is various and complex. It is clear that some of the Radical governments were indeed both extravagant and blatantly corrupt. Yet extravagance and corruption were common in this period in northern states and cities. Moreover, the Radical governments scored some real accomplishments, bringing to the South broader suffrage (for whites as well as Negroes), poor relief, and the beginnings of free, popular education.

Perhaps the key question to ask about Radical Reconstruction is whether it ever had a real chance of success; that is, could it have effected a permanent change in southern institutions and customs? The answer is complex. Successful Reconstruction would have demanded either prolonged northern occupation or some degree of cooperation between southern whites and Negroes. For the first alternative, the northern people proved to have no enduring appetite. The second seemed more promising initially. Many southern whites did make an effort to accept the new situation (though many did not). Contrary to legend, some "scalawags" were well intentioned, just as some carpetbaggers were honest and some Negro leaders well informed and moderate. yet any permanent alliance among these elements faced great difficulties. The cooperating southern whites were willing to accept Negro voting only under white leadership; the blacks demanded real political equality. Predictably, if not inevitably, the necessary coalition failed.

Violence against the Negroes and their political allies continued to break out on a larger and larger scale. At first determined to suppress the Ku Klux Klan and other terrorist organizations, Congress grew weary of the attempt. In one state after another, with differing degrees of forcible action, southern whites achieved victory at the polls. In 1877, when President Hayes withdrew the last federal troops, the cycle was complete; the South was again under the rule of native whites. At first, the new "lily-white" governments, mostly led by members of the prewar planter class, allowed Negroes some token participation in politics. Then in the nineties, governments claiming to represent poor whites came to power. Violently denouncing the alleged alliance of aristocrats and Negroes, these governments drove the southern blacks almost entirely out of politics. This was done partly by applying pressure and partly by enforcing ingenious suffrage requirements—grandfather clauses, literacy tests, and the like—against Negroes and not against whites.

SOCIAL RECONSTRUCTION

Since the Negroes never received the "forty acres and a mule" for which they had longed in 1865, they had to work for white landowners. As money to pay them was lacking, the only possible solution was some form of tenantry. The result was the sharecrop and the crop-lien systems. Throughout the South, sharecroppers, both white and black, received their seed, tools, and staple necessities from landlords to whom they turned over a third or a half of their produce. Most, and often all, of the rest of the produce went to pay long-standing debts accumulated by the tenants at country stores with high-monopoly prices and exorbitant rates of interest. The system was not slavery, and it got the crops planted and harvested. Yet the Negro farmer, forever in debt and unable to move, without education or political privileges, subject to white courts and terrorism, could hardly be called free.

In the 1880s, the white-ruled South put on a spectacular drive for industry. Heavy inducements were offered to attract capital, and much was accomplished in developing steel, lumbering, tobacco, and, especially, textile industries. However, by the turn of the century, the region had barely held its own; the South's percentage of the nation's industry was about that of 1860. Even this, in a rapidly expanding economy, was a considerable achievement. But the price was heavy. In southern mill towns, disease and child labor were endemic. Most of the profits of industry were flowing out of the section. Until World War II, the South remained both poor and overwhelmingly agrarian.

Perhaps the saddest chapter in all American history is the general acceptance, in the North, of the failure of so much effort. Thirty years after the war, most people took for granted a southern system that included not only disfranchisement and rigid social segregation of the Negro but also recurrent violence. In 1892 and 1893, for example, more than 150 Negroes were lynched each year, often with sadistic tortures.

How could the people who had defied the Fugitive Slave Act, fought the war, and voted for Radical Reconstruction accept this situation? For one thing, it was easy to emphasize the seamy side—and it was a large one—of Radical Reconstruction, the greed and corruption with which the process was executed. Moreover, most people were convinced that racial differences made political equality impossible. Government, according to nineteenth-century science and social science, could do very little to change customs or alter society. There was, moreover, a bright side to the story. A great Civil War had been settled without executions or confiscations, and the two sides were beginning to be reconciled. It was easy to forget that the Negro was paying most of the bill for this reconciliation.

Responsive in its way to the drift of public opinion, the Supreme Court made its peace with the new situation. In the Civil Rights cases (1883), it decided that the Fourteenth Amendment did not prevent *individuals,* as opposed to states, from practicing discrimination. In Plessy *vs.* Ferguson (1896), the Court held that "separate but equal" accommodations for Negroes in trains (and by implication in restaurants, hotels, and the like) did not violate their rights. Few inquired very carefully into whether accommodations were indeed equal.

The upshot, then, of the greatest struggle in American history seemed to be a tragic failure. Yet the story had not ended. The Negro had gained a few rights and a great many hopes. And neither in the North nor the South was the national conscience really at ease.

CONFLICTING HISTORICAL VIEWPOINTS

7. Was Reconstruction a Tragic Era?

Until the 1930s, historians generally agreed that Reconstruction was a period characterized by sordid motives and human depravity. It was the "Age of Hate," "The Blackout of Honest Government," "The Dreadful Decade," and "The Tragic Era." In 1939, however, Francis Butler Simkins, a distinguished southern scholar, urged his fellow historians to adopt "a more critical, creative, and tolerant attitude" toward the period. In a notable essay (Journal of Southern History *[1939]*)*, Simkins suggested that the traditional interpretation of Reconstruction was rooted in "the conviction that the Negro belongs to an innately inferior race."*

Until Simkins's time, most white students of Reconstruction did in fact approach their work with decidedly racist views. In the first serious history of the era, James Ford Rhodes's enormously influential History of the United States from the Compromise of 1850 *(7 vols., 1893–1906), blacks were described as "the most inferior race." Similarly, in John W. Burgess's* Reconstruction and the Constitution *(1902), Negroes were characterized as inherently inferior beings incapable of "subjecting passion to reason." Although Rhodes and Burgess were sharply critical of the motives and actions of congressional Radicals, the traditional interpretation of Reconstruction is best identified with the work of William A. Dunning. A Columbia University scholar and the author of* Reconstruction, Political and Economic *(1907), Dunning and his many students uncovered a wealth of factual information about the period. But their work was seriously marred by their prosouthern and anti-Negro biases. They portrayed the postbellum scene in darkly tragic hues of unrelieved brutality, scandal, corruption, and licentiousness. According to the Dunningites, Reconstruction was not only unnecessary but harshly cruel to the prostrate South and ruthlessly exploitive of the ignorant freedmen.*

Black scholars, most notably W. E. B. Du Bois, author of Black Reconstruction *(1935), vigorously disputed Dunning School conclusions. But in an age of virtually unchallenged white supremacy, few Caucasians thought to question simplistic characterizations of vindictive Radicals, venal carpetbaggers, reprobate scalawags, and barbarous darkies. A shift in the climate of racial opinion, however, ushered in a new era of Reconstruction historiography. Reflecting a growing national sensitivity to civil rights, historians since the 1930s have turned Dunning's conclusions inside out. First in a series of monographs and biographies, then later in such sweeping syntheses as John Hope Franklin's* Reconstruction After the Civil War *(1961) and Kenneth Stampp's* The Era of Reconstruction *(1965), revisionists discarded racial stereotypes and viewed the postbellum period in a generally favorable light. According to these modern scholars, traditional studies grossly exaggerated not only the extent of corruption, fraud, and black rule, but even the length of Radical control. Indeed, to both Franklin and Stampp, Reconstruction was a tragic era only in that it failed to insure blacks economic, political, and social equality.*

At present the revisionists are clearly in the ascendancy. But as Stampp has written, the revisionist's "ultimate and inevitable fate is one day to have its own revisions revised."

FOR FURTHER READING:

Herman Belz's *Reconstructing the Union* (1969) is a provocative study of Presidential Reconstruction. Representative traditional interpretations of Congressional Reconstruction include Walter L. Fleming, *The Sequel of Appomattox* (1919) and E. Merton Coulter, *The South During Reconstruction* (1947). H. K. Beale, *The Critical Year* (1930) and E. L. McKitrick, *Andrew Johnson and Reconstruction* (1960)* offer conflicting views of Lincoln's successor. La Wanda and John Cox, *Politics, Principle, and Prejudice* (1963),* David Donald's *The Politics of Reconstruction* (1965), and W. R. Brock, *An American Crisis: Congress and Reconstruction* (1963) are noteworthy revisionist works. Robert Cruden focuses on *The Negro in Reconstruction* (1969),* and Hans L. Trefousse sympathetically analyzes *The Radical Republicans* (1969). There are numerous state studies, but F. B. Simkins and R. H. Woody, *South Carolina During Reconstruction* (1932), Joel Williamson, *After Slavery* (1965), and V. L. Wharton, *The Negro in Mississippi, 1865–1890* (1947)* are among the best. C. Vann Woodward's justly celebrated trilogy, *Reunion and Reaction* (1951),* *Origins of the New South* (1951),* and *The Strange Career of Jim Crow* (1955),* and Paul Gaston's *New South Creed* (1970) are valuable for understanding the South during the post-Reconstruction period.

---

*Available in paperback edition.

Name Index

Adams, Charles Francis, 166, 189
Adams, Henry, 97, 98
Adams, John, 51, 52, 73, 77, 80, 81, 82, 85, 86
Adams, John Quincy, 96, 109, 121, 122, 142, 149
Adams, Samuel, 41, 43, 46, 51, 73
Addison, William, 30
Albion, Robert G., 113
Alden, John R., 45, 57
Alexander, Thomas B., 183
Allen, Ethan, 62
Andrews, Charles McClean, 13, 23, 44
Andros, Sir Edmund, 12
Anthony, Susan B., 147
Aptheker, Herbert P., 152
Arnold, Benedict, 49, 55
Atchison, David R., 177

Bacon, Nathaniel, 28, 34
Bailyn, Bernard, 45, 57
Baldwin, Joseph, 113
Baltimore, Lord, see Calvert, George
Bancroft, George, 44, 45, 69, 70, 71, 141
Barbour, Philip L., 13
Barnes, Gilbert H., 153
Bassett, John Spencer, 137
Beale, H. K., 206
Beard, Charles A., 70, 82, 182
Beard, Mary, 182
Becker, Carl L., 44, 57
Beecher, Lyman, 143, 145, 146
Bell, John, 181
Belz, Herman, 206
Bemis, Samuel Flagg, 82, 98, 123
Benson, Lee, 70, 138, 216
Berkeley, Sir William, 28

Beveridge, Albert J., 194
Biddle, Nicholas, 110, 131, 132
Bill, Alfred H., 168
Billington, Ray A., 113, 167,
Blassingame, John, 152
Bloomer, Amelia, 147
Boorstin, Daniel J., 34, 45, 153
Booth, John Wilkes, 193
Bowen, Catherine Drinker, 71
Braddock, General James, 22
Bradford, William, 13
Brant, Irving, 71, 98
Breckinridge, John C., 180, 181
Bridenbaugh, Carl, 34
Brock, W. R., 206
Brodie, Fawn M., 153
Brown, John, 178, 180
Brown, Joseph E., 190
Brown, Moses, 173
Brown, Richard M., 34
Brown, Robert E., 34, 35, 70
Brown, Wallace, 57
Bruckey, Stuart, 113
Buchanan, James, 176, 178, 179
Burgess, John W., 205
Burgoyne, General John, 54, 55
Burnside, Ambrose E., 188
Burt, A. L., 98
Calhoun, John C., 92, 93, 103, 109, 111, 121, 126-29, 159, 160
Calvert, George, 5
Calvert family, 19, 20
Cartwright, Peter, 153
Cash, W. J., 153
Cass, Lewis, 160, 165
Catton, Bruce, 194
Chambers, Clark, 27
Chambers, William N., 82, 138

Champlain, Samuel de, 21
Channing, Stephen A., 183
Charles I, 5, 6, 10
Charles II, 10, 12, 14-16
Charles, Joseph, 82
Chase, Samuel, 87
Chauncy, Charles, 31
Chesnut, Mary, 195
Chevalier, Michael, 139
Chingachgook, 141
Clay, Henry, 92, 93, 109, 121, 122,
    129, 131, 158, 159, 160, 166
Cleland, Robert G., 168
Clinton, DeWitt, 107, 119
Clinton, George, 77
Coddington, Edwin B., 195
Cole, Arthur C., 182
Coles, Harry L., 98
Commager, Henry Steele, 153
Commons, John R., 183
Cooper, James Fenimore, 141
Cornish, Dudley, 194
Cornwallis, Lord, 65
Coulter, E. Merton, 206
Cox, John and LaWanda, 206
Craven, Avery O., 182, 183
Craven, Wesley Frank, 13
Crawford, William H., 109, 120, 121
Crenshaw, Ollinger, 183
Crevecoeur, J. Hector St. John, 24,
    33, 34
Cromwell, Oliver, 10
Cross, Whitney R., 153
Cruden, Robert, 206
Cunliffe, Marcus, 82
Cunningham, Noble E., 82, 98
Current, Richard N., 194
Cutright, Paul R., 98

Dangerfield, George, 113
Dauer, Manning J., 82
Davidson, Edward H., 35
Davis, David Brion, 71, 153
Davis, Jefferson, 181, 188, 189, 193
Dawes, William, 43
Demos, John, 13
DeRosier, Arthur, 138
De Voto, Bernard, 98, 168

Diamond, Sigmund, 13
Dickerson, Oliver M., 23
Donald, David, 183, 194, 206
Douglas, Stephen A., 167, 177-81
Douglass, Elisha P., 57
Duberman, Martin, 154
Du Bois, W. E. B., 205
Dunning, William A., 205
Dwight, Timothy, 143

Eaton, Clement, 153, 194
Eaton, John, 126
Eaton, Peggy, 126
Edwards, Jonathan, 32
Elkins, Stanley, 152
Ellis, Richard E., 98
Emerson, Ralph Waldo, 141
Engerman, Stanley, 153

Ferguson, E. James, 71
Filler, Louis, 153
Fillmore, Millard, 167, 178
Finney, Charles Grandison, 143, 144,
    146, 148
Fischer, David H., 98
Fishlow, Albert, 113
Fiske, John, 69, 70
Fleming, Walter L., 206
Flexner, James T., 82
Fogel, Robert W., 113, 152
Foner, Eric, 183
Fourier, Charles, 145
Fox, Dixon Ryan, 123
Franklin, Benjamin, 22, 30, 31, 33,
    52, 55
Franklin, John Hope, 194, 205, 206
Frederickson, George M., 194
Freehling, William W., 138
Freeman, Douglas Southall, 57, 195
Frelinghuysen, Theodore J., 32
Fremont, John C., 178, 191
Frothingham, Octavius B., 153
Fuller, Margaret, 147
Fulton, Robert, 106

Gadsden, Christopher, 40
Gage, General Thomas, 43, 49, 50
Galloway, Joseph, 42

Garrison, William Lloyd, 148
Gaston, Paul, 206
Gatell, Frank Otto, 139
Gates, Horatio, 55
Gates, Paul W., 113
Genovese, Eugene, 152
George III, 38, 52
Gilbert, Sir Humphrey, 2
Gipson, Lawrence H., 23, 44
Goodrich, Carter, 113
Govan, Thomas P., 138
Graebner, Norman, 168
Grant, Ulysses S., 189, 192
Greeley, Horace, 145
Greene, Jack P., 23
Greene, Nathanael, 56
Gregg, Josiah, 168
Grenville, George, 38
Grimke, Angelina and Sarah, 147
Grund, Francis J., 139

Hacker, Louis, 97
Hamilton, Alexander, 64, 65, 67, 71,
    73, 74-77, 79-82, 85
Hamilton, Holman, 168
Hammond, Bray, 137
Hancock, John, 40, 43, 73
Hansen, Chadwick, 13
Hansen, Marcus Lee, 34, 183
Harrison, William Henry, 103, 142, 158
Hawthorne, Nathaniel, 141
Hayes, Rutherford B., 203
Heimert, Alan, 35
Helper, Hinton Rowan, 176, 183
Henry VII, 2
Henry VIII, 2
Henry, Patrick, 40, 50
Hooker, Joseph E., 188
Hooker, Rev. Thomas, 9
Horsman, Reginald, 98, 113
Houston, Sam, 159
Howe, Sir William, 54
Hudson, Henry, 15
Hunter, Louis C., 113
Hutchinson, Thomas, 57

Jackson, Andrew, 94, 96, 103, 121,
    125-38, 141, 142, 159

Jackson, Thomas J. ("Stonewall"), 188
Jacobs, Wilbur R., 35
James I, 3, 6
James II, 12, 15
James, Marquis, 168
Jameson, J. Franklin, 45
Jay, John, 56, 71, 79, 82
Jefferson, Thomas, 52, 60, 63, 69
    74, 76-82, 85-89, 150
Jensen, Merrill, 44, 57, 70
Johnson, Andrew, 191, 199-202
Johnston, Albert Sidney, 188
Johnston, Joseph E., 188
Jones, John Paul, 57
Jordan, Winthrop D., 34, 153
Josephson, Hannah, 183

Kammen, Michael, 23
Kearner, Stephen, 164
Kerber, Linda K., 98
Knollenberg, Bernhard, 46
Koch, Adrienne, 82
Kraditor, Aileen S., 153

Labaree, Leonard W., 34, 46
Lamb, Colonel John, 25
Lee, Richard Henry, 51
Lee, Robert E., 188, 192-93
Leisler, Jacob, 28
Levy, Leonard, 82, 98
Lewis, Meriwether, 88
Lincoln, Abraham, 179-81, 185-94,
    197, 199
Link, Eugene P., 82
Lipset, Seymour M., 82
Livingston, Robert R., 87
Locke, John, 30, 51
Louis XIV, 21
Louis XVI, 77
Lovejoy, Elijah, 149
Lowell, Francis Cabot, 174
Lundy, Benjamin, 148
Lynd, Staughton, 71
Lyons, Peter, 414

McClellan, George B., 188, 191
McCormick, Cyrus, 172
McCormick, Richard, 138

McDonald, Forrest, 70, 71
McDowell, Irvin, 188
McMaster, John B., 97
McPherson, James, 194
McWhiney, Grady, 206
Madison, James, 60, 64, 66, 71, 73, 76, 77, 81, 86, 89-97, 109, 111
Mahan, Alfred Thayer, 97
Maier, Pauline, 46
Main, Jackson T., 34, 57, 70
Malone, Dumas, 98
Mann, Horace, 145
Marshall, John, 86, 87, 111-12, 130
Martineau, Harriet, 139
Mason, James, 189
Mather, Cotton, 31, 33
Mayhew, Jonathan, 31
Mayo, Bernard, 98
Meade, George G., 188
Melville, Herman, 141
Merk, Frederick, 167, 168
Meyers, Marvin, 138
Middlekauf, Robert, 13
Miller, John C., 45, 46, 57, 82
Miller, Perry, 13, 35, 153
Miller, William, 144, 215
Milton, George Ford, 183
Mitchell, Broadus, 82
Monroe, James, 87, 96, 109
Montgomery, Richard, 49
Moore, Barrington, 182
Moore, Glover, 122
Morgan, Edmund S., 13, 45, 46
Morgan, Helen M., 46
Morison, Samuel Eliot, 12, 13, 57
Morris, Richard B., 57
Morris, Robert, 61, 64
Morrison, Chaplain, 168
Mott, Lucretia, 147

Nagel, Paul C., 71
Napoleon, 87, 92
Napoleon III, 189
Nelson, William, 57
Nevins, Allan, 168, 182, 194
Newton, Sir Isaac, 30
Nichols, Roy F., 183
North, Douglass C., 113, 215

North, Lord, 40, 56
Notestein, Wallace, 12
Noyes, John Humphrey, 144

Oglethorpe, James, 16
Olmsted, Frederick Law, 141
Owen, Robert Dale, 145
Owsley, Frank L., 153, 194

Paine, Thomas, 43, 52, 59
Pakenham, Richard, 159
Palmer, R. R., 71
Parkman, Francis, 23, 168
Parton, James, 137
Patrick, Rembert W., 194
Peare, Catherine O., 23
Peckham, Howard, 57
Penn, William, 15-19, 20, 23
Perkins, Bradford, 98
Perkins, Dexter, 98
Pessen, Edward, 137, 138
Peterson, Merril D., 98
Philbrick, Francis, 113
Phillips, Ulrich B., 151-52
Pierce, Franklin, 167, 176-78
Pinckney, Charles C., 88
Pinckney, Thomas, 79
Pitt, William, 22
Pole, J. R., 45
Polk, James K., 160-165
Pope, John, 188
Potter, David M., 194
Pratt, Julius W., 97
Pressly, Thomas J., 182
Prucha, Francis, 113, 139

Quarles, Benjamin, 153, 194

Raleigh, Sir Walter, 2
Randall, James G., 182, 194
Randolph, John, 97
Remini, Robert V., 123, 138
Revere, Paul, 43
Rhodes, James Ford, 182, 205
Risjord, Norman, 98
Ritcheson, Charles R., 82
Rohrbough, Malcolm, 113
Rolfe, John, 4

Rossiter, Clinton, 57, 71
Rothbard, Murray N., 122
Rowse, A. L., 12
Ruffin, Edmund, 195
Rutman, Darrett B., 13

Santa Anna, 164
Scarborough, William K., 153
Schlesinger, Arthur M., Jr., 137
Schlesinger, Arthur M., Sr., 45
Scott, Dred, 179
Scott, Winfield, 164, 167
Scroggs, William O., 183
Seager, Robert, II, 168
Sellers, Charles, 123, 168
Shays, Daniel, 60
Simkins, Francis Butler, 205, 206
Slater, Samuel, 173
Slidell, John, 189
Smelser, Marshall, 98
Smith, Abbott Emerson, 34
Smith, Henry Nash, 168
Smith, James M., 82
Smith, Joseph, 145
Smith, Timothy L., 153
Stampp, Kenneth M., 152, 205, 206
Stanton, Edwin, 202
Stanton, Elizabeth Cady, 147, 277
Starkey, M. L., 13
Starobin, Robert S., 153
Steele, Richard, 30
Stevens, Thaddeus, 190
Stinchcombe, William C., 57
Stone, Lucy, 147
Stowe, Harriet Beecher, 176, 183
Sumner, Charles, 190
Sydnor, Charles S., 57, 122

Taney, Roger B., 179
Tappan, Arthur and Lewis, 146, 148
Taylor, George R., 97, 113
Taylor, William R., 153
Taylor, Zachary, 164, 165-67
Tecumseh, 93
Temin, Peter, 138
Thomas, Benjamin P., 194
Tocqueville, Alexis de, 139
Tolles, Frederick B., 23

Townshend, Charles, 39
Trefousse, Hans L., 206
Trist, Nicholas P., 164
Trollope, Frances, 139
Turner, Frederick Jackson, 34, 35, 113, 122, 137
Turner, Nat, 150
Tyler, Alice Felt, 153
Tyler, John, 158

Van Buren, Martin, 122, 126-29, 134-36, 142, 159, 160
Vance, Zebulon B., 190
Van Deusen, Glyndon G., 138, 183
Vandiver, Frank E., 194, 195
Van Doren, Carl, 35
Van Tyne, C. H., 57

Wade, Richard C., 113
Wallace, Willard M., 57
Walpole, Sir Robert, 20
Ward, Harry M., 23
Ward, John W., 138
Warren, Charles, 71
Washburn, Wilcomb E., 34, 230
Washington, George, 22, 43, 49, 54-57, 64, 65, 73, 74, 76-80, 82
Webster, Daniel, 159
Weisberger, Bernard, 154
Weld, Theodore Dwight, 148
Wells, Tom Henderson, 195
Wertenbaker, Thomas J., 23
Wharton, V. L., 206
White, Laura A., 183
Whitefield, George, 32
Whitney, Eli, 104
Wiley, Bell I., 195
Wilkins, Thurman, 138
William and Mary, 12, 19
Williams, Kenneth P., 195
Williams, Roger, 9
Williams, T. Harry, 194
Williams, William A., 182
Williamson, Joel, 206
Wilson, Edmund, 195

Wiltse, Charles M., 138, 168
Winthrop, John, 7, 9, 13
Wish, Harvey, 154
Wolfe, James, 22
Wood, Gordon, 70
Woodward, C. Vann, 206
Woody, R. H., 206

Wright, Conrad, 35
Wyatt-Brown, Bertram, 153

Young, Alfred F., 82
Young, James Sterling, 123

Zobel, Hiller B., 46

Subject Index

Abolition, 148-53, 190-93
Acts of Trade and Navigation, 17
Agrarianism, 58, 69, 101, 127
Agriculture, 171-72
Alcoholism, 146
Alien and Sedition Acts, 81
American Anti-Slavery Society, 148
American Colonization Society, 148
American Home Missionary Society, 145
American Party, 178
American Revolution, 49-57
  background, 44-45
Anglo-French Wars, 21
Anti-Masons, 119, 135
Antislavery movement, 148-153
Articles of Confederation, 53-54, 64
Atlanta, 192

Bank, national, 75-77, 85
Bank notes, 108
Banks, 108, 115, 117, 119, 191
Barnburners, 166
Bill of Rights, 74
  in state constitutions, 53
Black Hawk War, 130
Black population, 25-26
Board of Trade, 19, 20
Bonus Bill of 1817, 111
Boston Massacre, 40
Boston *News-Letter*, 30
Boston Tea Party, 41

British imperialism, 37
Brook Farm, 145
Bunker Hill, Battle of, 49

Cabinet, 74
California, 157, 162
Canals, 107
Cape Cod, 6
Carolina, 14
Charleston, 14, 15
Cherokee claims, 129
Cherokee Nation v. Georgia, 130
Chesapeake, 89
Chesapeake Bay, 3, 5
Civil Rights Act (1866), 200, 201
Civil War, 185-95
  causes, 181-83
Coercive Acts, 41
Colleges, 30, 32
Commercial agriculture, 104, 105
Commercialism, 58, 101
Committees of correspondence, 40, 42
Committees of safety, 42
Common Sense, 52
Commonwealth, 10
Compromise of 1850, 166, 167
Compromise Tariff of 1833, 129
Confederate States of America, 181, 187-94
Confederation, 60-62, 64-65
Congregationalists, 143
Congress, 66
Connecticut, 9

Connecticut River Valley, 9
Constitution, 65
  criticisms of, 70
  state constitutions, 52
  to 1800, 73
Constitutional amendments
  Bill of Rights, 1-10, 74
  13th, 191
  14th, 201
  15th, 202
Constitutional Convention, 65-68
Continental army, 43
Continental Association, 42
Continental Congress, 41, 43, 51-53
Convention of 1818, 95
Convicts, 25
Corporate charters, 108
Cotton, 104
Cowpens, Battle of, 56

Dartmouth College vs. Woodward, 112
Declaration of Independence, 52
Deism, 30, 33
Democracy
  development of, 50-51
Democratic-Republicans, 122, 126
Democrats, 126, 176
  election of 1844, 160
  election of 1848, 165
  post-Civil War, 198
Depressions
  1785-1786, 60, 64
  1820's, 115
  1830's, 134
Discrimination, 204
Distribution Act, 133
Draft riots, 190
Dred Scott decision, 179
Dutch, 25
Dutch colonies, 15
Economic growth, 76, 101, 171
Economic specialization, 102
Education, 8-9, 30
Electoral college, 68
Emancipation Proclamation, 191
Embargo Act of 1807, 89
English Civil War, 10
Englightenment, 29-31, 140, 142
Erie Canal, 107

Federalists, 68, 71, 77, 79-82, 85, 86, 89, 109
Feminism, 147
First Continental Congress, 41
First Reconstruction Act, 201
Florida, 57, 61, 93
Florida accession, 95-96
Florida Treaty, 96
Force Act, 129
Fort Duquesne, 22
Fort Sumter, 187
France
  and American Revolution, 55
  in Canada, 21-23
Free Banking Act of 1838, 134
Free Soil party, 166
Freedmen, 198-200, 203
Freedmen's Bureau, 193, 200, 201
Freeport Doctrine, 180
French and Indian War, 21, 22
French Revolution, 77
Friends, Society of, 10

Gag rule, 149
General Court (Puritan government), 7-9, 12
Georgia, 16
German immigration, 24, 27
Gettysburg, 188
Gibbons vs. Ogden, 112
Governors, Colonial, 20
Great Awakening, 31-33
Great Britain
  and Civil War, 189
  and colonization of America, 2-12
Great Revival, 143-45
Guadelupe Hidalgo, Treaty of, 164
Guilford Court House, Battle of, 56

Harrison Land Act, 103
Hartford, 9
Harvard University, 9
Headright system, 4, 14
Homestead Act, 190
House of Burgesses, 4
House of Representatives, 67, 73
Huguenots, 25

Immigration, 173
Implied powers, 76, 87

Impost of 1781, 61
Impressment, 78, 79, 89
Indian conflicts, 103
Indians, 129-130
Industrial revolution, 102, 173
Inflation, 133
Intolerable Acts, 41

Jamestown, 4
Jay Treaty, 79-80
Joint-stock companies, 3
Judiciary Act of 1789, 74, 86

Kansas-Nebraska Act, 177
Kentucky, 63
Kentucky and Virginia resolutions, 81
King George's War, 21
King William's War, 21
King's Mountain, Battle of, 56
Know-Nothings, 178
Ku Klux Klan, 203

Labor movement, 119, 175
Land Act of 1820, 117
Land Act of 1841, 158
Land sales, 63, 103
  Specie Circular, 133
Lane Debate, 148
Lecompton Constitution, 179
Liberalism, 1
Liberator, The, 148
Libraries, 30
Local option, 146
Lords of Trade, 19
Lords Proprietor, 14, 19
Louisiana Purchase, 87, 88
Loyalists, 49

McCulloch vs. Maryland, 112
Macon's Bill No. 2, 92
Manufacturing, 173
Marbury vs. Madison, 86
Market Revolution, 101-3, 171
Massachusetts Bay Company, 7, 9, 12
  and the Quakers, 10
Mayflower, 6
Mayflower Compact, 6
Maysville Road bill, 127
Mercantilism, 17
Mexican War, 162-64

Mexico, 162
Midnight judges, 86
Minutemen, 43
Missouri, 116
Missouri Compromise, 116, 165
Mohawk River, 27
Molasses Act (1733), 18
Molasses Acts, 38
Money supply, 18
Monroe Doctrine, 96
Mormonism, 145, 167
Morrill Land Grant Act, 190-91
Morill Tariff Act, 190

Narragansett Bay, 9
National banking system
  Jackson, 130-32
  First National Bank closes, 109
  Second National Bank, 110, 112
National capital, 76
National debt, 127
National Road, 106
National Trades Union, 175
Navigation Acts, 17-19
Negroes, 198-99
  and abolition, 148-53
  and discrimination, 204
  and slavery, 190-93
  and suffrage, 201
Netherlands, 15, 55
Neutrality
  Jefferson, 88, 89
New Amsterdam, 15
New England, 6-12, 26-27
New Jersey, 15
New Jersey Plan, 66
New Hampshire, 9
New Haven, 9
New Mexico, 167
New Orleans, Battle of, 94
New York, 15
Newspapers, 30
Nonintercourse Act, 92
North Carolina, 28
Northwest Ordinance of 1787, 63
Northwest Territory, 63
Nullification, 128, 129

Old West, 26, 27
Ordinance of 1784, 63

Ordinance of 1785, 63
Oregon question, 160-62
Ostend Manifesto, 177

Panic of 1819, 110, 115
Panic of 1837, 134, 175
Paper money, 19, 60, 108, 117
Peace Democrats, 190
Pennsylvania, 16, 24, 27, 28
Perfectionist movements, 144
Philadelphia, 16, 41, 43
Piety, decline of, 31
Plessy vs. Ferguson, 204
Plymouth colony, 6, 7
Popular sovereignty, 120, 166, 178
Population, 24
Portuguese colonies, 2
Preemption, 158
Presbyterians, 143
Privy council, 19, 20
Prohibition
  state, 146
Proportionate representation, 66
Proprietary Colonies, 14
Protestant Reformation, 2
Puritanism, 31
Puritans, 6-9

Quakers, 10, 15, 16
Quebec Act of 1774, 41
Queen Anne's War, 21

Radical Reconstruction, 201-4
Radical Republicans, 190-93, 200
Railroads, 107, 172, 209
Reconstruction, 197-206
Regulators, 28
Republican Nationalism, 109-11
Republican Party, 177-81, 185, 198
Republicans, 79-82, 86-88, 109
  and election of 1824, 120
  and War Hawks, 93
Religion,
  and the antislavery movement, 148
  colonial, 31-33
  freedom of, 9
  in the independent states, 59
  and romanticism, 142-44

Restoration, 10
Revenue Act of 1764, 38
Revival movement, 32
Rhode Island, 9
Richmond, 187, 188, 192
Roanoke Island, 2
Romanticism, 140-44
Royal colonies, 19
Rush-Bagot Agreement, 95

Saratoga, 55
Savannah, 55
Saybrook, 9
Scotch-Irish, 24, 27
Secession, 181, 185-87
Second Bank of the United States,
  110, 112, 130-32
Second Confiscation Act, 191
Second Continental Congress, 43
Seminoles, 130
Senate, 67, 73
Separation of church and state, 9
Seven Year's War, 22
Shakers, 144
Sharecroppers, 203
Shays's Rebellion, 60, 64
Slave insurrections, 150, 151
Slavery, 5, 25, 116, 140-54, 175-83,
  190-93
  and abolition, 148-53
  and territorial expansion, 158
South, The, 175-83, 185-94
  and Reconstruction, 197-206
South Carolina, 28, 128, 181, 187
Spain, 55
Spanish colonies, 2
Specie Circular, 133
Spoils system, 125
Stamp Act, 38-39
State banks, 108, 110, 119, 131,
  132-34
State Constitutions, 52
State-rights, 128, 129, 158
Statute for Religious Freedom, 60
Steamboats, 106
Stuart Restoration, 14
Suffrage,
  colonial period, 29
  Negro suffrage, 201

Supreme Court, 74
Susquehanna, 27

Tariff of Abominations, 122, 127-29
Tariff of 1816, 111
Tariff of 1824, 117
Tariff of 1842, 158
Tariff of 1857, 179
Tariffs, 116, 127-28, 161
    Tyler, 158
Taxation, 38
Tea Act of 1773, 40
Temperance movement, 146
Temperance societies, 146
Ten percent plan, 193, 199
Tennessee, 62, 63
Tenure of Office Act, 202
Territorial expansion, 63
Texas, 157, 159-60, 162
Tobacco, 4, 5
Townshend Acts, 39
Trail of Tears, 130
Transcendentalism, 141, 145
Transcontinental Treaty, 96
Transportation, 105
Treaty of Paris, 62
Trent affair, 189
Triangular trade, 18
Turnpikes, 106
Two-party system, 73, 81, 118, 119,
    135, 136

Unions, 119, 174-75
Unitarianism, 143

Urbanization, 26, 174
Utah, 167
Utopian movements, 144

Valley Forge, 55
Vermont, 62
Virginia colonies, 3-5
Virginia Company, 3, 4
Virginia Plan, 66

Wade-Davis bill, 193
War Hawks, 92-94
War of 1812, 94
Webster-Ashburton Treaty, 159
West Indies, 11
Westward movement
    in the colonial period, 26-27
    to the Pacific, 157
    post-1812, 103
    under Jefferson, 88
    under the confederation, 62-64
Whigs, 50, 135, 176
    election of in 1844, 160
    election of in 1848, 165
    and Harrison and Tyler, 158
    and the Mexican War, 164
Whiskey Rebellion, 76
Wilmot Proviso, 165, 166
Witchcraft, 12
Women's rights, 146
Worcester v. Georgia, 130